Cognitive Therapy
and Dreams

Rachael I. Rosner, PhD, is a research associate at the Danielsen Institute at Boston University. She received her PhD in psychology in 1999 from York University and completed her post-doctoral fellowship in the Department of the History of Science at Harvard University in 2002. Her doctoral dissertation was a history of the emergence of Aaron T. Beck's cognitive therapy. She is a historian of psychotherapy who has authored articles on cognitive therapy and dreams, Franz Brentano and Freud, and methodological issues in the history of the neurosciences, as well as a chapter on the history of psychotherapy research at the National Institute of Mental Health (NIMH) for the forthcoming *Psychology and the NIMH* (Wade Pickren, Ed.).

William J. Lyddon, PhD, is professor of psychology and director of training of the American Psychological Association's accredited counseling psychology doctoral program in the Department of Psychology at the University of Southern Mississippi. He has served on the editorial board of several scholarly journals and is currently consulting editor of the *Counselling Psychology Quarterly*, assessing editor of the *Journal of Mind and Behavior*, and associate editor of the *Journal of Cognitive Psychotherapy*, published by Springer Publishing Company. Dr. Lyddon has published over 85 journal articles and book chapters and is the coeditor (with Dr. John V. Jones, Jr.) of *Empirically Supported Cognitive Therapies: Current and Future Applications* (2001), which is also available in Italian (2002) and Spanish (2003) editions.

Arthur (Art) Freeman, EdD, is professor and chair of the Department of Psychology and director of the doctoral program in clinical psychology at the Philadelphia College of Osteopathic Medicine; he is also on the core faculty of the Adler School of Professional Psychology. Art has published professional books and trade books on cognitive therapy, including *Woulda, Coulda, Shoulda: Overcoming Mistakes and Missed Opportunities*, and *The Ten Dumbest Mistakes Smart People Make, and How to Overcome Them*.

Cognitive Therapy and Dreams

Rachael I. Rosner, PhD
William J. Lyddon, PhD
Arthur Freeman, EdD
Editors

 Springer Publishing Company

Copyright © 2004 by Springer Publishing Company, Inc.

Springer Publishing Company, Inc.
536 Broadway
New York, NY 10012-3955

Acquisitions Editor: Sheri W. Sussman
Production Editor: Jeanne W. Libby
Cover design by Joanne E. Honigman

04 05 06 07 08/5 4 3 2 1

Library of Congress Cataloging-in-Publication Data

Cognitive therapy and dreams / Rachael I. Rosner, William J. Lyddon, Arthur Freeman, editors.
    p. ; cm.
    Expanded from a special issue of the Journal of cognitive psychotherapy.
    Includes bibliographical references and index.
    ISBN 0-8261-4745-3
    1. Cognitive therapy. 2. Dreams—Therapeutic use. 3. Dream interpretation.
    [DNLM: 1. Cognitive Therapy—Collected Works. 2. Dreams—Collected
Works. WM 425.5.C6 C6778 2004] I. Rosner, Rachael I. II. Lyddon,
William J. III. Freeman, Arthur, 1942– IV. Journal of cognitive psychotherapy.
    RC489.C63 C6478 2004
    616.89'42—dc22   2003067290

Printed in the United States of America by Integrated Book Technology.

Contents

Part III: Constructivist Approaches

Part IV: Future Directions

Contributors

João G. Barbosa, MA, studied psychology at the University of Poro and the University of Minho. He is currently director of Dynargie in Portugal and a clinical psychologist in private practice.

Deirdre Barrett, PhD, is a clinical assistant professor of psychology at Harvard Medical School specializing in brief psychodynamic psychotherapy, hypnotherapy, and dream work. She is the author of *The Committee of Sleep: How Artists, Scientists and Athletes Use Dreams for Creative Problem Solving—And How You Can Too* (2001) and *The Pregnant Man: And Other Cases from a Hypnotherapist's Couch* (1998), as well as editor of the book *Trauma and Dreams* (1996). She is past president of the Association for the Study of Dreams and editor-in-chief of the international journal *Dreaming.*

Aaron T. Beck, MD, is widely recognized as one of the founders of the cognitive therapy movement. He is university professor emeritus at the University of Pennsylvania School of Medicine and president of the Beck Institute for Cognitive Therapy and Research. He is the author or coauthor of 13 books on the use of cognitive therapy with a variety of disorders, including depression, substance abuse, anxiety disorders, personality disorders, and anger. His most recent book is entitled *Prisoners of Hate: The Cognitive Basis of Anger, Hostility, and Violence* (1999).

Rachel E. Crook, PhD, is an assistant professor in the Counseling Psychology and Special Education Department at Brigham Young University. She received her PhD in counseling psychology from the University of Maryland, College Park. She has authored two articles for the journal *Dreaming* (Journal for the Association for the Study of Dreams) and a book chapter on training therapists to work with the Hill Cognitive-Experiential model of dream work. Her other academic interests include training and supervising graduate students in counseling theories and practices, and teaching supervision theory.

Harold E. Doweiko, EdD, is a psychologist at the Gundersen-Lutheran Medical Center in LaCrosse, Wisconsin. He has published on the topics of substance abuse, neurobiology, and antisocial personality disorder and is the author of *Concepts of Chemical Dependency,* now in its fifth edition. He is currently working on the sixth edition, as well as on a text on crisis intervention scheduled for publication in 2005.

Óscar F. Gonçalves, PhD, is full professor and director of clinical psychology at the University of Minho, Portugal. He has written extensively on constructivism and narrative psychotherapy, including chapters on cognitive narrative psychotherapy for Michael Mahoney's *Cognitive and Constructive Psychotherapies: Theory, Research, and Practice* (1995), Neimeyer and Mahoney's *Constructivism in Psychotherapy* (1995), Neimeyer and Raskin's *Constructions of Disorder: Meaning-Making Frameworks for Psychotherapy* (2000), and Beutler and Malik's *Rethinking the DSM: A Psychological Perspective* (2002).

Clara E. Hill, PhD, is professor of psychology and codirector of the Counseling Psychology Program at the University of Maryland. Her major areas of research are psychotherapy process and outcome, dream interpretation, and counseling training and supervision. She is the author of *Therapist Techniques and Client Outcomes: Eight Cases of Brief Psychotherapy* (1989), *Working with Dreams in Psychotherapy* (1996), *Helping Skills: Facilitating Exploration, Insight, and Action* (1999), *Helping Skills: The Empirical Foundation* (2001), and *Working with Dreams in Therapy: Facilitating Exploration, Insight, and Action* (2003).

Barry Krakow, MD, is a board-certified internist and sleep specialist who has been active in the field of sleep, nightmares, insomnia, and mental health research since 1988. His research team, first at the University of New Mexico School of Medicine and now at the Sleep and Human Health Institute (SHHI) in Albuquerque, New Mexico, has developed a cognitive-imagery technique known as imagery rehearsal therapy (IRT) to treat chronic nightmares. IRT was developed with sexual assault survivors, crime victims, and disaster survivors, and these studies were published in *JAMA, Journal of Traumatic Stress, American Journal of Psychiatry,* and *Journal of Clinical Psychiatry.* IRT has been manualized, and a teaching program, "Turning Nightmares into Dreams," is available at *www.nightmaretreatment.com.*

Mia Leijssen, PhD, is professor in the Department of Psychology, Katholieke Universiteit, Leuven, Belgium, where she teaches experiential psychotherapy, integrative counseling skills, and professional ethics for psychologists. She has a practice in individual and group psychotherapy. She was trained as a client-centered therapist and received her training in focusing from Eugene Gendlin. Her doctoral research was on the effects of focusing training during ongoing short- and long-term psychotherapy. She has published many articles and book chapters on experiential psychotherapy and on professional ethics for psychotherapists. She has written *Gids voor Gesprekstherapie* (1999), a Dutch handbook on experiential psychotherapy.

Aaron B. Rochlen, PhD, earned his PhD in counseling psychology from the University of Maryland in 2000 and is now an assistant professor in the Department of Educational Psychology at the University of Texas. His areas of interest are career counseling, men's issues, and dream interpretation.

Beverly White is currently a fifth-year PsyD student at the Philadelphia College of Osteopathic Medicine.

Foreword

I am delighted to write the Foreword to *Cognitive Therapy and Dreams*, by Rosner, Lyddon, and Freeman. One might say, it's something I've always dreamed of! For many years, I have been interested in the expansion and development of cognitive therapy. I have observed and commented upon this expansion (Dowd, 2002) and participated in it (e.g., Dowd, 1997, 2000). Now Rosner, Lyddon, and Freeman—all three highly accomplished scholars—have carried it one step further.

Cognitive therapy has increasingly been seen as *the* integrative therapy (e.g., Alford & Norcross, 1991). Its conceptual power, research basis, and broad therapeutic technique armamentarium has placed it in the forefront of existing psychotherapies. Now its ability to incorporate one of the most psychodynamic of techniques—dream interpretation—without doing violence to the cognitive model has further demonstrated this considerable heuristic and technical power.

This book illustrates several polarities. Some of the chapters use dream interpretation as an extension of more standard cognitive therapy, looking for the cognitive distortions in this domain of human cognition as well. These might be called the "objectivist" chapters. Others describe the use of dreams from a more metaphorical meaning point of view. These might be called the "constructivist" chapters. Both polarities (and combinations in between) are now accepted and well-represented in the cognitive therapy literature. The book also nicely illustrates the phenomenon of "second-order change" within cognitive therapy (Dowd & Pace, 1989) and included in dream work.

Dream work also illustrates the power of experiential understanding and body work in cognitive therapy, described by Mahoney (1995). As Dowd (2000) has also written, cognitive therapy in the early 21st century is a great deal more than talk. It involves nonverbal cognitions (imagery) as well as embodiment techniques.

Dreams may be thought of as examples of tacit cognitive schemas (Dowd & Courchaine, 1996), core cognitive schemas (Beck, 1995), or Early Maladaptive Schemas (Young, 1999). As such, they are examples of what Freud might have called *primary processes* involving highly idiosyncratic and metaphorical, non-veridical cognitions and are at a considerable theoretical distance from the original notion that dream contents have standard meanings.

This book contains chapters by writers who are not part of the cognitive therapy literature. I was impressed with how easily their ideas (e.g., Focusing, Imagery Rehearsal Therapy) fit within the cognitive therapy model, once again demonstrating the integrative power of the model.

While not strictly a treatment manual, this book contains enough treatment descriptions and client-therapist typescripts so that a sophisticated reader will be able to understand and implement the techniques without too much difficulty. I was surprised how close some of the concepts and techniques were to those with which I was already familiar, e.g., hypnotherapy.

I urge all cognitive therapists whose clients have ever asked them about their dreams to read this book. They, as I was, will be impressed with this further expansion and development of the cognitive therapy model.

E. Thomas Dowd, Ph.D., ABPP
Department of Psychology
Kent State University

REFERENCES

Alford, B. A., & Norcross, J. C. (1991). Cognitive therapy as integrative therapy. *Journal of Psychotherapy Integration, 1,* 175–190.

Beck, J. S. (1995). *Cognitive therapy: Basics and beyond.* New York: Guilford.

Dowd, E. T. (1997). The use of hypnosis in cognitive-developmental therapy. In R. L. Leahy (Ed.), *Practicing cognitive therapy: A guide to interventions.* Livingston, NJ: Jason Aronson.

Dowd, E. T. (2000). *Cognitive hypnotherapy.* Livingston, NJ: Jason Aronson.

Dowd, E. T. (2002). History and recent developments in cognitive psychotherapy. In R. L. Leahy & E. T. Dowd (Eds.), *Clinical advances in cognitive psychotherapy: Theory and application.* New York: Springer.

Dowd, E. T., & Courchaine, K. E. (1996). Implicit learning, tacit knowledge, and implications for stasis and change in cognitive psychotherapy. *Journal of Cognitive Psychotherapy: An International Quarterly, 10,* 163–180.

Dowd, E. T., & Pace, T. M. (1989). The relativity of reality: Second-order change in psychotherapy. In A. E. Freeman, K. M. Simon, L. Beutler, & H. Arkowitz (Eds.), *Comprehensive handbook of cognitive therapy.* New York: Plenum.

Mahoney, M. J. (1995). Theoretical developments in the cognitive and constructivistic psychotherapies. In M. J. Mahoney (Ed.), *Cognitive and constructivistic psychotherapies: Theory, research, and practice.* New York: Springer.

Young, J. E. (1999). *Cognitive therapy for personality disorders: A schema-focused approach* (4th ed.). Sarasota, FL: Professional Resources Exchange.

Preface

The idea for this book germinated in the mind of a client in cognitive therapy and blossomed into a research idea as the therapist and client discovered, collaboratively, a framework for using dreams in a clinical context. The client was in treatment for depression and had begun to experience an increasing number of intense dreams as therapy progressed. The therapist had been trained in cognitive therapy and had only a rudimentary framework for incorporating dream work into the therapeutic agenda. The client nonetheless was keen to do dream work, and so over the course of treatment the therapist and client developed a series of hypotheses about what the dream images might mean, as well as a system for discovering and challenging automatic thoughts and cognitive distortions within the dream images. Dream work became a regular item on each week's session agenda and proved to be instrumental to the client's success in treatment. Both the client and the therapist noted, however, the absence of any systematic technique for working with dreams in cognitive therapy, and they agreed that this topic was worthy of much more theoretical, clinical, and experimental attention.

At the time this client was in treatment, virtually no research had been done on cognitive therapy and dreams. Indeed, until the early to mid-1990s cognitive therapists were much more concerned with putting cognitive therapy (and cognitive-behavioral therapy) on the map, distinguishing themselves from psychoanalysts, and demonstrating empirical support for this new treatment than with the pursuit of dreams and other perceived esoterica. Dreams, to many cognitive therapists, were a hallmark of the psychoanalytic method, which connoted the presence of an unconscious, of drives, wishes, motivations—the very constructs that cognitive therapists rejected. And yet clients didn't make the distinction between cognitive therapy and psychoanalysis, and not only were they dreaming but they were coming to therapy with the hope of making sense out of their dreams. Dreams were, and have continued to be, clinical data that cognitive therapists encounter. Until recently cognitive therapists have had the choice either of ignoring dream data entirely or of improvising a system on the spot for working with them, as did this therapist and client.

Inspired by clinical experience with this and other clients, I began to ask historical and theoretical questions about the relationship between cognitive therapy and dreams and about the history of cognitive therapy itself (Rosner, 1997). A literature search on cognitive therapy and dreams conducted in 1994 suggested that a few researchers from the mainstream of cognitive therapy, notably Beck (1971) and Freeman and Boyll (1992), had flirted with dreams in the formative and early years of the movement. By the mid-1990s an interest in dreams appeared to be blossoming within the emerging constructivist wing of cognitive therapy—in the hands, for instance, of Óscar Gonçalves (Gonçalves & Craine, 1992; Gonçalves, 1995) and David Edwards (Edwards, 1989), who were making arguments about dreams similar to George Kelly's personal construct theory of dreams in the 1950s (Kelly, 1991). Others, too, working at the intersection of cognitive therapy and experiential therapy, notably Clara Hill (Hill, 1996), had begun to develop impressive research programs on dreams. Deirdre Barrett, who was trained as a psychodynamic therapist, also was beginning to experiment with short-term, solution-focused dream work (Barrett, 1996).

In 1997, Bill Lyddon, associate editor of the *Journal of Cognitive Psychotherapy*, invited me to guest-edit a special issue on cognitive therapy and dreams—an invitation that offered an opportunity to bring together researchers from disparate research strands to introduce their work in this area to cognitive therapists (Rosner, Lyddon, & Freeman, 2002). With the publication of this volume, Bill Lyddon, Art Freeman, and I have been able to expand the previous forum to include the work of Barry Krakow (who is using imagery rehearsal to reduce nightmares), Mia Leijssen (who is expanding Gendlin's work on focusing and dreams), and Rachel Crook (who has surveyed the attitudes of cognitive therapists toward dreams and compared them with those of psychodynamic and eclectic therapists). This collection of projects is not exhaustive but rather representative of current work, and new projects continue to emerge, such as the article on "dream-mediated cognitive therapy" of Matsuda and Kasuga, which hopefully will be translated into English.

Looking back over the years since I first encountered dreams clinically, I am most struck by the fact that this new field has grown primarily in the hands of clinicians eager to expand beyond the traditional boundaries of cognitive therapy. There is something about dreams that penetrates deep into the heart of any theory of psychotherapy, including cognitive therapy, and those in pursuit of dreams have had to reexamine fundamental aspects of the cognitive model. Their integrative approaches to dreams, in turn, have begun to fill in some of the holes in the cognitive model itself. In addition, they offer a variety of ways of approaching dreams with theoretical, clinical, and experimental integrity while also retaining the distinctive qualities of the cognitive therapy treatment approach—practical, directive, and solution-focused. Many of the models and manuals herein have been built from the ground up, from the basis of clinical experience and clinical hypothesis, with a spirit of theoretical integration and technical eclecticism. I hope that this book will serve as the next step not only in introducing these researchers to each other but also in introducing them to clinicians and researchers more broadly. I also hope that it will foster continued efforts to build a comprehensive, integrative, and empirically supported foundation from which cognitive therapists can approach dreams with enthusiasm, confidence, and a spirit of collaborative adventure.

Rachael Rosner

REFERENCES

Barrett, D. (Ed.). (1996). *Trauma and dreams.* Cambridge, MA: Harvard University Press.

Beck, A. T. (1971). Cognitive patterns in dreams and daydreams. In J. H. Masserman (Ed.), *Dream dynamics: Science and psychoanalysis* (Vol. 19, pp. 2–7). New York: Grune & Stratton.

Edwards, D. J. A. (1989). Cognitive restructuring through guided imagery: Lessons from Gestalt therapy. In A. Freeman, K. M. Simon, L. E. Beutler, & H. Arkowitz (Eds.), *Comprehensive handbook of cognitive therapy* (pp. 283–297). New York: Plenum.

Freeman, A. (1981). Dreams and images in cognitive therapy. In G. Emery, S. D. Hollon, & R. C. Bedrosian (Eds.), *New directions in cognitive therapy* (pp. 224–238). New York and London: Guilford Press.

Freeman, A., & Boyll, S. (1992). The use of dreams and the dream metaphor in cognitive-behavior therapy. *Psychotherapy in Private Practice, 4,* 173–192.

Gonçalves, Ó., & Craine, M. H. (1992). *The use of metaphors in cognitive therapy.* Unpublished manuscript.

Gonçalves, Ó. F. (1995). Hermeneutics, constructivism, and cognitive-behavioral therapies: From the object to the project. In R. A. Neimeyer & M. J. Mahoney (Eds.), *Constructivism in psychotherapy* (pp. 195–230). Washington, DC: American Psychological Association.

Hill, C. (1996). *Working with dreams in psychotherapy.* New York and London: Guilford Press.

Kelly, G. (1991). *The psychology of personal constructs: Volume two—Clinical diagnosis and psychotherapy.* London and New York: Routledge.

Matsuda, E., & Kasuga, T. (1998). A new psychotherapeutic approach: A proposal of Dream Mediated Cognitive Therapy (DMCT). *Japanese Journal of Counseling Science, 31,* 310–319.

Rosner, R. I. (1997). Cognitive therapy, constructivism, and dreams: A critical review. *Journal of Constructivist Psychology, 10,* 249–273.

Rosner, R. I., Lyddon, W. J., & Freeman, A. (Eds.). (2002). Cognitive therapy and dreams. *Journal of Cognitive Psychotherapy, 16*(1)(Special issue).

Acknowledgments

An idea doesn't get very far without the support of a lot of people. Specifically, I would like to thank Bill Lyddon, who is most responsible for opening doors for this research and, ultimately, for the appearance of this book. His collaborative spirit and willingness to serve as mentor have been as instrumental in my development as a scholar as in the development of this book. Thanks to my parents and family for their support. Finally, I would like to thank Larry Denenberg, applied mathematician extraordinaire, who has an uncanny knack for recognizing distortions in thinking. He embodies what is best in the cognitive model every day.

RR

I want to extend my deep appreciation to the many students, colleagues, and mentors who have played a significant role in my personal and professional development. For their specific contributions to this book, I would like to thank Dodie Gillette for her painstaking attention to detail in the manuscript preparation process and to Darlys Alford for her helpful editorial assistance and suggestions throughout this project.

WJL

Special thanks are due to our editor, Sheri W. Sussman, who has helped keep us on track and whose steady hand on the tiller has helped bring this volume to completion.

I would like to thank my wife Sharon for her encouragement, keen eye, useful critique, and unconditional positive regard. She could give Carl Rogers lessons.

AF

PART I

Historical Contexts

CHAPTER 1

Cognitive Therapy and Dreams: An Introduction

RACHAEL I. ROSNER
WILLIAM J. LYDDON
ARTHUR FREEMAN

In the last few years cognitive therapists, particularly therapists working at the intersection of cognitive therapy and other therapeutic traditions, have found a new interest in dreams. One of the more interesting results of the current integrationist climate is that cognitive therapists have begun looking in directions previously considered taboo or irrelevant for their work—toward modern psychoanalysis, gestalt therapy, constructivist psychotherapy, and neurobiology, for instance—to explore topics traditionally outside the purview of cognitive therapy, including dreams. This trend is reciprocal; contemporary psychoanalytic researchers such as Drew Westen (Westen, 1991, 2000) or experiential therapists such as Clara Hill (Hill, 1996) have turned to cognitive therapy in the same spirit. The appearance of this book on a topic heretofore ignored in the cognitive therapy literature is an indication of the fruitful creativity, and of the shifting needs and interests, in a cognitive therapy community that is rapidly expanding its boundaries.

THEMES AND COMMENTARY

This volume contains a representative sample of some of the most interesting and promising work on dreams coming from therapists and researchers working at the crossroads of cognitive therapy and other systems—from a reprint of Beck's only article on cognitions and dreams (Beck, 1971) to the influence of modern neurobiology on the use of dreams in cognitive therapy. Consequently the contributions contained herein present a variety of arguments, sometimes contradictory, about how cognitive therapy is best equipped for using dreams clinically. Some of the contributors believe that the rational and logical manipulations of classical cognitive therapy should be used to challenge those assumptions and beliefs associated with a client's dream; others suggest that the client might more profitably benefit from an exploration of the subjective and metaphorical aspects of the dream. This difference parallels the contemporary distinction between objectivist and constructivist views in the cognitive therapy tradition (Lyddon, 1995; Mahoney, 1990; Neimeyer & Stewart, 2000). Because the authors tend to cluster into either the objectivist or constructivist positions, the book is organized around these two basic epistemologies. Our hope is that this organizational scheme will encourage readers to discover where the authors tend to diverge in their theoretical and epistemological commitments and, at the same time, where they tend to converge in their understanding and use of dreams in cognitive therapy (akin to highlighting common factors).

Section I, "Historical Contexts," sets the stage for the contemporary scene of cognitive therapy and dreams with an overview of the history and sociology of dream work in cognitive therapy. It begins with a historical look at the work of Aaron T. Beck, who developed a rudimentary cognitive theory of dreams in the late 1960s. Beck's cognitive dream theory was rooted in his early psychoanalytic dream research and was spurred by his interest in finding common factors between cognitive therapy and behavior therapy. Rosner (chapter 2) provides an overview of the intellectual and social history behind the development of Beck's dream theory and behind his decision to stop pursuing dream research in the early 1970s. Rosner's chapter is followed by a reprint of the only article that Beck published on cognitions and dreams (chapter 3), an article that was published originally in 1971 in the proceedings of the American Academy of Psychoanalysis. In this article Beck argues that dreams reflect the same constellation of cognitions about the self, the world, and the future that can be seen in waking ideation (automatic thoughts). Beck did not pursue any theoretical, clinical, or experimental work on dreams after 1971, and dreams drew a very small, if any, degree of clinical and experimental attention in the emergent cognitive-behavior therapy movement of the 1970s and 1980s. In chapter 4 Crook brings us to the present by opening a window onto contemporary attitudes toward dream work among cognitive therapists in private practice and comparing them with the attitudes of psychodynamic therapists and eclectic therapists.

Section II, "Objectivist Approaches," represents contemporary cognitive dream work coming out of the objectivist tradition, including those therapists most closely associated with mainstream cognitive and cognitive-behavioral approaches. Beck had suggested in 1971 that the dominant cognitive patterns (or schemata) of waking life not only structure the content of waking ideational experiences but also have the capacity to exert varying degrees of influence on dreams. As a result, he suggested, dream reports in clinical contexts might function as a kind of "biopsy" of the client's dysfunctional schemata. Doweiko (chapter 5) and Freeman and White (chapter 6), working in the Beckian tradition, suggest that the themes of a client's manifest dream content often reflect the client's waking cognitive distortions. The dreams, they argue, are amenable to the same cognitive restructuring and "reality" testing procedures that may be applied to the client's "nondream" realm of automatic thoughts and beliefs.

Consistent with Beck's 1971 conjecture, Doweiko (chapter 5) draws upon developments in the neurobiology of dreaming to point out that when a waking person relates the content of a dream, he or she will necessarily impose a structure onto the dream that will include the same cognitive distortions that he or she may use to interpret other aspects of experience. In this same vein, Freeman and White (chapter 6) integrate Adlerian dream theory into the objectivist cognitive model to suggest that clients should be encouraged to report their dreams in therapy as a way of understanding in greater depth the constellation of cognitive distortions that relate to their particular disorders.

Krakow (chapter 7) comes not from the tradition of Beck but from the perspectives of internal medicine and behavior therapy. His imagery rehearsal therapy (IRT) has been developed with groups of survivors of sexual abuse suffering from posttraumatic stress disorder (PTSD) to reduce the number, intensity, and intrusiveness of nightmares. IRT does not penetrate deep into the meaning and symbolism of dreams; rather, it works at the manifest behavioral level to help patients reduce the intrusiveness of nightmares. Krakow argues that while the original nightmare may have helped patients to process and assimilate traumatic experiences, recurrent nightmares are equivalent to noxious stimuli to which the patient becomes conditioned. Repeated rehearsals of alternate imagery offer the patients a feeling of mastery over the intrusive and noxious stimuli and help them sleep through the night. Improved sleep, Krakow suggests, is then instrumental in reducing other symptoms of PTSD.

The authors of the chapters in Section III, "Constructivist Approaches," by way of contrast, encourage clients to enter deep into the metaphorical, subjective, and affective experiences in their dreams, consistent with the constructivist perspective. Barrett (chapter 8) brings the perspective of modern psychodynamic theory to argue that (a) dreams function as powerful, condensed metaphors, and (b) modern, psychodynamic dream work may function as a useful shortcut for getting at a client's idiosyncratic cognitive patterns and meanings. Barrett illustrates the functional value of dreams with examples from the treatment areas of bereavement, depression, trauma, cross-cultural counseling, and behavioral medicine. From more of a decidedly constructivist (and specifically narrative-constructivist) perspective, Gonçalves and Barbosa (chapter 9) describe a cognitive, narrative approach to dream work designed to (a) expand the client's sensorial, emotional, and cognitive experience and (b) allow for the emergence of a coherent and meaningful dream narrative organized around a central or root metaphor. Once the metaphor is constructed, the client is encouraged to project an alternative and potentially more viable dream metaphor.

The last two chapters present contrasting integrations of experiential therapy and cognitive therapy that emphasize the use of dreams. Leijssen (chapter 10) brings the unique bodily perspective of Eugene Gendlin's focusing technique (Gendlin, 1996) to cognitive therapy by suggesting that the lived and "felt sense" of cognitions in dreams can enrich and deepen therapeutic work. Leijssen's five steps of entering, elaborating on, and challenging dream images introduce the experience of the body, as it tells and inhabits dreams, as an additional source of information in testing hypotheses. In a similar vein, Hill and Rochlen's cognitive-experiential model of dream work (chapter 11) underscores an active and creative role for clients as they explore their dreams, achieve insights into the meaning of their dreams, and take action by making changes in their dreams (and in their lives). It is important to note that in the methods suggested by Barrett, Gonçalves and Barbosa, Leijssen, and Hill and Rochlen, the therapist is *not* the expert who either knows the meaning of the dream or who can make judgments about the validity or rationality of the dream *content*. Rather, the therapist is the expert in the *process* of helping the client to explore and make meaning of the dream and to use this new meaning to guide future decisions and actions.

Contributors from both the objectivist and constructivist epistemological traditions, despite the differences in their theoretical backgrounds, tend to agree on a number of theoretical points about dreams from the cognitive perspective. Virtually all of them acknowledge that the dream generator is a primitive process that develops in childhood, that exists at the periphery of our consciousness, and that is superseded in waking life by higher-level processes. While Freud believed that the primitive process was a force against which the individual had to defend, all of the authors here adhere to the notion that the system that generates the dream speaks directly to us without the use of symbols. Indeed, while the contributors come from very different therapeutic traditions, they all agree that dreams reflect the concerns, worries, and desires of our conscious, waking lives. To them, dreams are neither mysterious nor secret symbols from a hidden, impulse-driven, and inaccessible place. Rather, they are messages from a part of our conscious selves that speaks verbally, visually, and metaphorically. Dreams are also connected to affective experiences, and so, we argue, cognitive therapists can appreciate dreams as the ultimate form of "hot cognition," densely packed morsels of cognitive and affective experiences that bridge the patterns of meaning making from our earliest preverbal experiences in childhood with the current thoughts and concerns of everyday life. They constitute a direct link—without the need of expert interpretation—to the clients' cognitive and affective schemata.

How might cognitive therapists draw practical conclusions out of this assortment of perspectives? First, contributors from both perspectives tend to use dreams as valuable diagnostic aids for determining problematic attitudes and beliefs. Furthermore, the contributors are virtually unanimous in arguing that reliving and/or restructuring dream themes in waking life has therapeutic value for clients in cognitive therapy. While they propose different manuals and techniques for accessing, experiencing, manipulating, and then acting on dream themes, these differences are variations on a theme, some emphasizing rational restructuring and others emphasizing subjective and lived experiences. All of these techniques for dream work, however, can be used in a manner consistent with cognitive, cognitive-behavioral, and integrationist therapeutic approaches. Many of the contributors offer further suggestions on how clinicians can modify their manuals to fit within the constraints of more time-limited and solution-focused therapeutic contexts.

Perhaps of equal importance is the fact that these chapters, when taken together, provide a kind of metatheory of dreams that is unique to the cognitive perspective. As such, they begin the process of generating a comprehensive cognitive model of dream work that includes cognitive, affective, physical, and behavioral features from which future research and clinical innovations can be built. On an even broader level, these authors are beginning to question with new eyes some of the most fundamental assumptions of cognitive therapy: What are the type of cognitions that cognitive therapy purports to modify—are they verbal, visual, body sensations, or all of the above? What is the relationship between emotions and cognitions when they are so intimately conjoined in phenomena like dreams? How do therapists and scientists approach a phenomenon that is particularly difficult to measure and manipulate?

Beck argued in 1970 that "cognitive therapy may be defined . . . as a set of operations focused on a patient's cognitions (verbal or pictorial) and on the premises, assumptions, and attitudes underlying these cognitions" (Beck, 1970, p. 187). All of the contributions to this book, despite the variety of traditions they represent, would meet Beck's criteria for cognitive therapy. It is our hope that they also shed light on some of the deeper and more neglected areas of the cognitive model itself.

REFERENCES

Beck, A. T. (1970). Cognitive therapy: Nature and relation to behavior therapy. *Behavior Therapy, 1*, 184–200.

Beck, A. T. (1971). Cognitive patterns in dreams and daydreams. In J. H. Masserman (Ed.), *Scientific proceedings of the American Academy of Psychoanalysis: Vol. 19. Dream dynamics: Science and psychoanalysis* (pp. 2–7). New York: Grune & Stratton.

Gendlin, E. T. (1996). *Focusing-oriented psychotherapy: A manual for the experiential method*. New York: Guilford.

Hill, C. E. (1996). *Working with dreams in psychotherapy*. New York: Guilford.

Lyddon, W. J. (1995). Forms and facets of constructivist psychology. In R. A. Neimeyer & M. J. Mahoney (Eds.), *Constructivism in psychotherapy* (pp. 69–92). Washington, DC: American Psychological Association.

Mahoney, M. J. (1990). *Human change processes*. New York: Basic Books.

Neimeyer, R. A., & Stewart, A. E. (2000). Constructivist and narrative psychotherapies. In C. R. Snyder & R. E. Ingram (Eds.), *Handbook of psychological change: Psychotherapy processes and practices for the 21st century* (pp. 337–357). New York: John Wiley & Sons.

Westen, D. (1991). Cognitive-behavioral interventions in the psychoanalytic psychotherapy of borderline personality disorders. *Clinical Psychology Review, 11*, 211–230.

Westen, D. (2000). Integrative psychotherapy: Integrating psychodynamic and cognitive-behavioral theory and technique. In C. R. Snyder & R. E. Ingram (Eds.), *Handbook of psychological change: Psychotherapy processes and practices for the 21st century* (pp. 217–242). New York: John Wiley & Sons.

CHAPTER 2

Aaron T. Beck's Dream Theory in Context: An Introduction to His 1971 Article on Cognitive Patterns in Dreams and Daydreams

RACHAEL I. ROSNER*

In 1995 at the outset of my dissertation research on the history of cognitive therapy I asked Aaron Beck if he might clarify several conundrums I had observed about his break from psychoanalysis. One of these conundrums involved his flirtation with dreams in the early years of cognitive therapy. The latest date for which I could find any publication on dreams was 1971, well beyond his break with psychoanalysis and the formulation of cognitive therapy, with his "Cognitive Patterns in Dreams and Daydreams." Yet he published this article in a psychoanalytic journal. Beck had argued only a

*The writing of this chapter was supported by a postdoctoral fellowship from the National Science Foundation. Research for the chapter was supported by a York University Dissertation Completion Grant and Ontario Scholarships. The author thanks Dr. Aaron T. Beck for access to his personal correspondence and Susan Lanzoni and Debbie Weinstein for comments on an earlier draft.

year before (Beck, 1970a) that cognitive therapy should be seen as a school separate from psychoanalysis. Why did he publish his most significant article on cognitive therapy and dreams in a psychoanalytic journal? Since the data were so limited, I asked him almost on a whim if there was any chance that he was working toward psychotherapy integration even in the early years of cognitive therapy.[1]

Beck's response was surprising. He indeed had hoped to find common ground with psychoanalysts in the early years of cognitive therapy and to "break out of the bondage of predefined approaches of psychoanalysis and behavior therapy."[2] This article, he indicated in his response, was part of that effort. But the psychoanalysts did not respond with enough enthusiasm to encourage his collaborative plans. My own research, drawn from personal interviews, his private correspondences, and his unpublished manuscripts, has borne out the answer he gave in 1995 (Beck, 1991; Rosner, 1999).

Still, questions remain about the place of dreams in cognitive therapy. This 1971 article seems to have had little impact on either psychoanalysis or cognitive therapy, given that it is rarely cited in the literature. And after 1971 Beck abandoned all work on dreams. Clearly, after 1971 he did not feel that dreams were particularly important for cognitive therapy. Thus, even if Beck was seeking common factors in the early years, the value of dreams for cognitive therapy remains unclear. What is the value of reprinting and giving so much historical attention to an otherwise forgotten article from his remote past? How can a historical analysis of Beck's early cognitive dream theory be of use to contemporary therapists?

I hope to show that this otherwise unknown article exposes dreams as essential instruments in the development of cognitive therapy itself and that Beck did not abandon dreams as much as it might appear. I will argue that there were two phases, or chapters, of Beck's career in which dreams played a pivotal role. First, Beck's early psychoanalytic dream research in the late 1950s and early 1960s was part of a broader effort to become proficient at large-sample social science research. The dream research inspired him to question the experimental and theoretical viability of drive theory, leading him to reject this central feature of psychoanalysis and to develop the cognitive model in response.

Second, Beck returned to the study of dreams in the late 1960s, after the cognitive model was in place, in an effort to find a community of like-minded therapists in which to plant the seeds of his new approach. In this context, he developed a rudimentary cognitive theory of dreams that emphasized common factors. Beck demonstrated to psychoanalysts that cognitive therapy was commensurate with neo-Freudian schools such as Adler and Horney. At the same time, he used these cognitive ideas about daydreams and fantasies to illustrate the compatibility of cognitive therapy with behavior therapy. The behavior therapy community embraced this work with more enthusiasm than the psychoanalytic community. Beck abandoned dreams, in part, because the pressures against psychoanalysis in behavior therapy were too great to overcome his common factors philosophy. Still, this article, when viewed in context, not only illustrates the depth of Beck's indebtedness to dreams for cognitive therapy but also shows that dreams fostered the enduring bond between cognitive therapy, psychoanalysis, and behavior therapy that has resurfaced in the common factors spirit of our own time. In this sense, Beck's story can inspire contemporary cognitive therapists to reach beyond their familiar theoretical territory to explore the clinical value of dream data.

BECK AND THE TRADITION OF EXPERIMENTAL DREAM RESEARCH IN PSYCHOANALYSIS

Beck began studying dreams in the late 1950s as a junior-level professor in the Department of Psychiatry at the University of Pennsylvania and as a psychoanalytic candidate at the Philadelphia Psychoanalytic Institute (Rosner, 1999). Beck's psychiatric training did not equip him particularly well for research. Psychiatrists in the 1950s were trained to be clinicians, and very few of them had any experimental research skills. Virtually all psychoanalytic research, when it was done, was based on the case study method. I mention Beck's early training (or lack thereof) in experimental research because his work on dreams is an outgrowth of what became an intense desire in his early professional life to become proficient in large-sample experimental science.

Beck did not enter the world of experimental dream research completely ill-equipped, however. He had inherited a protoexperimental tradition of dream study from Leon Saul, his psychoanalytic mentor (and training analyst) at the University of Pennsylvania, who had inherited it from his own mentor, Franz Alexander. Beck followed in a rather unique tradition that used quantitative methods to study psychoanalytic material. His mentors also were among the first analysts to study manifest dream themes, as they could be quantified and evaluated with greater ease than latent themes. Their interest in manifest content reflected an increasing interest in the ego rather than in the id and libido. Leon Saul extended some of Alexander's measures in the 1950s with a series of comprehensive rating systems of ego functions in manifest dream themes.[3] Saul was interested in articulating how the ego managed hostility in different diagnostic conditions, most notably hypertension (Saul, 1940; Saul et al., 1954; Saul & Sheppard, 1956).

Beck conducted his first scientific experiment on dreams as a member of Saul's research team (Beck & Hurvich, 1959). Beck and a graduate student in psychology, Marvin Hurvich, tested whether or not hostility might be manifest in depression. They hypothesized that depression was a form of inverted hostility and that themes of being thwarted, rejected, losing, and quitting would appear with statistical significance in the manifest dream themes of depressed patients. They built the Masochism Scale to determine the frequency of these themes. They found that the dreams of depressed patients did show a relatively higher frequency of unpleasant affect relative to nondepressed patients (Beck & Hurvich, 1959),[4] and they argued that manifest dreams of depressed patients supported the psychoanalytic postulate of inverted hostility. Beck replicated these findings with a larger study on dreams that was part of an NIMH-sponsored depression research project (Beck & Ward, 1961). Beck and his colleagues on this project suggested that masochistic dreams occurred in depressed patients even in the absence of an acute depressive episode. They argued that masochistic dreams could be "more properly regarded as related to certain personality characteristics of individuals who may develop depressions" (Beck & Ward, 1961, p. 70). Both of these studies supported the psychoanalytic propositions that depression was a form of inverted hostility and that depressed patients evidenced a wish to suffer.

I argued in my dissertation that Beck struggled during these years, however, to reconcile in his own mind the two worldviews of psychoanalysis and experimental science (Rosner, 1999). While he had been trained to raise psychoanalytic theory above the level of doubt, the epistemology of experimental science was requiring him to trust *data* rather than theory. Indeed, one of the most distinguishing features of Beck's early psychoanalytic dream research was not his psychoanalytic ideas per se but rather his commitment to modernizing psychiatric research with the more sophisticated statistical techniques and experimental methods of the social sciences. He hired Marvin Hurvich, for instance, particularly for his expertise in large-sample experimental research methods. At this stage of his career, Beck remained committed to psychoanalytic theory. But these psychoanalytic dream studies belied a central tension in Beck's mind between psychoanalysis and science that he had not yet fully resolved (Rosner, 1999).

Ultimately, I would like to argue, Beck privileged experimental science over psychoanalysis. In other words, he privileged method over theory, and this decision set the stage for the emergence of cognitive therapy. In the 1960s, Beck was extraordinarily committed to a worldview that privileged the place of the scientist. Two particularly instructive examples of the depth of

Beck's commitment to experimentalism in the 1960s illustrate the increasing inseparability of the epistemology of experimental science from his clinical and theoretical innovations: His decision to use experimental techniques inside the therapy room for clinical purposes in the early 1960s and his decision in the mid-1960s to reevaluate and reinterpret the findings of his psychoanalytic dream research.

Cognitive therapists are intimately aware of the basic techniques of cognitive therapy; they usually are not as aware, however, of the historical conditions that fostered their development. Beck had been making clinical observations about the role of cognitions in psychopathology since the late 1950s.[5] He had even published some of those observations in an article on psychodynamics in 1961 (Beck & Stein, 1961). I would like to suggest that Beck did not initiate clinical innovations based on those observations until he had decided that the future of his professional life depended on embracing wholeheartedly the worldview of scientific research—after he and Hurvich had published their dream monograph and under the influence of his large NIMH-sponsored depression research project.

His clinical innovations based on those observations, which he undertook with considerable urgency in the late 1960s, brought the ethos of the laboratory directly into the therapy room. In the early 1960s Beck, like George Kelley before him, began to teach patients to become scientists in their own mental laboratories.[6] Cognitive therapy from its inception, it could be argued, was a program of scientific training (Beck, 1967, p. 569; Rosner, 1999). Beck taught his patients first to identify their cognitive distortions, otherwise known as automatic thoughts (clinical observation), and then to recognize that these distortions were beliefs that could be tested objectively. He trained his patients to reexamine and challenge the evidence (experimental testing). Finally, he encouraged them to espouse a new and more objective interpretation of the facts (theory).[7]

The second example is from a project begun in 1962 that included, but was not limited to, the dream research. At the close of his NIMH depression research project in 1962, Beck decided to summarize his findings, including his dream research and some of his very early cognitive formulations, in monograph form.[8] This monograph would situate his depression research within the broader medical and psychological literature and point the way to future theories and research projects. Beck also approached the book with a missionary zeal to provide his psychiatric colleagues with a guidebook on how to conduct proper experimental science.[9] He wanted the monograph, therefore, not to follow a chronological progression of his discoveries about depression but rather to follow "a sequence of steps in the development of the research project . . . in terms of the specific conceptual and methodological problems. These would be taken up in a systematic way and the various techniques used in solving these problems would be discussed."[10]

The monograph in question became Beck's 1967 *Depression: Clinical, Experimental, and Theoretical Aspects*, reprinted in 1970 as *Depression: Causes and Treatment* (Beck, 1967, 1970d). The book's narrative followed the signposts of its subtitle: Beck took the readers on a journey from clinical observation to large-scale experimental testing to the emergence of a grounded theory with clinical applications—the very steps necessary for systematic experimental research. It is unfortunate that Beck modified the subtitle of his book when it was reprinted in 1972; the original subtitle offered a wealth of information about the centrality of methodological considerations to his expertise in depression. But cognitive therapy owes its existence in part, I am arguing, to Beck's decision to give the greatest weight to the epistemology of experimental science. Beck positioned cognitive therapy in the 1967 book as the theoretical (and clinical) result of having followed these stages of scientific research.

Beck's ongoing dream research was one of the central locations in which he transformed himself scientifically. Indeed, one of the most significant events in the evolution of cognitive therapy was his decision to reexamine and reinterpret the dream data from the NIMH project in 1962 that he documented publicly in 1967 (Beck, 1967). Beck discovered that the data did not necessarily validate the inverted hostility hypothesis, as he and his colleagues had previously believed. While the depressed subjects did have unpleasant dreams with masochistic content, the manifest themes did not show any *wish* to suffer (Beck, 1967). The data only supported the fact that depressed patients suffered. Beck (1967) reported that "since the (wish) could not be demonstrated directly in the clinical material, the (psychodynamic) formulations could not be subjected to direct test" (p. 171).

Beck decided to address this problem by making a methodological change in his research. "As the research developed," he wrote, "I attempted to circumvent these methodological problems by . . . [staying] at the level of the patient's experiences [rather] than to infer some underlying process" (Beck, 1967, p. 171). Beck decided not to look for wishes at all but rather merely to generate hypotheses about the patients' experiences that could easily be identified, quantified, and evaluated. But this decision had theoretical consequences for Beck. Not only were wishes inaccessible methodologically, he concluded, but they were simply not there to be found. Without the cornerstone of a wish, "the whole formulation of the need to suffer collapses" (p. 171). Beck rejected drive theory altogether, including the existence of defense mechanisms and symbolism. "The focusing on the material," he wrote, "in terms of the patient's perception of himself and of external reality gradually shifted the emphasis from a motivational model to a cognitive model" (p. 172). He argued that his new clinical approach, what he was calling "Cognitive (Insight) Psychotherapy," reflected more accurately the clinical and experimental data he had collected (Beck, 1967, p. 318). The 1967 book marked Beck's first public admission that he was moving away from psychoanalysis toward a new cognitive therapy, and his dream research and the epistemology of experimental science played central roles in that journey.

BECK'S 1971 "COGNITIVE PATTERNS IN DREAMS AND DAYDREAMS" IN CONTEXT

Beck devoted much less time to dream research after the publication of his 1967 book on depression. He had briefly considered conducting a series of experiments on the dreams of depressed and suicidal patients as part of a larger project for which he had received new NIMH funding in the late 1960s. Beck also wanted to test the hypothesis that there was a continuity between the manifest content of dreams and EEG records collected during the night.[11] But these studies would have required the use of a sleep laboratory, which exceeded the proposed budget for his NIMH grant, and they were never conducted.[12] For these and other reasons dreams receded into the periphery of his gaze as a scientist.

However, Beck drew on his expertise as a psychoanalytic dream researcher and clinician to reach his broader goal of finding a community for cognitive therapy. In the late 1960s Beck began to publish on dreams again, this time elaborating a cognitive theory of dreams that, I am arguing, he used in two contexts and for two purposes: to establish himself as a neo-Freudian revisionist and to articulate the value of cognitive therapy for behavior therapists. Beck worked on the theory relatively briefly, from 1968 to 1971, and he published only two articles on cognitions and dreams specifically, the more significant of which is reprinted here (Beck, 1969,[13] 1971). Nonetheless, the new dream theory was an extremely valuable tool as he searched for an audience for his new school of psychotherapy. He used dreams as a way of demonstrating the virtues of common factors, or what he was calling a "broad-spectrum" approach. This philosophy was instrumental in Beck's success in bringing cognitive therapy to national attention.

Beck's new cognitive dream theory argued that dreams were ideational cousins of automatic thoughts, sitting along a continuum of irrational cognitions, otherwise known as schemas, that follows a unique pattern specific to particular disorders (Beck, 1971). He believed there was a continuity between the idiosyncratic cognitive patterns in waking life, which take the form of automatic thoughts and daydreams at the periphery of consciousness, and in the manifest themes of dreams during sleep. In 1971 he wrote: "A useful way of presenting the hypothesis is in terms of a continuum as follows: Moving from the verbal to the visual, we have 'automatic thoughts'— spontaneous daydreams—drug-induced hallucinations—dreams" (Beck, 1971, p. 7). Beck suggested that the press of reality puts the irrational content of waking fantasies such as automatic thoughts and daydreams in check. During sleep, however, when "external input is withdrawn, the cognitive pattern exerts a maximum influence on the content of dreams" (p. 7). Dreams were discrete examples of the same processes at work in the production of automatic thoughts and were therefore valuable as a "kind of biopsy of the patient's psychological processes" (p. 6). He distanced himself from classical analysis by arguing that dreams served no psychic function, such as guarding sleep, and did not require intricate interpretation to be understood.

Beck published this theory in the proceedings of the American Academy of Psychoanalysis, a breakaway group from the American Psychoanalytic Association that fostered free and scientific exchange of psychoanalytic ideas. It is curious that Beck decided to return to organized psychoanalysis—even if to a liberal group of analysts—with his cognitive ideas. Not only had he rejected drive theory, the cornerstone of mainstream psychoanalysis, but also "psychoanalysis" appeared to have rejected him. His application for membership in the American Psychoanalytic Association was rejected in 1960,[14] and he never reapplied. His presentation of the dream theory was almost devoid of references to psychoanalytic theory. Still, Beck returned with a fair degree of commitment. He joined the Academy in 1968, was voted a trustee in 1969,[15] and chaired a midwinter conference the same year on depression and suicide[16] in which he presented a paper on the cognitive triad (Beck, 1970b). In 1971, Beck responded to a call for papers for a midwinter conference on dreams and dreaming.[17] His paper was received enthusiastically, at least by the psychiatrist chosen to provide a written response.[18]

How might we understand Beck's return to psychoanalysis? His interest may have derived from the close relationship that his mentors and colleagues enjoyed with the academy. Leon Saul was a founding member of the academy, as were followers of Karen Horney and Harry Stack Sullivan. Roy Grinker, the editor of the *Archives of Psychiatry* who had published many of Beck's articles, including the depression inventory (Beck, Ward, Mendelson,

Mock, & Erbaugh, 1961), his second article on dreams (Beck & Ward, 1961), and his first two articles on thinking and depression (Beck, 1963, 1964), was also a founding member and active participant.[19] Beck may have turned to the community he knew best for support for his new model.

A complimentary interpretation of the significance of this venue for the dream article is that Beck saw a close relationship between cognitive therapy and the schools of neo-Freudianism that had found comfortable homes there away from the orthodoxy of the American Psychoanalytic Association. Beck remembers that "first, I called this ego psychology, [and then I felt this was] the psychoanalysis of the '60s, this was neo-analysis. What I am saying is that [cognitive therapy] is consistent to this day with Adler and Horney and so on. I kind of identified myself with the so-called neo-analytic school" (Beck, 1990). The academy was home to many neo-Freudians, including students of Adler, Horney, and Sullivan, among others, who had put aside drive theory in favor of ego- and environmentally oriented approaches. Beck drew analogies in both of his academy papers between his model and certain features of Freud's primary and secondary processes, arguing in the dream article, for example, that the hyperactive schema was analogous to Freud's preconscious state (Beck, 1971). In his unpublished notes Beck had imagined a system of reality testing[20] analogous to the ego that mediated between primitive impulses and the press of reality. Given the direction of his own theoretical and clinical work, Beck reasonably could have assumed that neo-Freudian schools would have been receptive to his ideas about dreams.

DREAMS AND BEHAVIOR THERAPY

This second interpretation is consistent with a project called "broad-spectrum psychotherapy" with which Beck was very active at the time of his involvement in the Academy. The broad-spectrum philosophy urged therapists to look for common factors and to overcome theoretical boundaries to make all techniques accessible to all therapists. In 1967 Beck established a new course for medical students at the University of Pennsylvania entitled "Broad Spectrum Psychotherapy." His aim was to position the major schools of psychotherapy, among which he now counted cognitive therapy, not in opposition to each other but in relation to each other on a spectrum of specific interventions. Psychotherapists, he argued, felt compelled to embrace only one theory and employ only those techniques articulated by that theory.[21] In contrast, he suggested, we try to avoid getting hung up on theoretical disputation. . . . We start with the assumption that each of the systems of psychotherapy have [*sic*] some merit. We attempt to select the general type of psychotherapy that seems to be indicated on the basis of patient variables. . . . The pragmatic approach is: if a particular form of therapy works (and there is no contraindication for its use), then use it. Once the practitioner is freed from his conformist attitude to a particular school of psychotherapy, he is then free to select the appropriate technique from a wide variety of available techniques.[22]

Beck's desire to conceptualize different schools of psychotherapy as complementary to each other, rather than as antagonistic to each other, could well have inspired him to seek friendly intellectual relations with members of some of the liberal wings of psychoanalysis.

But his work on broad-spectrum psychotherapy also brought him into contact with leading behavior therapists in Philadelphia, notably Joseph Wolpe and Arnold Lazarus at Temple University. Wolpe disagreed with Beck's ideas about the existence of cognitive mediators, but Lazarus found Beck's ideas very interesting. By the late 1960s the younger generation of behavior therapists, led by Lazarus, initiated a process of what Michael Mahoney calls the "Cognitive Inquisition" (Mahoney, 1974). Dissatisfied with the limitations of the strict stimulus-behavior paradigm they had inherited from Wolpe, they began to mine the theories of other systems for an operationalizable cognitive mediator they could place between the stimulus and the response. Lazarus and a small community of behavior therapists soon emerged in the late 1960s with the common goal of using the broad-spectrum philosophy to find this cognitive mediator (Brown, 1967, 1969; Sloane, 1969; Ward, 1968).

Beck began to look for more specific areas of overlap between cognitive therapy and behavior therapy. Lazarus had been arguing for several years that behavior therapy would benefit from recognizing that some fear reactions were not responses to observable stimuli but responses to the potential meaning of those stimuli. He discovered that the technique of time projection with positive reinforcement, by which the therapist induced the client to imagine doing pleasurable activities over consecutive weeks, could lift depression (Lazarus, 1968). He stressed emphatically that the most successful clients were "able to picture vivid images" (Lazarus, 1968). Lazarus himself may have offered the first olive branch in the quest for a common factors approach. Beck was impressed with Lazarus's ability to manipulate his patients' moods through the use of induced fantasies and noticed some overlap with his own hypotheses about the value of weighing all the evidence and considering alternative hypotheses.[23] He found a point of overlap with Lazarus by suggesting that his own theory of automatic thoughts could be extended to include *visual* thoughts, such as the induced images in Lazarus's clinical experiments.

Beck soon generated several comparative papers rooted in the broad-spectrum philosophy that outlined how cognitive therapy could explain the cognitive processes at work in induced imagery and systematic desensitization. One of the more influential of these papers was his "Cognitive Therapy: Nature and Relation to Behavior Therapy" (Beck, 1970a), which appeared in the first volume of the journal *Behavior Therapy*. Beck (1970a) wrote:

> Substantial amplification of the nature of cognitive processes is necessary to account adequately for clinical phenomena and for the effects of therapeutic intervention. A greater emphasis on the individual's descriptions of internal events can lead to a more comprehensive view of human psychopathology and the mechanisms of behavior change. By using introspective data, the cognitive theorist has access to the patient's thoughts, ideas, attitudes, dreams, and daydreams. These ideational productions provide the cognitive theorist with the raw materials with which he can form concepts and models. (pp. 193–194)

Introspective data, he continued, demonstrated "the existence of complex organizations of cognitive structures . . . composed of primitive systems consisting of relatively crude cognitive structures (corresponding to Freud's notion of primary process), and of more mature systems composed of refined and elastic structures (corresponding to the secondary process). Some of the conceptual elements may be predominantly verbal, whereas others may be predominantly pictorial" (p. 194). He concluded that cognitive therapy should be seen as a separate system from behavior therapy, but that behavior therapists could benefit from employing some of his assumptions about the nature and role of cognitions in psychopathology.

A subset of these comparative papers investigated specifically the roles of fantasies, dreams, and daydreams in psychotherapy. The earliest of these was an unpublished manuscript on fantasy in broad-spectrum psychotherapy.[24] Beck argued in this manuscript (1968) that Wolpe's description of systematic desensitization was too limited in scope and failed to account for the "wide range of potential uses of fantasy in psychotherapy" (Beck, unpublished manuscript, 1968, p. 2). He outlined the ways in which he was using spontaneous and induced fantasies in cognitive therapy, without the need for relaxation or focusing exclusively on anxiety, to gain more information about the nature of his patients' problems and to effect change. For instance, Beck (unpublished manuscript, 1968, pp. 9–10) suggested that

> by discussing the patient's spontaneous fantasies experienced previous to the psychotherapeutic interview, it is possible to determine more precisely the content of

the particular problem. In some ways this procedure is analogous to reporting and associating to dreams. By focusing on the material elaborated in association to the fantasy, the therapist and the patient can gain a great understanding of the particular psychological problem.

Beck demonstrated that this technique was of equal use in psychodynamic psychotherapy as in other therapies because the therapist, whatever his or her persuasion, "can elicit reports of the patient's pictorial fantasies in much the same way as he elicits reports of dreams and other ideational material" (Beck, unpublished manuscript, 1968, p. 28).

He presented an even more comprehensive discussion of these ideas in an article on fantasies in the *Journal of Nervous and Mental Disease* (Beck, 1970c), and the similarity between this article and the 1971 dream article is striking. Beck directed this article, like the unpublished manuscript on fantasy, to the inadequacies of Wolpe's system. But he offered the very same argument about the nature of cognitions and dreams that appeared in his paper to the American Academy of Psychoanalysis. He argued, for instance, that

> the similarity between the content of the verbal and the pictorial cognitions suggests that they arise from the same conceptual system. The cognitive response to a situation is shaped by the specific cognitive pattern that has been activated. When a particular cognitive pattern is hyperactive (as in the various psychopathological states), then the content of the spontaneous verbal cognitions and the spontaneous pictorial cognitions tend to be determined by this hyperactive cognitive pattern. (Beck, 1970c, p. 13)

As in the 1971 article, he suggested "a continuity in the manifest content of dreams, daydreams, and verbal cognitions. . . . A theoretical construct that may explain this continuity among ideational phenomena is that they are the derivatives of the same hyperactive cognitive pattern" (Beck, 1970c, p. 13). Beck tailored this discussion to the concerns of behavior therapists by demonstrating that "there is convincing clinical evidence that unrealistic pictorial images exert significant influence not only on affect and motivation but also on the patient's overt behavior" (p. 15). But this article, when compared to the dream article of 1971, demonstrates clearly how Beck was able to reach both groups with a model of cognitive processes that highlighted the common factors it shared with each.

Historical circumstance, more than anything else, pushed Beck closer to the behavior therapists and farther away from the psychoanalysts. The behavior therapists moving in a cognitive direction responded with much greater urgency and enthusiasm to his work than did the psychoanalysts. Beck was invited to participate in small conferences with behavior therapists such as

Gerald Davison and at annual meetings of both the Society for Psychotherapy Research (SPR) and the Association for the Advancement of Behavior Therapy (AABT). Members of AABT and SPR quickly catapulted Beck into a leadership role in the emerging national cognitive-behavioral therapy (CBT) movement. He simply did not enjoy the same kind of enthusiastic and professionally stimulating relationship with members of the academy.

Perhaps the most momentous of the CBT invitations was David Barlow's suggestion that Beck participate in a panel on cognitive behavior modification with Donald Meichenbaum and Michael Mahoney at the annual AABT meeting in 1974. Beck spoke on "new trends in cognitive therapy" and received an extremely enthusiastic welcome.[25] Barlow (personal interview, March, 1999) recalls that Beck had brought along "maybe twenty to twenty-five hand-outs. And we had put him, thinking he was reasonably popular, in a larger room that maybe held one hundred people. And something like two hundred to three hundred people [appeared] . . . and he was absolutely blown away." Beck's appeal, Barlow suggests, was in his clinical expertise:

> There were many people who were doing psychotherapy day in and day out and were dissatisfied with psychoanalysis, but in the consulting room with the prevailing standards of seeing people for an hour, [they] couldn't just have them walk up and down the room and watch their behavior. Obviously they were talking to them, they were examining their assumptions, looking at the cognitive foundations of their psychopathology. Here was a fellow who was clearly no longer a psychoanalyst and yet was proposing something that people could do in a consulting room, something that they could adapt to their customary kinds of therapeutic practice.[26]

These kinds of sentiments helped to secure for Beck a permanent place in the cognitive-behavioral therapy community, which he has enjoyed up to the present time.

Beck did not publish any other articles on fantasies or dreams after this surge of activity in the late 1960s. Indeed, dreams disappeared entirely from the cognitive model after 1971. Why might this have been the case? One answer may lie in Beck's pragmatic spirit. Beck didn't need to study dreams anymore to make his case for the value of cognitive therapy. He offered behavior therapists a comprehensive and compelling argument without compromising their shared commitment to experimental science. They offered him a supportive community of scientist-practitioners with a solid infrastructure that could bring cognitive therapy to a national audience. This was an excellent marriage from which each party benefited enormously, and Beck simply followed the most pragmatic course.

This alliance with behavior therapists also fostered, I would argue, a certain kind of politics of "forgetting." In the early 1970s, considerable animosity remained between behavior therapists and psychoanalysts, despite the efforts of the broad-spectrum psychotherapists. The behavior therapists certainly would not have encouraged Beck to explore the more psychodynamic features of his model, and Beck may not have been particularly keen to point them out either. Beck had become extremely frustrated with a psychoanalytic politics of personal loyalty that had permeated the Department of Psychiatry at the University of Pennsylvania in the mid-1960s (Rosner, 1999). It may have been politically expedient for both Beck and the behavior therapists, once their alliance had proven so fruitful, simply to ignore the psychoanalytic elements of his work. I am arguing that the broad-spectrum philosophy may not have been sufficiently powerful—or compelling—to overcome the political forces in behavior therapy that raged against psychoanalysis. Beck nurtured those features of his model that he shared with behavior therapists while he let other features, such as dreams, fall aside until they disappeared from public view. In a way Beck had come full circle—he privileged method over theory just as he had done in 1962. By privileging the behavior therapists, he chose the community with whom he shared more scientific and *method-ological* interests and let ties dissolve with the community with whom he shared (increasingly tenuous) theoretical interests. He never rejected the value of dreams, nor even abandoned them, but merely put them out of view.

CONCLUSION

Beck's work on dreams was extremely important in the development of cognitive therapy. His early psychoanalytic dream research taught him how to conduct scientific experiments, spurred him to reevaluate the experimental viability of long-standing psychoanalytic hypotheses about depression, and catalyzed his interest in cognitive processes. His cognitive dream theory, rooted in the early dream research, was forged in a broad-spectrum spirit that argued with compelling evidence that cognitive therapy could function both as a form of neo-Freudianism and as an ally of behavior therapy. Beck, with his background in both psychoanalysis and science, was able to speak directly to the concerns of both groups.

I would like to use this last observation as a point of departure for discussing the relevance of this historical analysis for contemporary therapists. Most cognitive therapists who work with dreams sit at the crossroads of cognitive therapy and other systems, whether psychoanalytic or gestalt or interpersonal. Beck sat in a similar place in the early years of cognitive therapy. The history of his 1971 article on dreams shows that cognitive therapy was the product of psychoanalytic, cognitive, and behavioral ideas about human nature and its ideational processes, including dreams. Beck achieved national recognition for his dream work precisely because he sought areas of overlap between different therapeutic techniques.

The boundaries between therapeutic models in our own time often obscure a wealth of valuable clinical data for practitioners of any one school, particularly data that might come from the elicitation and elaboration of dreams. The common factors and psychotherapy integration philosophies of our own time have focused on rectifying this problem. It can be no surprise then that Beck has been, once again, at the forefront of the psychotherapy integration movement of more recent times (Beck, 1991), revisiting his early link to the neo-Freudians and pursuing his commitments to "clinical and experimental investigations" rather than to one theory or another (p. 197). His work, both then and now, has encouraged practitioners to make clinical data their highest priority, even if the data—such as dreams, one might argue—do not fit easily into their preferred theoretical system. When taken in context, Beck's 1971 article clearly points the way to the integrative environment of our own time that has encouraged anew an interest in cognitive therapy and dreams. Perhaps Beck's story can inspire cognitive therapists to reach beyond their familiar domains to claim the same kind of pragmatic creativity that gave birth to his own cognitive dream theory.

NOTES

[1]Letter from author to Dr. Aaron T. Beck (hereafter ATB), June 8, 1995.
[2]Letter from ATB to the author, July 20, 1995.
[3]Undated, typewritten draft of chapter entitled "Patterns in Dreams of Depressed Patients." Dated ca. 1968. Personal Collection, ATB.
[4]This article was reprinted in an edited volume on abnormal psychology, and the Masochism Scale was reprinted separately in a large volume on the content analysis of dreams (Hall & van de Castle, 1966; Sarbin, 1961).
[5]Lecture notes for Second-Year Course in Psychodynamics, Lecture 9, "Nuclear Emotional Constellations," ca. 1958. Beck wrote in his notes about "deeply rooted emotional attitudes and expectations which are expressions of (a) early conditioning, (b) wish fulfillments, (c) unreasonable fears, or (d) defense against a deeper attitude. Consist of warped evaluations and expectations of self and others, which have not been corrected by personal experience. Tend to be extreme and absolute; Black and White, no shades of grey." Personal Collection, ATB.

[6]Letter from ATB to Seymour Feshbach, January 18, 1963. Personal Collection, ATB.

[7]See letters from patients to Dr. Beck, February 4, 1963, October 25, 1964, and November 7, 1964. These letters are handwritten homework assignments in which patients list their feelings and their rational and unreasonable responses to them in tables. See also patient letter to Beck, September 28, 1966. Personal Collection, ATB.

[8]Letter from ATB to Albert J. (Mickey) Stunkard, September 26, 1962. Personal Collection, ATB.

[9]Letter from ATB to Leon J. Saul, March 8, 1962. Personal Collection, ATB.

[10]Letter from ATB to Seymour Feshbach, March 8, 1962. Personal Collection, ATB.

[11]Undated typewritten note, ca. 1968, "Study No. 2. Dreams and Daydreams of Depressed, Suicidal Patients." Personal Collection, ATB.

[12]Personal communication, ATB.

[13]The other piece Beck published on dreams was a three-page discussion of a chapter by Rosalind Cartwright on dreams and REM sleep. Beck briefly mentioned his new cognitive dream model. Rosalind Cartwright has become one of the foremost dream researchers of the last thirty years.

[14]Letter from Gerhart Piers, chairman, Committee on Membership, American Psychoanalytic Association, August 1957. Personal Collection, ATB.

[15]Letter from Harold I. Lief, chairman, Nominating Committee, to Drs. Frances Arkin, Robert A. Cleghorn, Ralph M. Crowley, and Morton Enelow, December 15, 1969. American Academy of Psychoanalysis (History Committee), Box 1, ff. 6. Courtesy of the Oskar Diethelm Library, History of Psychiatry section, Department of Psychiatry, New York Hospital and Cornell University Medical College.

[16]American Academy of Psychoanalysis, Box 1, ff. 16. Courtesy of the Oskar Diethelm Library.

[17]Ullman, Montague (undated). Call for papers for the theme of the midwinter meting, December, 1970: Dreaming and Dreams: Recent Clinical Perspectives. American Academy of Psychoanalysis Papers, Box 1, Folder 4. Courtesy of the Oskar Diethelm Library.

[18]Shainberg, D. (1971). Discussion of papers of Aaron T. Beck, M.D., and John L. Schimel, M.D. In J. H. Masserman (Ed.), *Dream dynamics* (pp. 20–23). New York: Grune & Stratton.

[19]Beck acknowledged his indebtedness to Grinker with a contribution to a *Festschrift* in Grinker's honor (Beck, 1972).

[20]See, for instance, his handwritten notes dated May 19 and November 7, 1964. Personal Collection, ATB.

[21]Letter from ATB to Dr. Robert Toborowsky, January 11, 1969. Personal Collection, ATB.

[22]Unpublished paper on "broad-spectrum psychotherapy," undated but in a file entitled "Broad Spectrum Psychotherapy: Important Notes." Personal Collection, ATB.

[23]Letters from ATB to Dr. Arnold Lazarus, July 1 and August 9, 1967. Personal Collection, ATB.

[24]Unpublished manuscript "Use of Fantasy in Broad Spectrum Psychotherapy," February, 1968. Personal Collection, ATB.

[25]Notes entitled "Panel on New Trends in Cognitive Therapy: Presented to the Annual Meeting of the Association for the Advancement of Behavior Therapy, November 2, 1974." Courtesy of the Center for Cognitive Therapy, University of Pennsylvania.

[26]Personal interview with Dr. David Barlow, March 1999.

REFERENCES

Beck, A. T. (1963). Thinking and depression: 1. Idiosyncratic content and cognitive distortions. *Archives of General Psychiatry, 9* (October), 324–333.

Beck, A. T. (1964). Thinking and depression: II. Theory and therapy. *Archives of General Psychiatry, 10* (June), 561–571.

Beck, A. T. (1967). *Depression: Clinical, experimental, and theoretical aspects.* New York: Hoeber Medical Books.

Beck, A. T. (1969). Dreams as compared to other forms of fantasy: Discussion. In R. M. Whitman, M. Kramer, B. J. Baldridge, & P. H. Ornstein (Eds.), *Dream psychology and the new biology of dreaming* (pp. 373–376). Springfield, IL: Charles C. Thomas.

Beck, A. T. (1970a). Cognitive therapy: Nature and relation to behavior therapy. *Behavior Therapy, 1,* 184–200.

Beck, A. T. (1970b). The core problem in depression: The cognitive triad. In J. H. Masserman (Ed.), *Depression: Theories and therapies* (pp. 47–55). New York: Grune & Stratton.

Beck, A. T. (1970c). Role of fantasies in psychotherapy and psychopathology. *Journal of Nervous and Mental Disease, 150*(1), 3–17.

Beck, A. T. (1970d). *Depression: Causes and treatment.* Philadelphia: University of Pennsylvania Press.

Beck, A. T. (1971). Cognitive patterns in dreams and daydreams. In J. H. Masserman (Ed.), *Dream dynamics: Science and psychoanalysis* (Vol. 19, pp. 2–7). New York: Grune & Stratton.

Beck, A. T. (1972). The phenomena of depression: A synthesis. In D. F. Offer & D. X. Freedman (Eds.), *Modern psychiatry and clinical research: Essays in honor of Roy R. Grinker* (pp. 136–158). New York: Basic Books.

Beck, A. T. (1990). *Interview with Paul Salkovskis, November 2, 1990* [Transcript of Interview]. San Francisco: 24th Annual Convention of the Association for the Advancement of Behavior Therapy.

Beck, A. T. (1991). Cognitive therapy as *the* integrative therapy. *Journal of Psychotherapy Integration, 1*(3), 191–205.

Beck, A. T., & Hurvich, M. S. (1959). Psychological correlates of depression: 1. Frequency of "masochistic" dream content in a private practice sample. *Psychosomatic Medicine, 21*(1), 50–55.

Beck, A. T., & Stein, M. (1961). Psychodynamics. In R. Service (Ed.), *Encyclopedia of medicine, surgery, specialties: Vol. XI. Revision service* (pp. 422C–422KK). Philadelphia: F. A. Davis.

Beck, A. T., & Ward, C. H. (1961). Dreams of depressed patients: Characteristic themes in manifest content. *Archives of General Psychiatry, 5*, 462–467.

Beck, A. T., Ward, C. H., Mendelson, M., Mock, J., & Erbaugh, J. (1961). An inventory for measuring depression. *Archives of General Psychiatry, 4*, 561–571.

Brown, B. M. (1967). Cognitive aspects of Wolpe's behavior therapy. *American Journal of Psychiatry, 124*(6), 854–859.

Brown, B. M. (1969). The use of induced imagery in psychotherapy. *Psychotherapy: Theory, Research and Practice, 6*(2), 120–121.

Hall, C. S., & van de Castle, R. L. (1966). *The content analysis of dreams.* New York: Appleton-Century-Crofts.

Lazarus, A. A. (1968). Learning theory and the treatment of depression. *Behavior Therapy and Research, 6*, 83–89.

Mahoney, M. (1974). *Cognition and behavior modification.* Cambridge, MA: Ballinger Publishing.

Rosner, R. I. (1999). *Between science and psychoanalysis: Aaron T. Beck and the emergence of cognitive therapy.* Unpublished doctoral dissertation, York University, Toronto, Ontario.

Sarbin, T. R. (Ed.). (1961). *Studies in behavior pathology: The experimental approach to the psychology of the abnormal.* New York: Holt, Rinehart & Winston.

Saul, L., Sheppard, E., Selby, D., Lhamon, W., Sachs, D., & Master, R. (1954). The quantification of hostility in dreams with reference to essential hypertension. *Science, 119*, 3090.

Saul, L. J. (1940). Utilization of early current dreams in formulating psychoanalytic cases. *Psychoanalytic Quarterly, 9*(1), 453–469.

Saul, L. J., & Sheppard, E. (1956). An attempt to quantify emotional forces using manifest dreams—a preliminary study. *Journal of the American Psychoanalytic Association, 4*, 486–502.

Sloane, R. B. (1969). The converging paths of behavior therapy and psychotherapy. *International Journal of Psychiatry, 8*, 493–501.

Ward, C. H. (1968). Psychotherapy categories: A spectrum approach. *American Journal of Psychiatry, 124*(12), 131–133.

CHAPTER 3

Cognitive Patterns in Dreams and Daydreams*

AARON T. BECK

Dreams and their meanings have challenged man for thousands of years. Numerous theories of dreams have had their day in the sun and then died. Among contemporary writers, certain assumptions seem to dominate. The major assumption is that dreams have some meaning. Stemming from this major premise, other assumptions or hypotheses have been advanced.

1. Dreams are wish fulfillment. Alternatively, following Freud, dreams are the guardian of sleep.
2. Dreams are an attempt at problem solving. This has been particularly elaborated by French.
3. Dreams are a manifestation of certain psychological processes of which the dreamer is totally unaware; that is, dreams spring from the unconscious.
4. The content of dreams is continuous with the content of the individual's waking ideation and behavior (Adler). Or the opposite view has been advanced, namely that the content of the dream is reciprocal to the waking behavior.

*Reprinted with permission. Originally published in J. H. Masserman (Ed.), *Dream dynamics* (pp. 2–7). New York: Grune & Stratton.

As an exercise, it is useful to put aside these assumptions—some of which are by no means verifiable at this stage of our development and start with the simplest proposition: a dream is a visual phenomenon occurring during sleep. Its content is relatively uninfluenced by the immediate external environment. The interpretation of dreams, unlike certain other phenomena, is so dependent on the introspective report of the subject that there is no inter rater reliability regarding the phenomenon of the dream itself. In other words, it is a "private"—as opposed to a "public"—experience.

Starting from this point, what can be said about dreams? There are many obvious dream characteristics that do not require elaboration. In brief, anything can happen in a dream—from a simple prosaic repetition of an event that occurred during the daytime to the most fantastic, grotesque imagery of which the human mind is capable.

An important issue to explore is whether the dream has anything to do with the dreamer; that is, is the dream more than just a random sequence of images that bear no relationship to the psychological life of the individual? Is the dream merely an epiphenomenon dependent upon random neuronal activity, or is it related in some way to the personality or life experiences of the dreamer himself? Do dreams have any characteristics that are specific for the individual dreamer? Although clinical evidence would answer that there is a relationship between the dream and the individual's personality, such evidence may be biased by the assumptions of the dream collector.

However, we have done a number of controlled systematic studies that support this proposition. In a study of depressed patients whose waking ideation and fantasies contained particular themes, we were able to isolate similar themes in their dreams. For instance, the theme of a negative outcome of any activity that the individual engages in was common both to dream and waking life (Beck, 1967). The sense of passivity and frustration was particularly obvious in the dreams of these patients and was also represented in the waking ideation.

Another study relevant to this question investigated the dreams of convicts. We found a significant preponderance of dream themes relevant to the particular crime that was committed. For instance, sex offenders tended to have a significantly higher proportion of themes involving sexual deviation for which they were convicted than did a control group of other convicts (Goldhirsh, 1961).

An example drawn from my clinical practice was a delinquent boy who, in response to my inquiry about dreams, recounted a dream in which he planned and executed an elaborate crime. Enough features peculiar to dreams were present to warrant my accepting this as a dream rather than a fabrication.

While describing the dream, he did not seem to realize he was exposing himself. When I started to explore the relation of dream content to waking ideation, he immediately became unwilling to discuss the subject. Later (after he had broken treatment), he, indeed, carried out a crime that followed in broad outline what he had described in the dream.

Similarly, in a pilot study we have scored the themes reported in the daydreams of hospitalized patients and found that these could be correlated with their dreams. There appears to be continuity in some dreams between the dream theme and an individual's waking experiences. At times, however, the dream seems to be quite different from the waking conceptualizations; the dream themes may be reciprocal to the conscious preoccupations. For example, Jean Miller (1970) has indicated that severely depressed patients often report relatively pleasant or neutral dreams but the dreams take on an unpleasant content as the patient emerges from his depression.

Now to return to the question: do dreams have meaning? In man's thirst for meaning, he has attached esoteric significances to dreams, for example, prophetic power. It is doubtful that every dream of an individual can throw light on his conflicts, difficulties, impulses, life style, or personality. However, certain pathognomonic or idiosyncratic dreams may effect an understanding of a particular nosological category or crystallize a patient's specific problems. When a single dream does not reveal this crystal, a sequence of dreams may.

In terms of psychopathology in general, certain patterns in dreams appear to correlate with particular diagnostic categories. If a series of dreams is studied, for instance, one can find that certain themes differentiate one psychiatric group from another. Depressed patients, as mentioned previously, will have dreams of being defeated, thwarted, and, as Miller (1970) has pointed out, coerced. The coercion theme seems to be related to the depressed patient's passivity. Paranoid patients, on the other hand, are more likely to have dreams in which there is some kind of persecution or unjustified abuse. Manic patients tend to have dreams with more expansive themes; anxiety neurotics have an excess of dreams of danger.

Further, a single dream *may* provide a quick clarification of a patient's problem. Even in a preliminary diagnostic interview, dreams may present rich information. On the basis of the patient's report of his current life situation and his past history, a series of alternative hypotheses may be set up. The dream can then serve to support one or the other hypothesis, modify a hypothesis, or offer completely different possibilities.

For example, some time ago I was asked to make a quick evaluation of a college student who was depressed. She gave a history of not getting any gratification out of activities in college or from her relationships with men;

however, she could not account for this fact. I then asked her to tell me her most recent dream and she presented the following:

> I was going to give a piano recital [she was in fact a good pianist]. I arrived late for the recital—about one-half hour late. I sat down at the piano. I could not find my notes. I started to play anyhow. Then I started to strike the wrong keys. I tried to play the piece from memory but I couldn't really remember it. I was disgusted with myself and everybody was disgusted with me. I got up from the piano and ran out.

When I explored how this dream related to her everyday life, her life style emerged. It appeared that whenever she started an activity in college she expected to do badly even though she had previously been very successful in her undertakings. She generally was late for extracurricular activities and dates (since she expected rejection, she would stall until the very last minute). When she overcame her expectations of failure, she could become involved. However, any slight error or faux pas became magnified into major reversals—as in her dream of striking the wrong keys on the piano and not being able to remember the score. After exaggerating her minor problems into major disasters, she would "cop out." This was analogous to her running away from the piano recital in the dream.

In brief, the reasons for this patient's lack of enjoyment can be understood as follows: First, she expected to do badly in activities or relationships and consequently held herself back from participating. Second, once she became involved, she selectively abstracted any inefficiencies or exaggerated them. These interpretations confirmed (for her) that she was, indeed, inadequate and that nothing would work out for her. Third, she would break off the relationship or the activity. She always quit before she had a chance to obtain any satisfaction from it.

I discussed the foregoing formulation with the patient and she was struck by its accuracy. Further support for the interpretation was derived from her subsequent behavior. When she later decided to persevere in her activities and relationships, she began to get some favorable feedback from her performance. Her view of herself as an ineffectual, undesirable person changed and she began to anticipate greater success. In technical terms, her cognitive appraisal of herself and the future changed from negative to positive.

A COGNITIVE MODEL OF DREAMS

There is no doubt that some dreams seem to be clear-cut wish fulfillments. One experiment, for instance, indicated that subjects deprived of food had a higher incidence of dreams of eating than did a control group. However, on the basis of our research, I have concluded that this may not always, or even generally, be the case.

A more parsimonious way of approaching dream reports is to regard their interpretation as a kind of biopsy of the patient's psychological processes. The cognitive model provides a useful framework for analyzing these processes. According to this model, the pathognomonic dream dramatizes the way the individual sees himself, his world, and his future. In the course of an individual's waking experiences, certain cognitive patterns peculiar to that individual are activated, but may be obscured by the input of external stimuli. When the external stimuli are cut off during sleep and a certain state of arousal is reached, these patterns (or schemata) exert a maximum influence on the individual's thinking and are manifested in the thematic content of the dreams.

Cognitive patterns or schemata exert a varying degree of pull on the individual's dreams. Although some dreams seem to be a prosaic reflection of daytime events, pathognomonic dreams, which are often the repetitive dreams, point to a particular type of conceptualization.

The conceptualizations apparent in dreams also seem to influence the emotions and behavior of waking life. In his waking experience, an individual may conceptualize a situation in a variety of ways. He is most aware of the realistic conceptualization; however, the unrealistic one, based on more primitive cognitive patterns, may have a greater influence on both his waking emotions and his dreams, in which it emerges dramatically. The kind of stuff that dreams are made of may be obtained by training a patient to observe not only his realistic appraisal of a situation but also the automatic, unrealistic evaluations that seem to be at the fringe of awareness. I have described these elsewhere as "automatic thoughts" or distorted cognitions, a kind of ideation probably analogous to what Freud called the preconscious. These cognitions are much more closely related to the pathognomonic or idiosyncratic dream than are the usual realistic cognitions at the center of the person's awareness.

In psychopathology, however, unrealistic cognitions are dominant in the waking ideation, and in severe cases, occur at the center of the cognitive field. The depressed patient perseverates in thinking about his inadequacies, losses, and bleak future. The anxiety neurotic is preoccupied with hypothetical dangers. The paranoid patient dwells on the theme of abuse by others. These dominant patterns in the waking mentation exert their influence in the dreams. Thus, the depressive, anxiety neurotic, and paranoid patients are prone to dream respectively of themes of failure, danger, or abuse.

SUMMARY

In a study of night dreams and waking fantasies we found a significant association between the manifest content of the fantasies and of the dreams.

A useful way of presenting the hypothesis is in terms of a continuum as follows: Moving from the verbal to the visual, we have "automatic thoughts"—spontaneous daydreams—drug-induced hallucinations—dreams.

According to the cognitive model of dreams, certain cognitive patterns structure the content of the waking fantasies and other waking ideational experiences as well as the content of the dreams. These cognitive patterns are specific to the individual; in the case of psychiatric patients they represent idiosyncratic ways of conceptualizing themselves and the outside world. When the individual is asleep and external input is withdrawn, the cognitive pattern exerts a maximum influence on the content of dreams. This particular model offers an alternative to Freud's dictum that dreams serve as the guardian of sleep or as a wish fulfillment.

REFERENCES

Beck, A. T. (1967). *Depression: Clinical, experimental, and theoretical aspects.* New York: Hoeber.

Goldhirsh, M. I. (1961). Manifest content of dreams of convicted sex offenders. *Journal of Abnormal Social Psychology, 63,* 643–645.

Miller, J. B. (1970). Waking and dreaming conceptualization in depression. In J. Masserman (Ed.), *Depressions: Theories and therapies.* New York: Grune & Stratton.

CHAPTER 4

A Comparison of Cognitive, Psychodynamic, and Eclectic Therapists' Attitudes and Practices in Working with Dreams in Psychotherapy

RACHEL E. CROOK

In this chapter, I review findings from a survey conducted by Crook and Hill (in press) of clinicians' experiences in working with dreams. I place special emphasis on the experiences of cognitively oriented clinicians. The rationale for the study is discussed first, followed by a description of the method used in the study. The responses of cognitive therapists are then compared to those of therapists from other orientations in terms of personal characteristics, training in dream interpretation, time spent on dreams in therapy, types of dream activities used, and functions of dreams. Finally, I suggest implications of these findings for cognitive therapists.

RATIONALE FOR THE STUDY

Although working with clients' dreams was an important element of psycho-therapy for the early psychoanalytic therapists (e.g., Freud, 1900/1965; Jung,

1974), it was not often used by therapists from other theoretical orientations in the United States during much of the 20th century, perhaps because dream interpretation was considered by many to be a lengthy and unscientific process irrelevant to everyday life (Erikson, 1954; Cartwright, 1993). However, in the last 20 years, proponents of dream interpretation in various theoretical orientations have begun developing approaches to working with clients' dreams (e.g., Gendlin, 1986; Hill, 1996; Cartwright & Lamberg, 1992; Johnson, 1986; Mahrer, 1990; Weiss, 1986). Working with dreams in therapy is important, these proponents argue, because many clients want to understand their troubling dreams and nightmares. In addition, working with dreams often provides therapists with a means of navigating around therapeutic obstacles and quickly getting to core issues. Hence there seems to be a renewed and revitalized interest in dream interpretation from a variety of theoretical orientations, including cognitive therapists.

However, other than from laboratory studies and several brief surveys, not much is known about therapists' attitudes toward dream interpretation and their ways of working with dreams in therapy. In the laboratory, for instance, Hill and her colleagues have found that clients consistently rate working alliance, insight, and session quality significantly higher in dream interpretation sessions than in regular therapy sessions (Cogar & Hill, 1992; Diemer, Lobell, Vivino, & Hill, 1996; Falk & Hill, 1995; Heaton, Hill, Petersen, Rochlen, & Zack, 1998; Hill, Diemer, & Heaton, 1997; Hill, Diemer, Hess, Hillyer, & Seeman, 1993; Rochlen, Ligiero, Hill, & Heaton, 1999; Wonnell & Hill, 2000; Zack & Hill, 1998). These findings suggest that dream interpretation may be a useful clinical tool to explore issues, help clients gain insight, and develop the therapeutic relationship.

Outside the laboratory, only three field studies were found that focused on clinicians' experiences in working with dreams in therapy. Keller et al. (1995) found that most of the therapists in their sample (83%, $N = 228$) reported working with dreams in therapy at least occasionally and were most likely to use Freudian and Gestalt approaches. Similarly, Schredl, Bohusch, Kahl, Mader, and Somesan (2000), in their sample of German therapists, found that most of those clinicians who worked on dreams reported using a Freudian or Jungian approach. Schredl et al. also noted that psychodynamic therapists were more likely than humanistic and cognitive-behavioral therapists to consider work with dreams to be valuable for clients. In the third study, Fox (2002) learned that most clinicians in her sample (83%, $N = 265$) worked with dreams to some extent in therapy. Hence these findings suggest that therapists are somewhat likely to work with dreams in therapy and that psychodynamic therapists are more likely to do so than therapists of other theoretical orientations.

However, little is known about how therapists from different theoretical orientations actually work on dreams in therapy with clients. Perhaps a cognitive therapist simply listens to the client describing dream images, whereas a psychodynamic therapist might focus on unconscious wishes, encourage the client to reexperience the feelings in the dream, and use the dream as a metaphor later in therapy. Although both therapists are working with dreams in therapy, they are using very different approaches and may be doing so with different self-evaluations of competency. Because cognitive therapists may prefer to tailor specific interventions to specific client problems, they may prefer to work on dreams with specific types of clients and under specific therapeutic situations. In addition, factors such as attitudes toward dreams and dream recall may affect how likely cognitive therapists are to work with dreams. Research shows, for example, that volunteer clients with positive attitudes toward dreams are more likely to desire to participate in dream interpretation experiments and to benefit from dream interpretation sessions (Rochlen et al., 1999). Cognitive therapists, then, with positive attitudes toward dreams may be more likely to work with dreams in therapy than cognitive therapists with negative attitudes toward dreams.

The primary purpose of this chapter, therefore, is to examine Crook and Hill's (in press) findings on cognitive therapists' attitudes, beliefs, and practices in regard to working with dreams in ongoing therapy. In addition, I compared the experiences of cognitive therapists to those of therapists from other theoretical orientations. Clinicians were asked about their attitudes toward dreams, training in dream interpretation, and feelings of competence in working with dreams, as well as the number of clients who brought dreams into psychotherapy. Types of dream interpretation activities used by therapists in working with clients—such as asking clients to describe dream images in greater detail and working with conflicts represented in dreams—were also assessed. In addition, indications and contraindications for therapists' use of dream interpretation with certain types of clients and in certain situations were explored. Finally, given the controversy in the field about the function of dreams, therapists were asked to discuss their beliefs about the function of dreams (e.g., random firings of the brain vs. messages from the unconscious).

METHOD

Participants

Participants were 129 clinicians (88 men, 41 women; 107 Caucasian, 4 African American, 4 Latino(a), 1 Asian American, and 4 other) from the

American Psychological Association's Division 42 (Independent Practice), all of whom held doctoral degrees in psychology. These clinicians had an average of 21.54 (SD = 10.82) years of clinical experience after their highest degree and were, on average, 55.83 years old (SD = 11.17 years). The majority of participants (n = 108) indicated private practice as their primary work setting; the rest identified an agency (n = 8) or academic work setting (n = 9). In the past year, participants had seen clients for an average of 22.18 (SD = 14.04) hours a week.

In comparison to norms, the age of therapists in this sample was found to be similar to the Division 42 mean at the time of the survey, given that 59% of Division 42 members were between the ages of 45 and 59. Number of years of clinical experience for this sample was also similar in that 22.10 (SD = 9.80) years was the average for Division 42 members since their last degree. The representation of gender and race among participants was also similar to those of the entire Division 42 at the time of the survey (38% female, 62% male; 87% white, 2% Hispanic, 1% black, 1% Asian, and 8% other) (APA Division Services). Hence the sample appeared to reflect closely the population from which it was drawn.

Using 5-point Likert scales (5 = high), clinicians rated themselves as believing and adhering an average of 3.92 (SD = 1.12) to the theory and techniques of cognitive-behavioral orientations, 3.26 (SD = 1.08) to humanistics orientations, and 3.08 (SD = 1.35) to psychodynamic orientations. To differentiate therapists along lines of theoretical orientation, a cluster analysis was performed on the data, and a three-cluster solution was found. In the first cluster, 40 clinicians rated themselves as believing and adhering an average of 1.63 (SD = 0.70) to the theory and techniques of psychodynamic orientations, 2.88 (SD = 0.94) to those of humanistic orientations, and 4.78 (SD = 0.42) to those of cognitive-behavioral orientations. The first cluster, then, was labeled as the *cognitive therapist cluster*. In the second cluster, 27 clinicians rated themselves as believing and adhering an average of 3.93 (SD = 0.83) to the theory and techniques of psychodynamic orientations, 2.48 (SD = 0.85) to humanistic orientations, and 2.74 (SD = 1.06) to cognitive-behavioral orientations. The second cluster was identified as the *psychodynamic therapist cluster*. In the third cluster, 45 clinicians rated themselves as believing and adhering an average of 3.71 (SD = 0.94) to the theory and techniques of psychodynamic orientations, 4.11 (SD = 0.68) to humanistic orientations, and 3.91 (SD = 0.95) to cognitive-behavioral orientations. Thus the final cluster was labeled the *eclectic cluster*. Seventeen participants failed to complete the theoretical orientation ratings and hence were not included in the cluster analysis.

Instruments

The Therapist Dream Questionnaire was developed by Crook and Hill (in press). Preliminary items were reviewed by three advanced graduate students in counseling psychology who had experience in dream work, and changes were made to the questionnaire on the basis of their comments. The Dream Questionnaire was then pretested on a sample of 25 therapists randomly selected from APA's Division 42 and again revised according to their suggestions. The final version included six parts with 71 items.

Part 1 included items about therapists' age, gender, primary racial/ethnic identification, professional training, level of experience, theoretical orientation, beliefs concerning the function of dreams, work on their own dreams, and own dream recall. Estimated dream recall was measured using a two-question format. The first question, taken from Hiscock and Cohen (1973), was "During the last 2 weeks, immediately upon waking up in the morning, how often could you recall dreaming?" Respondents checked one of eight possibilities: every morning, just about every morning, most mornings, about every other morning, about two mornings a week, about one morning a week, once during the 2 weeks, and not once. The highest recall response was scored as 7 and the lowest as 0. The second question, taken from Robbins and Tanck (1988), was "How often do you usually have dreams you remember?" Participants checked one of five possibilities: about every night, two to three times a week, almost once a week, one to two times a month, and less than once a month. The most frequent recall response was scored as 4, and the least frequent recall response was scored as 0. Because of the strong correlation found between the two recall items, $r(360) = 0.72$, $p < 0.001$ (Hill et al., 1997), the practice of summing the two dream recall items has been used in several studies (e.g., Rochlen et al., 1999) and was also used in the present study.

Part 2 centered on clinicians' training in dream interpretation and measured the number of clients who brought dreams into therapy and the time spent in therapy working on clients' dreams. Training in dream interpretation was assessed by asking clinicians to rate how much training they had received (i.e., workshops, supervision, reading, graduate courses) on a 5-point Likert scale (1 = no training, 5 = extensive training). Also, participants were asked to estimate the percentage of their clients who had presented dreams in therapy in the past year and to estimate the percentage of time spent in therapy working with clients' dreams.

Part 3 contained 22 items, measured using a 5-point Likert scale (1 = never, 5 = frequently), about therapeutic dream activities and strategies that therapists might consider using in working with clients' dreams (Crook & Hill, in press). The first eight items related to the exploration of dreams (listen if clients bring in dreams, explore connections of dream images to waking life, ask clients to describe dream images in greater detail, collaborate with clients to construct a dream interpretation, work with conflicts that are represented in dreams, encourage clients to associate to dream images, encourage clients to reexperience feelings in dreams, and use dream images as metaphors later in therapy). The next eight items focused on helping clients gain insight into the meaning of the dream (interpret dreams in terms of waking life experiences, interpret dreams in terms of past experiences, interpret dreams in terms of the therapy relationship, interpret the dream for the client, interpret dreams according to the client's unconscious wishes, interpret dreams in spiritual terms, ask clients to act out different parts of dreams, and interpret dreams according to archetypes). The final six items were action-oriented and directive (invite clients to tell dreams, collaborate with clients to make changes based on dreams, explain how one works with dreams, suggest changes clients could make based on learnings from the dream, mention that one is willing to work with dreams, and help clients to try to change dreams).

Part 4 included 9 items, measured using a 5-point Likert scale (1 = not likely, 5 = very likely), about the likelihood of participants working on clients' dreams under different therapeutic conditions (e.g., client presents recurrent dreams; client presents troubling dreams or nightmares; client is interested in learning about his or her dreams; client is at an impasse in therapy; therapist has a dream about the client; client is being seen for long-term therapy; client is willing to work with dreams; client presents dreams as a way of avoiding important life issues; client presents a pleasant dream).

Part 5 contained 10 items, measured using a 5-point Likert scale (1 = not likely, 5 = very likely), about the likelihood of respondents working on dreams in therapy with different types of clients (e.g., client who is psychologically minded, client with posttraumatic stress disorder, client who is healthy and seeking growth, client with adjustment disorder, client with depression/anxiety, client with a personality disorder, client with substance abuse problems, client who is not psychologically minded, client with recurrent nightmares, and client with schizophrenia/psychoses).

Part 6 assessed therapists' attitudes toward dreams using the Attitudes Toward Dreams—Revised scale (ATD-R; Hill et al., 2001). The ATD-R is a 9-item self-report measure of an individual's attitudes about dreams. Participants responded to all items on a 5-point Likert scale (5 = high). Hill et al. (2001) showed that the revised scale had an internal consistency alpha of 0.88, was highly correlated with the original scale (0.91), and had a 2-week test-retest reliability of 0.92. For the present study, an internal consistency alpha of 0.90 was found for the ATD-R.

Procedure

Clinicians ($N = 257$) were randomly selected from the American Psychological Association's Division 42 (Independent Practice) and sent a packet containing the Therapist Dream Questionnaire and a self-addressed stamped return envelope. Although all participants were asked to complete Parts 1 and 6, only those therapists who had worked with clients in the previous 5 years (and thus were more likely to be accurate in reporting working with dreams in therapy) were asked to complete Parts 2–5. Therapists who did not return the packet were sent two reminder postcards as well as another copy of the Therapist Dream Questionnaire as follow-up measures. Of the 257 packets that were mailed, 129 were completed and returned and 28 could not be delivered, yielding a response rate of 58% (129/224). The return rate of 58% is comparable to that of other studies on clinicians in private practice (e.g., Fox, 2002, studied the dream interpretation experiences of 625 mental health clinicians and obtained a usable return rate of 42%; Keller et al., 1995, surveyed 500 psychologists' work with dreams in therapy and obtained a usable return rate of 46%). Of the 129 therapists who returned the questionnaire, 10 completed only Parts 1 and 6 because they had not seen clients in the previous 5 years.

RESULTS AND DISCUSSION

Demographic Variables

To determine whether cognitive therapists differed from psychodynamic or eclectic therapists on demographic variables, a series of one-way analyses of variance (ANOVA) was performed. Results showed no effects for age, gender, client hours per week, years of clinical experience, and work setting. Hence cognitive therapists generally had the same level of experience, saw the same number of clients, and worked in the same settings as therapists from other theoretical orientations in this sample.

Attitudes Toward Dreams, Dream Recall, and Personal Work on Dreams

All items reported in this section were measured on a 5-point Likert scale (where 5 = high), with the exception of dream recall scores, which were measured on an 11-point Likert scale (11 = high). Concerning attitudes toward dreams, results of a one-way analysis of variance with attitude toward dreams scores as the dependent variable and theoretical cluster as the independent variable showed that therapists' theoretical orientation was significantly related to attitudes toward dreams, $F(2, 109) = 26.95$, $p < 0.01$. Tukey's post hoc test revealed that therapists in the cognitive cluster had lower attitude toward dream scores ($M = 3.18$, $SD = 0.75$) compared to therapists in the psychodynamic cluster ($M = 4.33$, $SD = 0.55$) or the eclectic cluster ($M = 4.07$, $SD = 0.73$) (see Table 4.1). It is worth mentioning, however, that although cognitive therapists had lower attitudes toward dream scores than therapists in other theoretical orientations in this sample, the average score of cognitive therapists was about the midpoint on the attitude scale. Thus, overall, cognitive therapists seemed to have neutral attitudes toward dreams.

With respect to the dream recall of therapists, results of a one-way analysis of variance with estimated dream recall as the dependent variable and theoretical cluster as the independent variable showed that therapists' theoretical orientation was not significantly related to dream recall, $F(2, 109) = 2.22$, $p = 0.11$. Cognitive therapists reported that they recalled their dreams most mornings ($M = 4.68$, $SD = 3.08$), as did therapists in the psychodynamic cluster ($M = 6.19$, $SD = 2.37$) and the eclectic cluster ($M = 5.22$, $SD = 2.98$). It is important to note that although the means appear quite different, the standard deviations are very high in all three groups, suggesting significant variability in clinicians' ability to remember their dreams. On average, however, cognitive therapists in this sample were about the same as psychodynamic and eclectic therapists in terms of their reported dream recall.

Regarding personal work with dreams, results of a one-way analysis of variance with trying to figure out one's own dream scores as the dependent variable and theoretical cluster as the independent variable showed that therapists' theoretical orientation was significantly related to how often they tried to figure out their dreams on their own, $F(2, 106) = 8.11$, $p < 0.01$).

Tukey's post hoc test revealed that therapists in the cognitive cluster less frequently tried to figure out their own dreams ($M = 2.59$, $SD = 1.26$) than did therapists in the psychodynamic cluster ($M = 3.74$, $SD = 1.10$) or the eclectic cluster ($M = 3.44$, $SD = 1.25$).

Likewise, results of a one-way analysis of variance with talking about one's dream with a colleague, friend, or partner scores as the dependent

TABLE 4.1   Comparison of Clinicians' Attitudes Toward Dreams, Dream Recall, and Personal Work on Dreams

| | Theoretical cluster | | | | | |
| | Cognitive ($n = 40$) | | Psychodynamic ($n = 27$) | | Eclectic ($n = 45$) | |
	M	*SD*	*M*	*SD*	*M*	*SD*
Attitudes[1]	3.18	0.75	4.33	0.55	4.07	0.73
Dream recall[2]	4.68	3.08	6.19	2.37	5.68	2.69
Own dream work[3]	2.59	1.26	3.74	1.10	3.44	1.25
Training[4]	1.98	1.03	3.26	1.10	2.58	1.13
Competence[5]	2.13	1.14	3.44	1.09	3.18	0.97
Importance[6]	2.28	0.96	3.37	1.11	3.16	0.93
Clients[7]	14.03	18.14	44.08	26.49	24.26	23.78
Therapy time[8]	4.73	6.54	12.23	8.10	7.70	6.28

[1]Attitudes toward dreams scores (ATD-R; Hill et al., 2001). High scores indicate high levels on all variables.

[2]Estimated dream recall scores (Hill et al., 2001).

[3]Therapists' attempt to figure out their dreams on their own, where 5 = high frequency.

[4]Participants were asked to respond to the following question: "Rate how much training you have had in dream interpretation. Include in your estimate such things as workshops, supervision, reading, and graduate courses" on a 5-point Likert scale where 1 = no training, 5 = extensive training.

[5]Participants were asked to respond to the following question: "How competent do you feel as a therapist working with dreams in therapy?" on a 5-point Likert scale where 1 = not at all competent, 5 = extremely competent.

[6]Participants were asked to respond to the following question: "Overall, how important do you think it is to work with dreams in therapy?" on a 5-point Likert scale where 1 = not important, 5 = very important.

[7]Participants' estimate of the percentage of their clients who had brought dreams into therapy in the past year.

[8]Participants' estimate of the percentage of time they spend in therapy working on clients' dreams.

variable and theoretical cluster as the independent variable showed that therapists' theoretical orientation was significantly related to how often they sought help to figure out their dreams, $(F(2, 107) = 4.66, p < 0.01)$. Tukey's post hoc test revealed that therapists in the cognitive cluster less frequently sought help from others to figure out their own dreams ($M = 2.26$, $SD = 1.19$) compared to therapists in the psychodynamic cluster ($M = 3.08$, $SD = 1.23$) or the eclectic cluster ($M = 2.91$, $SD = 1.18$). An interesting finding was that cognitive clinicians were similar to therapists in other theoretical clusters in that they were unlikely to keep a current dream journal, $(F(2, 105) = 0.72, p = 0.49)$.

Hence, although there were no differences among therapists with respect to estimated dream recall, cognitive therapists had less positive attitudes toward dreams and were less likely to figure out their dreams on their own or to talk about their dreams with other people than were therapists with a psychodynamic or eclectic orientation.

Training, Competence, and Importance of Dream Interpretation

In order to interpret the data comparing training, competence, and the importance of dream interpretation, it was determined a priori that any mean ≥ 3.5 would indicate high endorsement, any mean between 2.5 and 3.49 would indicate moderate endorsement, and any mean ≤ 2.49 would indicate low endorsement of the item by participants. Thus cognitive therapists reported having a low amount of training in dream work ($M = 1.98$, $SD = 1.03$), with 17 therapists (43%) reporting having had no training. Results of a one-way analysis of variance with training in dream interpretation as the dependent variable and theoretical cluster as the independent variable showed that therapists' theoretical orientation was significantly related to training, $(F(2, 109) = 13.40, p < 0.01)$. Tukey's post hoc test revealed that therapists in the cognitive cluster had lower training scores ($M = 1.98$, $SD = 1.03$) compared to those of therapists in the psychodynamic cluster ($M = 3.26$, $SD = 1.10$) or the eclectic cluster ($M = 2.71$, $SD = 0.97$) (see Table 4.1).

Similarly, cognitive clinicians reported feeling low competence in dream interpretation ($M = 2.13$, $SD = 1.14$). A closer examination of the data for cognitive therapists showed that 15 clinicians (38%) reported feeling no competence in working with dreams, and no clinician in the cognitive cluster had high perceived competency. Results of a one-way analysis of variance with perceived competency in dream interpretation as the dependent variable and theoretical cluster as the independent variable showed that therapists' theoretical orientation was significantly related to perceived competency, $(F(2, 108) = 15.72, p < 0.01)$. Tukey's post hoc test revealed that therapists in the cognitive cluster had lower perceived competency scores ($M = 2.13$, $SD = 1.14$) compared to those of therapists in the psychodynamic cluster ($M = 3.44$, $SD = 1.09$) or eclectic cluster ($M = 3.18$, $SD = 0.97$) (see Table 4.1).

Finally, in terms of the importance of working with dreams, cognitive therapists on average gave a low endorsement to the importance of dream interpretation in therapy (M = 2.28, SD = 0.96), with 8 therapists (20%) specifying that it was not important and 1 therapist indicating that it was very important to work with dreams. Results of a one-way analysis of variance with belief about the importance of working with dreams in therapy as the dependent variable and theoretical cluster as the independent variable showed that therapists' theoretical orientation was significantly related to the importance of working with dreams, ($F(2, 109)$ = 12.59, $p < 0.01$). Tukey's post hoc test revealed that therapists in the cognitive cluster had lower scores for the importance of working with dreams (M = 2.28, SD = 0.96) compared to scores of therapists in the psychodynamic cluster (M = 3.37, SD = 1.11) or the eclectic cluster (M = 3.16, SD = 0.93).

Cognitive therapists, then, reported significantly less training in dream interpretation (e.g., workshops, supervision, readings, and/or graduate courses), reported significantly lower perceived competency in working with dreams, and gave less importance to working with dreams than did therapists in the psychodynamic cluster or eclectic cluster. Using the a priori determinations, cognitive therapists reported low amounts of training, low feelings of competence, and low endorsement on the importance of working with dreams. It is interesting to speculate about the relationship between training, competency, and perceived importance of working with dreams in therapy for cognitive therapists. For instance, cognitive therapists appear to have less training than therapists in other theoretical orientations, which could affect their feelings of competence in working with dreams in therapy. If a therapist has little training in working with dreams, then it is not surprising that she or he would feel less than competent when confronted with the task of helping a client understand a dream. One cognitive therapist in the sample reported, "I am not competent [in dream interpretation]." Similarly, another cognitive clinician revealed, "I don't work with dreams because it is not an area of competence." Likewise, one cognitive therapist mentioned that he did not work with dreams because of "lack of specific training." With little or no training and low perceived competency, it is no wonder that cognitive therapists thought it was less important to work on dreams in therapy than did therapists in other theoretical orientations. Fox (2002), for example, showed that clinicians' training in dream interpretation positively correlated with self-perceived level of competence in dream interpretation and efficacy of dream interpretation. Alternatively, perhaps cognitive therapists who believe that working with dreams in therapy is not important are less likely to seek out training opportunities and develop competencies in dream interpretation. Further research is needed to tease out the possible dynamics between training, competency, and perception of the importance of dream interpretation for cognitive therapists.

Amount of Time Therapists Spent Working
on Dreams in Therapy

An in-depth analysis along lines of theoretical orientation showed some differences in the amount of time clinicians in this sample worked with dreams. For instance, results of a one-way analysis of variance with time in therapy spent on dream interpretation as the dependent variable and theoretical cluster as the independent variable showed that therapists' theoretical orientation was significantly related to time in therapy focused on dream work, (F(2, 107) = 9.50, $p < 0.01$). Tukey's post hoc test revealed that therapists in the cognitive and eclectic clusters had lower estimated time percentage spent on dreams in therapy ($M = 4.73$, $SD = 6.54$; $M = 7.70$, $SD = 6.28$, respectively) compared to therapists in the psychodynamic cluster ($M = 12.23$, $SD = 8.10$) (see Table 4.1). Similarly, results of a one-way analysis of variance with percentage of clients bringing in dreams as the dependent variable and theoretical cluster as the independent variable showed that therapists' theoretical orientation was significantly related to the percentage of clients bringing dreams into therapy, ($F(2, 106) = 14.00$, $p < 0.01$). Tukey's post hoc test revealed that therapists in the cognitive and eclectic clusters had lower percentages of clients bringing in dreams ($M = 14.03$, $SD = 18.14$; $M = 24.26$, $SD = 23.78$, respectively) compared to therapists in the psychodynamic cluster ($M = 44.08$, $SD = 26.49$) (see Table 4.1).

Psychodynamic therapists, then, reported spending significantly more time in therapy working on clients' dreams and had a significantly higher percentage of clients bringing in dreams than did either cognitive or eclectic clinicians. The difference in therapy time devoted to dream interpretation and the percentage of clients bringing in dreams between clinicians in the psychodynamic and cognitive clusters makes sense given that psychodynamic clinicians in the sample had more positive attitudes toward dreams, had more training in dream interpretation, felt more competent in working with dreams, and placed more importance on working with dreams in therapy than did cognitive clinicians. Although there were differences between the psychodynamic and cognitive therapists, it is worth highlighting that cognitive therapists indicated spending at least some time in therapy on dreams (about 5%) and reported having a sizable percentage of their clients (14%) bring in dreams to therapy during the last year. For example, one cognitive therapist in the sample noted that if "dreams come up, I work with them." Hence the results indicate that some cognitive therapists are spending time on dream work in therapy.

Dream Activities in Therapy

Table 4.2 shows the means and standard deviations for the dream activity items across the three therapist clusters. In addition, Table 4.2 shows the

TABLE 4.2 Comparison of Clinicians' Dream Activities

Indicate how much you do the following activities in individual therapy:

| | Theoretical cluster | | | | | | | |
| | Cognitive | | Psychodynamic | | Eclectic | | F value | Sig |
	M	SD	M	SD	M	SD		
Listen if clients bring in dreams	4.13	1.12	4.59	0.89	4.47	0.94	1.97	.15
Explore connections of dream images to waking life	3.21	1.32	4.15	0.91	3.96	1.22	6.08	.01
Ask clients to describe dream images in greater detail	2.68	1.40	3.93	0.87	3.87	1.06	13.69	.01
Encourage clients to reexperience feelings in dreams	2.63	1.50	3.19	1.36	3.42	1.37	3.30	.04
Collaborate with clients to construct dream interpretation	2.61	1.24	3.81	1.08	3.93	1.12	15.54	.01
Interpret dreams in terms of waking life experiences	2.61	1.08	3.41	0.89	3.64	1.19	9.95	.01
Work with conflicts that are represented in dreams	2.55	1.11	3.78	0.97	3.58	1.22	12.19	.01
Encourage clients to associate to dream images	2.42	1.45	3.67	1.36	3.36	1.37	7.50	.01
Interpret dreams in terms of past experiences	2.26	1.01	3.44	0.85	3.36	1.13	15.07	.01
Use dream images as metaphors later in therapy	2.21	1.07	3.22	1.25	3.16	1.13	9.04	.01
Invite clients to tell dreams	2.05	1.09	2.96	1.22	2.80	1.08	6.67	.01
Collaborate with clients to make changes based on dreams	1.84	1.10	2.70	1.10	2.91	1.31	8.84	.01

(continued)

TABLE 4.2 *(continued)*

Indicate how much you do the following activities in individual therapy:

| | Theoretical cluster | | | | | | | |
| | Cognitive | | Psychodynamic | | Eclectic | | *F* value | Sig |
	M	*SD*	*M*	*SD*	*M*	*SD*		
Help clients try to change dreams	1.82	1.09	1.96	1.19	1.96	1.09	0.20	.82
Explain how you work with dreams	1.74	1.00	2.33	0.95	2.76	1.25	8.88	.00
Interpret the dream for the client	1.74	0.89	2.67	0.96	2.47	1.06	8.76	.01
Suggest changes clients could make based on dream learning	1.63	0.79	2.11	1.12	2.40	1.16	5.73	.01
Interpret dreams in spiritual terms	1.58	0.72	2.15	1.17	2.07	0.99	3.73	.03
Interpret dreams according to unconscious wishes	1.55	0.72	2.63	1.21	2.42	1.22	10.05	.01
Interpret dreams in terms of the therapy relationship	1.39	0.64	3.19	0.92	2.47	1.06	33.12	.01
Ask clients to act out different parts of dreams	1.39	0.79	1.52	0.75	2.07	1.21	5.46	.01
Mention that you are willing to work with dreams	1.37	0.75	2.44	1.34	2.04	1.04	9.12	.01
Interpret dreams according to archetypes	1.24	0.49	1.70	0.91	1.87	1.06	5.70	.01

Note. Dream activity items were arranged in order of decreasing frequency according to cognitive therapists' responses. High scores indicate high endorsement of dream activities in therapy on a 5-point scale (1 = never, 5 = frequently). Means > 3.5 = high endorsement, means < 3.49 and > 2.5 = moderate endorsement, means < 2.49 = low endorsement.

results of a series of one-way ANOVAs with dream activity items as the dependent variables and therapist cluster as the independent variable. Results indicated that cognitive therapists were less likely to use most types of dream activities than were psychodynamic or eclectic clinicians. However, there were no differences between therapist clusters in listening to a client's dream: cognitive, psychodynamic, and eclectic clinicians all strongly affirmed that they would listen if a client brought a dream into therapy. Likewise, there were no differences between therapists on helping the client to change the dream: cognitive, psychodynamic, and eclectic clinicians all reported being unlikely to use that particular dream activity in session. Although they generally reported engaging in dream activities less frequently than clinicians from other orientations, results from Table 4.2 show that cognitive therapists did engage in some dream activities. For example, items receiving moderate endorsement by cognitive therapists included exploring connections of dream images to the client's waking life, asking the client to describe dream images in greater detail, and collaborating with the client to construct a meaning for the dream. Cognitive therapists reported low endorsement for such dream activities as interpreting the dream for the client, helping the client change the dream, and inviting the client to tell a dream. As one cognitive therapist reported, "On a seldom basis, usually with difficult clients, I may ask them to talk about their dreams." Thus the data suggest that cognitive therapists would at least listen if a client brought in a dream and were likely to use some exploratory activities with moderate frequency, but are not likely to go into much depth in working with clients' dreams or to initiate working with dreams.

It is interesting to review the information in Table 4.2 with the understanding that almost half of these cognitive therapists (43%) reported having received no training in dream interpretation. Therapists with little or no training would probably be unlikely to mention that they are willing to work with dreams or to explain to clients how they work with dreams. Likewise, they would almost certainly not engage in complicated dream activities such as asking the client to act out different parts of the dream. Hence, training (or lack of it) may relate to cognitive therapists' likelihood of using certain dream work activities.

Therapy Situations and Client Types

Table 4.3 shows the means and standard deviations for therapists' responses to dream situations and client types. In addition, Table 4.3 shows the results

TABLE 4.3 Comparison of When Clinicians Work With Dreams

Indicate how likely you would be to work with dreams in the following situations:

	Cognitive		Psychodynamic		Eclectic		F value	Sig
	M	SD	M	SD	M	SD		
Client presents troubling dreams or nightmares.	3.82	1.09	4.63	0.74	4.27	1.01	5.62	.01
Client presents recurrent dreams.	3.66	1.21	4.63	0.74	4.22	1.06	7.03	.01
Client has recurrent nightmares.	3.37	1.20	4.30	1.07	4.09	1.06	6.71	.01
Client has posttraumatic stress disorder (PTSD).	2.97	1.33	4.06	1.02	3.91	1.14	8.86	.01
Client is interested in learning about his/her dreams.	2.74	1.41	4.33	0.78	3.80	1.20	15.60	.01
Client is psychologically minded.	2.64	1.32	4.30	0.95	3.96	1.07	20.72	.01
Client has adjustment disorder.	2.50	1.27	3.74	1.16	3.58	1.14	11.54	.01
Client is seeking growth.	2.42	1.24	4.00	1.07	3.84	1.21	19.47	.01
Client has depression/anxiety.	2.37	1.15	3.77	1.04	3.58	1.14	16.53	.01
Client presents a pleasant dream.	2.29	0.87	3.41	1.05	3.37	1.20	13.27	.01
Client is willing to work with dreams.	2.26	1.03	4.11	1.09	3.62	1.25	24.40	.01
Client is being seen for long-term therapy.	2.13	1.04	4.11	1.05	3.67	1.17	31.44	.01
Client presents a dream as a way of avoiding important life issues.	2.10	0.95	3.33	1.27	3.29	1.33	12.64	.01
Client has a personality disorder.	1.97	0.97	3.25	1.23	2.96	1.15	12.57	.01
Client is at an impasse in therapy (i.e., is stuck).	1.95	0.96	3.48	1.16	3.00	1.19	17.09	.01
Client has substance abuse problem.	1.79	0.86	3.15	1.18	3.07	1.22	17.88	.01
Client has schizophrenia/psychosis.	1.61	0.92	1.81	0.68	2.07	1.10	2.47	.09
Client is not psychologically minded.	1.50	0.73	3.11	1.22	2.47	0.94	23.81	.01

Note: Therapy situation and client type items were arranged in order of decreasing frequency according to cognitive therapists' responses. High scores indicate high endorsement of working with dreams in various situations on a 5-point scale (1 = not likely, 5 = very likely). Means > 3.5 = high likelihood, means < 3.49 and > 2.5 = moderate likelihood, means < 2.49 = low likelihood.

of a series of one-way ANOVAs with therapy situation and client items as the dependent variables and therapist cluster as the independent variable. Results indicated that, overall, cognitive therapists were less likely to use dreams in most therapy situations and with most clients than were psychodynamic or eclectic clinicians. One exception to this pattern was in the case of working on dreams with a schizophrenic or psychotic client. There were no differences in responses between cognitive, psychodynamic, and eclectic therapists—all clinicians endorsed that they were unlikely to conduct dream interpretations with those types of clients.

Although cognitive therapists showed themselves to be less likely to work on dreams in various therapy situations and with various types of clients in comparison to therapists from other orientations, cognitive therapists did seem willing to work on dreams in certain conditions and with certain clients. For instance, Table 4.3 indicates that cognitive therapists were very likely to work on dreams when clients presented troubling dreams, nightmares, or recurrent dreams. Cognitive therapists indicated that they were moderately likely to conduct dream interpretation when clients seemed interested in their dreams, were insightful, or were diagnosed with a condition, such as posttraumatic stress disorder (PTSD), that involved distressing dreams. One cognitive therapist, for example, reported that on a client diagnosed with PTSD she used imagery techniques focused on the client's recurring nightmares. Similarly, another cognitive therapist noted that it was helpful to work on dreams with a Vietnam veteran client who had severe PTSD. Hence cognitive therapists said that they were more likely to work on dreams in therapy when clients presented dreams as a troubling issue than when clients were distressed in other areas. Moreover, it seems that, regardless of their theoretical orientation, therapists were unwilling to work on dreams with clients whose perceptions of reality were distorted and thus may have had difficulty differentiating between dreaming and waking-life activities.

Functions of Dreams

Table 4.4 shows the means and standard deviations for therapists' beliefs about the functions of dreams. In addition, Table 4.4 shows the results of a series of one-way ANOVAs with dream functions as the dependent variables and therapist cluster as the independent variable. Results indicate some variability among therapist clusters regarding the functions of dreams. For instance, cognitive clinicians were less likely than clinicians from other clusters to endorse that dreams were attempts at problem solving, reflections of waking

TABLE 4.4 Comparison of Clinicians' Beliefs About the Functions of Dreams

| | Theoretical cluster | | | | | | | |
| | Cognitive | | Psychodynamic | | Eclectic | | F value | Sig |
	M	SD	M	SD	M	SD		
Dreams are attempts at problem solving.	3.10	0.93	3.81	1.04	4.07	0.81	12.49	.01
Dreams reflect waking life.	3.05	1.06	3.63	0.88	3.78	1.02	5.94	.01
Dreams represent unconscious messages.	2.71	1.18	4.22	0.89	4.02	1.00	23.72	.01
Dreams represent the brain's attempt to purge unneeded connections.	2.48	1.36	2.07	1.21	2.20	1.12	0.97	.38
Dreams are due to random firings of the brain.	2.28	1.22	1.81	0.83	2.07	1.10	1.45	.24
Dreams are meaningless.	1.80	1.07	1.26	0.53	1.31	0.56	5.59	.01
Dreams are messages from external sources (i.e., God, devil, deceased relatives).	1.18	0.45	1.52	1.05	1.41	0.82	1.78	.17

Note: Dream function items were arranged in order of decreasing frequency according to cognitive therapists' responses. High scores indicate high endorsement on the function of dreams on a 5-point scale (1 = strongly disagree, 5 = strongly agree). Means > 3.5 = high endorsement, means < 3.49 and > 2.5 = moderate endorsement, means < 2.49 = low endorsement.

life, or representations of unconscious messages. Furthermore, cognitive therapists were more likely than other therapists to indicate that they considered dreams as meaningless. There were no differences between therapists along lines of theoretical orientation on beliefs that dreams are due to random firings of the brain, are attempts to purge connections, or are messages from external sources—all therapists in the sample gave low endorsements to those beliefs.

These results may be a bit misleading, however, if one considers cognitive clinicians' responses in the context of the a priori determinations (see Table 4.4). Hence although their endorsements were not as strong as those of other clinicians, cognitive therapists moderately agreed that dreams are attempts at problem solving, reflect waking life, and represent unconscious messages. Moreover, cognitive therapists indicated low agreement with the statement that dreams are meaningless. Overall then, cognitive therapists are unlikely to believe that dreams serve a biological function or are the result of supernatural causes. They are more likely to consider that dreams are not meaningless events but have some value or worth.

Implications for Cognitive Therapists' Training and Practice

Results from this survey of clinicians in private practice indicate that cognitively oriented therapists have less training in working with dreams than do therapists from other theoretical orientations. Similarly, cognitive therapists have lower perceived competency in working with clients' dreams as compared to psychodynamic and eclectic therapists. Two implications of this finding are that cognitive therapists may want to seek out training in working with dreams and that training programs may want to consider opportunities in dream work for students. Also, it seems important for cognitive therapists to have some kind of rationale for working with clients' dreams. As one cognitive clinician in this sample noted, "If I were trained to understand how [dream interpretation] might be helpful to people, I might use some of this." Training in dream interpretation, therefore, appears to be a crucial factor in encouraging dream work among cognitive therapists.

Another important finding from this study is that clients are bringing in dreams to cognitive therapists, and cognitive clinicians are spending some time in therapy working on clients' dreams. Cognitive therapists seem willing to at least listen if a client brings in a dream, and they will engage in some activities of an exploratory nature but are unlikely to focus on more complex dream work activities or to invite clients to tell dreams. As one cognitive therapist reported, "I usually allow the client to bring [dreams] up. If they do, then I'm willing to explore the dream." In a similar manner, another cognitive clinician noted, "I don't use [dreams] unless a client brings them up (not often)." Likewise, a therapist in the cognitive cluster mentioned, "I don't ask about dreams and people don't volunteer in my experience." It may be that cognitive therapists are reluctant to engage in more complicated dream activities because they lack the necessary training. Again, training may be the key to expanding the skills and activities of cognitive therapists in dream activities.

In conclusion, the findings of this study indicate that although cognitive therapists are less inclined and oriented to work with dreams in therapy than therapists from other orientations, there appears to be some evidence that cognitive clinicians who engage in some dream activities believe that dreams have potential value and are willing to work on dreams with clients who present troubling dreams or nightmares in therapy. Additionally, there seems to be an interest among cognitive therapists in this sample to receive more training in working with clients' dreams. As a result, resources (such as the current book) specifically designed for cognitive therapists may be an important first step in encouraging cognitive clinicians to incorporate dream work into their therapy sessions.

REFERENCES

Cartwright, R. D. (1993). Who needs their dreams? The usefulness of dreams in psychotherapy. *Journal of the American Academy of Psychoanalysis, 21*(4), 539–547.

Cartwright, R. D., & Lamberg, L. (1992). *Crisis dreaming: Using your dreams to solve your problems.* New York: HarperCollins.

Cogar, M., & Hill, C. E. (1992). Examining the effects of brief individual dream interpretation. *Dreaming, 2,* 239–248.

Crook, R. E., & Hill, C. E. (in press). Working with dreams in psychotherapy: The therapists' perspective. *Dreaming.*

Diemer, R. A., Lobell, L. K., Vivino, B. L., & Hill, C. E. (1996). Comparison of dream interpretation, event interpretation, and unstructured sessions in brief therapy. *Journal of Counseling Psychology, 43*(1), 99–112.

Erikson, E. (1954). The dream specimen of psychoanalysis. In R. Knight & C. Friedman (Eds.), *Psychoanalytic psychiatry and psychology* (pp. 131–170). New York: International Universities Press.

Falk, D. R., & Hill, C. E. (1995). The effectiveness of dream interpretation groups for women undergoing a divorce transition. *Dreaming, 5*(1), 29–42.

Fox, S. A. (2002). A survey of mental health clinicians' use of dream interpretation in psychotherapy. *Dissertation Abstracts International: Section B. The Sciences & Engineering, 62*(7-B), 3376.

Freud, S. (1965). *The interpretation of dreams* (J. Strachey, Trans.). New York: Avon. (Original work published 1900)

Gendlin, E. T. (1986). *Let your body interpret your dreams.* Wilmette, IL: Chiron Publications.

Heaton, K. J., Hill, C. E., Petersen, D., Rochlen, A. B., & Zack, J. (1998). A comparison of therapist-facilitated and self-guided dream interpretation sessions. *Journal of Counseling Psychology, 45,* 115–122.

Hill, C. E. (1996). *Working with dreams in psychotherapy.* New York: Guilford.

Hill, C. E., Diemer, R. A., & Heaton, K. J. (1997). Dream interpretation sessions: Who volunteers, who benefits, and what volunteer clients view as most and least helpful. *Journal of Counseling Psychology, 44,* 53–62.

Hill, C. E., Diemer, R., Hess, S., Hillyer, A., & Seeman, R. (1993). Are the effects of dream interpretation on session quality, insight, and emotions due to the dream itself, to projection, or to the interpretation process? *Dreaming, 3*(4), 269–280.

Hill, C. E., Kelley, F. A., Davis, T. L., Crook, R. E., Maldonado, L. E., Turkson, M. A., et al. (2001). Predictors of outcome of dream interpretation sessions: Volunteer client characteristics, dream characteristics, and type of interpretation. *Dreaming, 11,* 53–72.

Hiscock, M., & Cohen, D. B. (1973). Visual imagery and dream recall. *Journal of Research in Personality, 7*(2), 179–188.

Johnson, R. A. (1986). *Inner work: Using dreams and creative imagination for personal growth and integration.* San Francisco: Harper & Row.

Jung, C. G. (1974). *Dreams* (R. F. C. Hull, Trans.). Princeton, NJ: Princeton University Press.

Keller, J. W., Brown, G., Maier, K., Steinfurth, K., Hall, S., & Piotrowski, C. (1995). Use of dreams in therapy: A survey of clinicians in private practice. *Psychological Reports, 76,* 1288–1290.

Mahrer, A. R. (1990). *Dream work in psychotherapy and self-change.* New York: Norton.

Robbins, P. R., & Tanck, R. H. (1988). Interest in dreams and dream recall. *Perceptual and Motor Skills, 66,* 291–294.

Rochlen, A. B., Ligiero, D. P., Hill, C. E., & Heaton, K. J. (1999). Effects of training in dream recall and dream interpretation skills on dream recall, attitudes, and dream interpretation outcome. *Journal of Counseling Psychology, 46,* 27–34.

Schredl, M., Bohusch, C., Kahl, J., Mader, A., & Somesan, A. (2000). The use of dreams in psychotherapy: A survey of psychotherapists in private practice. *Journal of Psychotherapy Practice and Research, 9*(2), 81–87.

Weiss, L. (1986). *Dream analysis in psychotherapy.* New York: Pergamon.

Wonnell, T. L., & Hill, C. E. (2001). Effects of including the action stage in dream interpretation. *Journal of Counseling Psychology, 47*(3), 372–379.

Zack, J. S., & Hill, C. E. (1998). Predicting outcome of dream interpretation sessions by dream valence, dream arousal, attitudes toward dreams, and waking life stress. *Dreaming, 8*(3), 169–185.

PART II

Objectivist Approaches

Dreams as an Unappreciated Therapeutic Avenue for Cognitive-Behavioral Therapists

HAROLD E. DOWEIKO

> It is not our body which feels, not our mind which thinks, but we, as single human beings, who both feel and think.
> —St. Thomas Aquinas (Adels, 1987)

The dream experience, long the mainstay of psychoanalytic inquiry, has essentially been abandoned by psychotherapists whose training was completed in the last quarter of the 20th century. At the same time, traditional psychoanalytic theory has been banished to the outermost reaches of therapy and is viewed with suspicion by most present-day therapists. While it is not the task of this chapter to determine whether psychoanalytic theory should or should not have been virtually banished from the realm of psychotherapy, it is suggested here that in relegating psychoanalysis to the hinterland of therapeutic inquiry, the cognitive-behavioral schools of psychotherapy have also dismissed a potentially useful tool in working with the client: dream therapy. It is the purpose of this chapter to suggest a model within which dream therapy might be integrated into cognitive-behavioral therapy.

THE NEUROBIOLOGY OF DREAMING

During the decade of the 1990s, or the "decade of the brain," more was learned about how the brain functions than had been discovered in all of the preceding centuries (Damasio, 1999). Partly as a result of the remarkable discoveries in neuroscience made during this single decade, scientists have come to accept the theory that there are three basic states of existence: (1) full waking, (2) sleep, and (3) the phases of sleep in which dreaming takes place. Further, scientists have come to understand that each state of existence is quantitatively different from the others in form and function (Hobson, 1999a).

The average individual spends eight hours of each day asleep, but the process of sleep is not static. Rather, researchers have identified four main stages in the phenomenon known as sleep; the individual glides through these stages in a cycle that last between 60 and 90 minutes. When in the deepest stage of sleep, Stage 4 (or "Delta") sleep, the sleeper will develop a psychomotor activity known as rapid eye movement (REM) sleep. There is a known relationship between REM sleep and the third state of existence: dreaming. About 70% of those individuals who are awakened from REM sleep will report having experienced a dream (Gillin, Seifritz, Zoltoski, & Salin-Pascual, 2000). Such REM-stage dreams are usually vivid, bizarre, and filled with complex imagery (Hobson, 1999a). However, individuals awakened from non-REM (NREM) sleep stages, especially the deeper stages of NREM sleep, also report dream experiences about 10% to 20% of the time (Gillin et al., 2000). These NREM dreams tend to be dull, analytical, without the vibrant imagery noted in REM dreams.

Researchers have utilized electroencephalographic (EEG) studies of the brain wave patterns during REM and NREM dream states and have discovered that during NREM dreams the cortex of the brain is relatively inactive as compared to REM sleep (Hobson, 1999b). Given the fact that REM and NREM dreams occur at different phases of the sleep cycle, with different patterns of cortical arousal during each phase, it should not be surprising to learn that the REM and NREM dreams reported to scientists are quite different in nature (Flanagan, 2000; Hobson, 1999b).

Typical dream reports include calm acceptance of imagery and behaviors that are nothing short of bizarre. The dreamer casually walks across bodies of water or through walls, or calmly accepts an instantaneous switch in dream location from one site to another a thousand or more miles away. One reason why dreams might seem so bizarre is that although the average person spends 1.5 to 2 hours per night in the dream state, she or he is lucky to remember more than a few minutes' worth of the dream (Hobson, 1999a, 1999b). Another reason why the REM dream experience involves bizarre experiences is that, during this phase of sleep, the frontal cortex is, in effect, "switched off" (Hobson, 1999a, 1999b). In effect, the waking memory of the dream is the outcome of a process in which the now fully awakened brain attempts to make sense of the dream process (Hobson, 1999a, 1999b).

The Importance of Dreaming

During REM sleep, and especially during the REM dream state, acetylcholine levels closely approximate those seen in the waking brain. At the same time, brain serotonin and norepinephrine levels are drastically reduced, with the result being that the individual experiences a form of temporary insanity during REM sleep (Hobson, 1999a, 1999b). This process of temporary-insanity-while-in-REM-sleep is one characteristic of the human species. If the average individual lives to the age of 70, he or she will spend approximately 50,000 hours of his or her life dreaming (Hobson, 1989). In other words, the average individual might spend 1/12th of his or her lifetime in the dream state. From an evolutionary standpoint, any activity that occupies 1/12th of the organism's time must be of critical importance to the survival of the organism. This theory is supported by the observation that rats who are deprived of REM sleep for extended periods of time will die from a metabolic dyscontrol syndrome. Humans who have been deprived of normal REM sleep time, either because of illness or the abuse of certain chemical compounds that interfere with REM sleep, will experience "REM rebound" when the condition that prevented normal REM sleep is removed (Hobson, 1999b). Subjectively, the experience of REM rebound involves vivid, often frightening dreams, which might be so intense that the individual will resume the abuse of chemicals in order to be able to sleep again (Doweiko, 1999).

STATEMENT OF THE PROBLEM

Sleep is a complex phenomenon, and EEG studies have identified four distinct stages in the sleep cycle. The first stage of sleep is a short, transitional phase that normally makes up 5% or less of the individual's sleep time (Gillin et al., 2000). Electrical activity during Stage 1 sleep is marked by low-voltage activity over a number of frequencies and slow eye movements. The sleeper is easily awakened from Stage 1 sleep and will not report any dream activity after being awakened.

Unless prevented from being able to progress, the sleeper enters Stage 2 sleep within a short period of time. Stage 2 normally comprises 45% to 75% of total sleep time and is identified by the presence of "sleep spindles" and

K-complex waves in the sleeper's EEG (Gillin et al., 2000). The individual is less easily awakened from Stage 2 sleep, and upon waking will not report having experienced any dreams before being disturbed by insensitive researchers. If left asleep, the individual will eventually progress to Stage 3 sleep. In Stage 3 sleep, "Delta" wave patterns are first noted in the EEG, while Stage 4 (or "Delta") sleep is marked by periods where more than 50% of the electrical activity is marked by Delta wave activity.

During Stage 4 sleep, the individual will experience short periods of REM sleep. REM periods also increase in length with each subsequent cycle through stages. The EEG will show characteristic patterns of low voltage and fast frequency activity, and the eyes will flit back and forth under the closed eyelids almost as if the dreamer were watching a movie on his or her personal movie screen. During this stage of sleep, the dreamer will lose control over major muscle groups and, if awakened rapidly enough, will report having experienced a dream. If left alone, the sleeper will cycle through all four stages, approaching (but normally not entering) Stage 1 sleep again every 60 to 90 minutes before starting another cycle.

The most memorable component of the sleep experience is, for most persons, the *dream state*. The experience of dreaming has been quite moving for many persons, often being cited as the cause of panic attacks, the source of new insights into problems facing the dreamer, or a period in which the dreamer might experience memories of past events or contact with lost family members. Events of such importance have been viewed as being of importance to the individual, and scientists have long struggled to understand the forces that initiated the dream experience and their significance for the dreamer. Early attempts to understand the dream experience were guided by Freudian (1965) theory, which rested upon the neurological paradigms of the late 1800s. Freud (1965) viewed the dream experience as being shaped primarily by internal psychological forces and established an eloquent theory of dreams, their meaning for the dreamer, and their analysis. Unfortunately, although Freudian (1965) dream theory forms the foundation upon which countless books, journal articles, and stories in the popular press are based, this theory is no longer accepted by most neurobiologists. In spite of the lack of acceptance by the present generation of neurologists, modifications of traditional Freudian theory continue to be advanced as explanations for the dream experience. For example: "Dreams are attributed the function of incorporating emotionally salient elements from the dreamers' waking life and treating them in ways that mitigate the strong affect in a restorative or adaptive manner" (Newell & Cartright, 2000, p. 34). While this perspective presents a very enticing armchair appeal, it fails to take into account neurobiological research findings suggesting that the dream experience is the result of an extremely complex process of neuronal activation and suppression in the sleeper's brain. During the period of dreaming, certain regions of the brain are selectively "switched off," while other regions of the brain become exceptionally active (Hobson & McCarley, 1977; Hobson, 1989, 1999a, 1999b). These studies suggest that dream imagery itself is nothing more than a form of "noise" created by the brain's activities during certain phases of sleep. Up until this time, and herein lies the crux of this chapter, cognitive-behavioral therapists have virtually ignored the dream state in their efforts to help their clients.

In an earlier paper (Doweiko, 1982), this author suggested a way that the dream might be utilized by the cognitive-behavioral therapist. This article met with little acceptance, possibly because of a basic misunderstanding surrounding the use of the dream experience within cognitive-behavioral therapy. In brief, although the dream experience itself is shaped by neurobiological factors that lie well outside the range of cognitive-behavioral psychotherapies, and although the dream occurs in an altered state of existence that also lies outside the scope of cognitive-behavioral psychotherapy, *the dreamer's interpretation of his or her dreams takes place while he or she is in a normal waking state.* In other words:

> . . . we can't actually do the science on dreams themselves because we have no means of spying directly on the movie being played in the mind of the dreamer. Instead, we must rely on the dreamer's subsequent reports. And dream reports, by virtue of the fact that the dreamer must put whatever images and sensations he or she can recall into words, have already been interpreted. (Hobson, 1999b, p. 181)

This is actually a strength when cognitive-behavioral therapies are applied to the process of dream interpretation. As Hobson (1999a) noted, the process of dream interpretation is quite risky—what "we see, feel, and do in our dreams reveals our specific and personal predilections" (p. 93). In other words, when the dreamer relates the content of her or his dream, she or he either consciously or unconsciously will impose some form of structure on that dream (Flanagan, 2000). This takes place while the dreamer is in the waking state. Thus the logic that the dreamer will use to reconstruct the dream will include the same cognitive distortions that she or he (mis)uses to interpret external reality.

It is suggested here that cognitive-behavioral therapists, in avoiding the perceived heresies of dream interpretation, have failed to appreciate the fact that the process of dream recall and discussion takes place in the waking state of mind and not while the dreamer is asleep. The individual's reported memory of the dream experience will thus utilize the same cognitive distortions that the individual uses to support his or her waking psychopathology, since he or she developed the memory while awake. Failing to understand this has prevented the cognitive-behavioral schools from being able to harvest the rich source of data about the client found in his or her dream life.

This is not to suggest that the cognitive-behavioral therapists take a step (or steps) back to the relatively simplistic work of Freud's (1965) interpretation of dreams. Rather, it is suggested that, because the modern neurobiological theory of dreams postulates that dreams are separate states of existence from the waking state, the cognitive-behavioral therapist is delivered from the need to address what happens *during* these periods in the individual's life. At the same time, modern neurobiological theory allows the cognitive-behavioral therapist to explain some of the client's experiences during the dream state, making them less frightening and incomprehensible. For example, the therapist might inform the client that during the dream state, the amygdala, which is where fear seems to be generated, is especially active. This seems to explain why so many dreams have themes of danger, fear, or threats built into them. It is necessary to recall that the architecture of sleep evolved in an era when humans, and their ancestors, were vulnerable to attacks from any number of predators. It would thus make sense that the nervous system would prime the individual for fight or flight situations at night when the individual was asleep and thus at increased vulnerability to possible attack. When this is explained to the client, his or her dream becomes less frightening and more understandable. But the individual's reported memories of his or her dreams are interpreted during the conscious state, which is, by an amazing coincidence, the same state of awareness in which cognitive-behavioral therapy is conducted. This makes them legitimate areas of therapeutic inquiry and intervention, although in a different manner than is utilized during Freudian (1965) dream analysis. The cognitive-behavioral therapist does not need to ignore, or worse yet, shrink in horror from, the client's reports of dream memories. Neither does the cognitive-behavioral therapist need to dismiss the client's dreams as being unworthy of therapeutic interest.

This is true because we all have an "innate tendency to project meaning onto stimuli" (Hobson, 1999a, p. 93). The individual's dream experience provides a stimulus field onto which she or he will project her or his unique meaning(s) when she or he is conscious. Within this context, the "dream" experience is, in reality, an attempt on the part of the individual to interpret and impose some measure of order upon the chaotic sensory impressions left over from the dream state that existed while the individual was asleep (Hobson, 1989). For example, Beck and Ward (1961) found that, when compared to nondepressed persons, depressed persons tended to report significantly more dreams that were "an expression of a persistent need to inflict suffering on the self" (p. 66). It is now possible to conclude that the depressive themes found in these dreams might have been an artifact of the conscious recollection of dream memories made by depressed patients who tend to view life with cognitive distortions that enhance and support their state of mind (Weiss, 1986).

THE "5 Ps" OF DEPRESSION

To illustrate the above process, consider the state of depression. The cognitive-behavioral therapist might first explain to a depressed client that there are certain characteristic, cognitive distortions that are both representative of, and that contribute to, the state of depression. These are: (1) perfectionism ("I must be perfect in everything that I do—99% is not good enough!"); (2) personalizing ("If anything bad happens, I am at fault"); (3) pessimism ("Nothing that I do ever works out"); (4) perpetuating ("It will never get better"); and, especially in extreme cases of depression, (5) paranoia ("People don't like me . . . they look at me all the time"). The therapist will have explained that not every depressed client has all five of the forms of cognitive distortion discussed here, but that most people have at least two, if not more, of these habitual ways of viewing self and others. It would have been explained that these cognitive rules would then "flavor" the way that we interpret not only the social environment but also our dreams. Having established the concept of cognitive distortion as an element that is both characteristic of, and which contributes to, depression, the cognitive-behavioral therapist then is free to address dreams that might be remembered by the client.

What follows is a segment of a therapy session in which a client being treated for depression spontaneously reported having a memory of a dream from the night before.

Patient: I was in the conference room, doing some paperwork. I don't know why I was working there rather than in my office, but I was all alone. Suddenly, John, Matt, and Sue and some people that I did not know came in with a student. They sat the student down and then sat down around him. I asked Matt whether or not I should move and he said "yes." So, I gathered up my papers and started to leave the conference room. Then John said that I should not go very far. After they finished with the student, Sue and I had to go to meet with an administrator and somebody who had complained about my work. Then I woke up.

Therapist: How did you feel when you woke up?

Patient: Initially, I felt bummed out. Then I remembered that it was only a dream, and I started to feel better.

Therapist: Good! Remember: the dreaming mind is worlds away from the waking mind. But I'm curious about what made you feel bummed out.

Patient: I was upset because somebody had complained about my work. I try to do a good job. I really do! Yet somebody complained about how I do my job. It made me feel a sense of shame . . . worthlessness.

Therapist: So you bring the same demand for perfection into your dreams that you do into your waking mind? Notice that in this dream fragment, you do not know the nature of the complaint or even if it is your fault or not. Yet it seems that you are holding yourself to the standard of perfection ("Nobody should complain about me!"), and it seems that you are personalizing the blame ("If there is a complaint, *I* must have done something wrong") in this dream fragment. These are some of the same issues that we have discovered contribute to your feelings of depression.

In this second example, the therapist is working with a patient who is in the early stages of recovery from an alcohol problem. Although warned that he would have "using" dreams that might be quite intense, the patient reported to his aftercare support group that he had a dream of unusual intensity that left him feeling quite anxious and upset when he awakened. The therapist asked him to relate his dream to the group in order to help the group members understand why it was so distressing to the patient.

Patient: I was in Sam's bar, with my brother and a couple of friends. We were playing pool. Everybody was drinking beer, except for me. I was drinking [soda] pop. There was a band playing, and I remember thinking that it would be nice to have a can of beer. I remember watching Tom drink his beer and thinking to myself that it *looked* good. I could almost taste it. I woke up and thought that I had actually had some beer to drink because I could taste it in my mouth.

Therapist: How did you feel in the instant that you woke up?

Patient: I was covered in sweat . . . I was scared . . . was shaking . . . it seemed so real that I woke up thinking that I had drank some beer . . . I could almost taste it, and it was so intense that it scared me.

Therapist: Remember what we discussed earlier about how a part of the brain called the amygdala is quite active during that part of sleep where we dream. The name of that part of the brain isn't important. What *is* important, however, is that you remember that this is the region of the brain where fear seems to be generated. So, when this region of the brain is active in sleep, you will have dreams that are quite frightening. This is natural. It is a carryover from thousands of years ago when there were many reasons to avoid sleeping too deeply. Back then, things that went "thump" in the night could hurt you, and so it was useful to stay anxious. That gave you a head start when it came to dealing with things that might sneak up on you while you were asleep, since you were already anxious from the dream(s) that you were having. You could wake up and be almost instantly ready to defend yourself, or run for your life, because you are preparing to deal with a crisis situation even while you are asleep. So now, what would make a recovering alcoholic the most nervous, being chased by a monster, or, being tempted to drink?

Patient: Being tempted to drink, I suppose.

Therapist: Right! So the amygdala generates "fear" signal, and your unconscious mind matches that signal with the one thing that would make you most anxious: being close to a relapse. That is a natural process in dreaming: we match memories with the emotions that the sleeping brain generates. Yet there is something that I think you are overlooking about the dream. When you were tempted to drink, your unconscious was strong enough to wake you up. In effect, your unconscious took you out of the situation where you were in danger of relapsing. You seemed to react to the dream as if you were helpless. Yet, in the dream you did not take the drink. You found a way to cope with the temptation to drink and woke yourself up. I wonder if this is not a message that you are doing better than you have given yourself credit for, at this point.

Patient: Well, I had not looked at it that way. It seemed so real. But I did wake myself up before I actually drank the beer. I guess I will have to think about this one, for a while.

In this manner, the therapist helps the patient: (a) reframe the dream from one where he is supposedly helpless (terrified that he would drink) to (b) a normal, albeit uncomfortable, part of the recovery process in which (c) the patient did *not* drink in spite of his fears, but (d) in which he found a way to cope with the dreaded situation in which he is tempted to drink (he woke himself up). The therapist might also emphasize other coping mechanisms that the patient might employ (leave the dangerous situation, etc.).

In each of these two examples, the cognitive-behavioral therapist was able to address the client's dream memory and use it to illustrate how his or her cognitive "set" influenced how he or she interpreted the dream. In some cases, especially with repetitive dreams, it might prove useful to have the client attempt to alter the course of the dream through the application of "lucid" dreaming teachniques (Green & McCreery, 1994). If the client is able to learn to use lucid dreaming techniques to alter or control what she or he perceives as going on in the dream, then she or he might feel empowered and less victimized by the memories of dream experiences. Although the lucid dreamer does not have *total* control over his or her dreams, it is often sufficient for the individual to be able to change *some* aspect of the dream experience to become empowered. For example, one client, troubled by nightmares, "programmed" himself to simply wake up if he found that the dream imagery was too intense to allow him to rest peacefully. Just being able to terminate the dream, and awaken, was enough to help this client feel less threatened by the nightmares, and consequently he was able to sleep more restfully.

SUMMARY AND CONCLUSIONS

The Freudian model of dream interpretation, once the centerpiece of psychiatric practice, was based on the neurobiological models of the 1870s and 1880s. Research into the neurobiology of sleeping and the dream state that develops in the deepest stages of sleep, however, has shown that they are far more complex than Freudian theory postulated. For example, research suggests that these states of mind are quite unlike that of waking. Both the process of sleeping and the dream experience that occurs in the deepest stages of sleep involve neurological and cognitive processes that do not occur in the waking state.

From a developmental standpoint, it is safe to assume that sleep and the experience of dreaming are of importance to the individual, or else he or she would not spend approximately 1/12th of his or her life in this state of existence. However, for the most part, cognitive-behavioral therapists have tended to overlook the experience of sleep, and especially the client's recollections about the dream state, as being outside the realm of their practice. It is the purpose of this chapter to suggest that since the process of dream recall and discussion takes place during the waking state, the cognitive "set" used by the client to remember details about the dream and to interpret the dream memories will contain the same characteristic distortions that she or he normally uses to interpret external reality. This offers the cognitive-behavioral therapist a chance to use the dream memory as an additional avenue to address the client's concerns.

REFERENCES

Adels, J. H. (1987). *The wisdom of the saints.* New York: Oxford University Press.

Adler, A. (1956). *The individual psychology of Alfred Adler* (H. L. Ansbacher & R. R. Ansbacher, Eds., Trans.). New York: Harper & Row.

Beck, A. T., & Ward, C. H. (1961). Dreams of depressed patients: Characteristic themes in manifest content. *Archives of General Psychiatry, 5,* 462–467.

Damasio, A. R. (1999). How the brain creates the mind. *Scientific American, 281,* 112–117.

Doweiko, H. (1982). Neurobiology and dream theory: A rapprochement model. *Individual Psychology, 38,* 55–61.

Doweiko, H. (1999). *Concepts of chemical dependency* (4th ed.). Pacific Grove, CA: Brooks/Cole.

Flanagan, O. (2000). *Dreaming souls.* New York: Oxford University Press.

Freud, S. (1965). *The interpretation of dreams: Complete psychological works* (J. Strachey, Trans.) (standard ed., Vols. 4 and 5). London: Hobarth Press.

Gabbard, G. O. (2000). Psychoanalysis. In B. J. Sadock & V. A. Sadock (Eds.), *Comprehensive textbook of psychiatry* (7th ed., pp. 563–606). New York: Lippincott Williams & Wilkins.

Gillin, J. C., Seifritz, E., Zoltoski, R. K., & Salin-Pascual, R. J. (2000). Basic science of sleep. In B. J. Sadock & V. A. Sadock (Eds.), *Comprehensive textbook of psychiatry* (7th ed., pp. 199–208). New York: Lippincott Williams & Wilkins.

Glasser, W. (1985). *Control theory.* New York: Harper & Row.

Green, C., & McCreery, C. (1994). *Lucid dreaming.* New York: Routledge.

Hobson, J. A. (1989). Dream theory: A new view of the brain-mind. *Harvard Medical School Mental Health Letter, 5,* 3–5.

Hobson, J. A. (1999a). *Dreaming as delirium.* Cambridge, MA: MIT Press.

Hobson, J. A. (1999b). Order from chaos. In R. Conlan (Ed.), *States of mind* (pp. 179–199). New York: John Wiley & Sons.

Hobson, J. A., & McCarley, R. W. (1977). The brain as a dream state generator: An activation-synthesis hypothesis of the dream process. *American Journal of Psychiatry, 134*(12), 1335–1348.

Jung, C. (1971). *The portable Jung* (J. Campbell, Ed.). New York: Penguin Press.

Newell, P. T., & Cartwright, R. D. (2000). Affect and cognition in dreams: A critique of the cognitive role in adaptive dream functioning and support for associative models. *Psychiatry, 63,* 34–44.

Rogers, C. (1980). *A way of being.* Boston: Houghton Mifflin.

Singer, J. (1972). *Boundaries of the soul: The practice of Jung's psychology.* New York: Anchor Press.

Weiss, L. (1986). *Dream analysis in psychotherapy.* New York: Pergamon Press.

Wernick, R. (1989). From out of the past comes thundering hoofbeats of the demon "nightmare." *Smithsonian, 19,* 72–83.

CHAPTER 6

Dreams and the Dream Image: Using Dreams in Cognitive Therapy

ARTHUR FREEMAN
BEVERLY WHITE

> Dream a little dream with me. . . .
> —(The Mamas and the Papas, 1968)

INTRODUCTION

Dreams have been part of the human experience throughout recorded history. In the book of Genesis, Joseph, the youngest and most favored son of Jacob, is described as a dreamer. Joseph's first dream gets him in trouble when he dreams that the wheat sheaves of his brothers are bowing to his. This makes his brothers so angry that they jealously begin to consider getting rid of him. They do just that by selling him into slavery in Egypt. Later, Joseph's ability to interpret dreams allows him to offer an explanation of the pharaoh's dreams. This ability brings Joseph status, power, and riches and prevents the Egyptian people from succumbing to a famine that has affected the rest of the region.

Over the years, popular music has extolled the virtues and wonders of the dream. Whether they are of a lover ("Dream Lover"), a desired location ("California Dreaming"), or a lost lover ("Lover Come Back to Me"), dreams have been a cornerstone of our musical tradition.

In Dickens's classic, *A Christmas Carol*, Ebenezer Scrooge is confronted by the specter of Joseph Marley, his late partner. Scrooge is challenged by the specter to believe his own senses and accept that the apparition is indeed Joseph Marley. Scrooge, ever contrary, refuses to believe his eyes, because, he says, "a little thing affects them. A slight disorder of the stomach makes them cheats. You may be an undigested bit of beef, a blot of mustard, a crumble of cheese, a fragment of an underdone potato. There's more of gravy than grave about you, whatever you are." With this scene as prologue, Ebenezer Scrooge begins his long Christmas night. Dickens's view may be equally applied to dreams. Maybe they are nothing more than the undigested remains of a Whopper or a Big Mac. Maybe our dreams are simply the result of acid reflux.

However, when one thinks of dreams as part of the raw material for psychotherapy, one must immediately think of Freud and his "royal road to the unconscious." Dreams have been an important part of psychotherapeutic treatment since the days of the early pioneers in the development of psychotherapy. Freud, Adler, Jung, and others, despite major disagreements on the foci or overall goals of treatment, all agreed on the importance, if not the primacy, of the dream as one of the most essential psychotherapeutic tools. Freud's notion was that through an understanding of the dream theme, content, images, and subsequent associations the analyst could understand the workings of the patient's unconscious. Conflicts as yet unspoken or dynamics not fully understood (by patient or analyst) could be clarified through the interpretation of the symbols of the dreams. For Jung, the dream symbol was important because it reflected not only the personal unconscious of the individual but also the collective unconscious of the group.

The basic premise of Freud's early lectures on dreams and his later elaborations through several editions of his classic volume *The Interpretation of Dreams* (1999) was that the dream involved wish fulfillment. The dream became the pathway used by the individual to satisfy the unrestricted demands and desires of the id, thereby allowing accumulated "energies" to be discharged. The dream became the way of fulfilling desires that could not otherwise be fulfilled during the waking life for any of a number of reasons. This window into the underlying and unconscious world allowed the skilled psychoanalytic interpreter to understand the interplay of the patient's psychic structures. The patient's defenses and the conflicts that were the bases of the patient's dysfunctional or maladaptive behaviors, affect, and thoughts could all be understood by the careful and systematic interpretation of the patient's dreams. Dreams were therefore an expected part of the analytic process, and production and recollection of the dreams were an important part of the analytic material. In fact, patients who did not report their dreams or claimed that they did not dream were seen as resisting the analysis.

Since dreams might reflect the symbolized turmoil of the primitive personality structures, they were, for Freud, the normal person's loss of reality. Dreams were a psychotic-like state that allowed dreamers to speak and consort with persons long dead, fantasy objects, or persons presently in their life. The dream activities were not hindered by external social contracts, violations of legal standards, or issues of interpersonal appropriateness, but only by limitations self-imposed by the schema of the dreamer. The dream could have an impact and manifestation in the individual's waking state that might affect his or her postdreaming mood state (e.g., feeling down), behavior (tremulousness), pleasure (arousal and sexual release), or cognition (being scared).

For Adler (1927), however, the dream life corresponded directly and entirely to the dreamer's world picture or lifestyle. It was Adler's view that in the sleep state the individual's sense of and contact with reality were diminished but not extinguished. The dream state, according to Adler, was part of a continuum of consciousness that allowed for problem solving when the demands of reality were far less pressing or demanding. Ideally, this would allow for the possibility of more creative problem solving without the constraint of reality. Further, dreams put dreamers in touch with feelings that they may have neglected or avoided in the waking state. Adler states: "The purpose of dreams must be in the feelings they arouse. The dream is only the means, the instrument to stir up feelings" (p. 127). This was in direct conflict with the Freudian notion of the dream as being specifically focused on the unconscious and not on the conscious. The early theorists and their followers regarded dreams and dream work as a normal part of human experience and of great value as a therapeutic tool. They were much more contentious when they discussed the purpose and the source of the dreams or the "proper" way of understanding and using the dream in psychotherapy.

The issue at hand is not whether people dream. They do. Certainly no therapist, whatever his or her theoretical orientation, could deny the existence of dreaming without failing to recall subjective experience of just the night before. Whether they are upsetting and frustrating or gratifying and pleasurable, patients may bring their dreams to the therapy work. They do this because they expect they are supposed to based on their previous therapy experience or their understanding of what happens in therapy. As any practicing clinician will affirm, dreams are commonly mentioned or referred to in therapy. This can present a dilemma for any therapists who have limited training in the use of dreams. They may, in fact, end up in the dilemma described by Shonbar (1968):

She further confounded me by reporting a dream one day. As a client-centered therapist I'd had little experience with dreams. . . . When my patient told me her dream I felt handcuffed; my limited armamentarium gave me no way to deal with it meaningfully, apart from a comment on the mood or feeling of the dream. I felt as if something valuable had been brought into the room and just shoved aside into a corner—or, more properly, that it lay between us untouched, thus depriving her of its potential value. (p. 55)

The fact that dream work has not been a well-used or well-researched technique of cognitive-behavioral therapy (CBT) up to the present point might be explained by a number of factors.

1. Cognitive therapists generally come from a more behavioral tradition and orientation. Their clinical training might have had little or no reading, training, or supervision in the use of dreams in the therapeutic encounter.
2. Since dreams may have no direct behavioral component, the therapist might have been taught that dreams ought to be avoided.
3. Those CBT therapists who have had psychodynamic training may refrain from using dreams as a way of further distancing themselves from their early psychodynamic influences or may think that the use of dreams in therapy will be seen as "backsliding" by their CBT colleagues.
4. Some cognitive therapists avoid using dreams in therapy because of their belief that dream work is of no value (Ellis & Harper, 1975).
5. There are few guidelines for using dreams. There has been no manual developed for CBT dream work.
6. Since dream content is hard to study, research data have been sparse.
7. With limited time allowed for therapy by many funding sources, dream work has been seen as a poor use of valuable time.
8. Dreams are regarded as unconscious and therefore not appropriate for a CBT focus.
9. Dreams may be seen as the result of a physiological rather than psychological process and therefore more akin to Scrooge's "undigested piece of beef."
10. Dreams are seen as merely an interesting, though valueless, artifact.

Regardless of the underlying reason, the avoidance of dream work as part of therapy causes the loss of extremely valuable cognitive and affective data regarding patients, their perceptions, their schemas, and their automatic thoughts and images. As another source of data, the dream can become a valuable tool in the overall CBT armamentarium and a fruitful area for exploration (Mahoney, 1974). The issue for the present discussion is not who dreams, how often they dream, or where dreams come from, but whether and how dreams can be made useful parts of the CBT process.

CONSCIOUSNESS AND AWARENESS
OF DREAM THEMES

From the classical psychoanalytic perspective, two types of dream content were identified: manifest content and latent content. The latent content reflected the unconscious conflicts while the manifest content was the way the dream appeared to the dreamer, a much more direct and conscious focus. For both types of content, the therapist would explore the associated thoughts and memories that were triggered by the dream. The latent content, according to dynamic theory, contained the repressed or hidden meaning that was available only upon interpretation. The latent content was generally uncovered by the analyst's interpretations of the dream symbols and of the patient's associations to the dream images and symbols. The patient's defenses, and the conflicts that were the basis of the patient's dysfunctional or maladaptive behaviors, affect, and thoughts, could all be understood by the careful and systematic psychoanalytic interpretation of the patient's dreams.

For the more classical analyst, manifest content would be discarded as introductory, covering, or stimulus material, with the latent content being the "essence" of the dream. (Of course, one might argue that as soon as the patient identifies a symbol and discusses and describes associations to it, the previously latent content becomes manifest and should therefore be discarded.) The primary focus on the latent content shifted attention away from the manifest content, and the manifest content was virtually ignored by classical analysts (Fine, 1990). In fact, however, a great deal of psychodynamic information is available from the manifest dream content. Erikson (1954), Alexander and Selesnick (1966), and others all believed that the dream's manifest content was valuable in and of itself, and they offered guidelines and suggestions for its analysis.

By focusing on the latent or unconscious symbols and their meaning, the therapist may lose much of the important meaning(s) of the dream. His or her interpretation may not only be off the target but may move the cognitive stream in ways the patient does not see. It is necessary to view dreams as reflecting the cognitions and affective responses of waking experience and of the patient's life in general rather than as mysterious reflections of so-called deeper issues.

DREAMS AND CBT

The first CBT outline for dream work was formulated by Beck (1971). He outlined a cognitive model of dreams based partly on his early classical psychoanalytic training and partly on his extensive clinical experience demonstrating the potential value of the dream. Beck originally regarded dreams as a snapshot or sort of biopsy of the patient's psychological process and processing style. Later, he saw the patient's dreams as idiosyncratic and dramatic expressions of the patient's view of self, the world, and the future (what Beck termed the "cognitive triad"). Given that the dream material reflected the cognitive triad, it would follow that the dream would also embody the patient's cognitive distortions in those three broad areas. Beck (1967) pointed out that concentrating on the manifest content (the aware and easily described aspect of dreams) is far more satisfactory than attempting to infer underlying processes that may be vague or unreachable. Since the manifest content is readily available to the dreamer and can be reported to the therapist, it is available for immediate use in the therapy session. Utilizing material that is readily available, the patient can obtain a sense of mastery and self-knowledge without depending on the therapist to interpret the symbolism of the dream. Beck states: "If the patient has a dream in which he perceives other people as frustrating him, it would be more economical to simply consider this conception of people as being frustrating rather than to read into the dream an underlying 'masochistic wish' " (p. 180).

Further, Beck (1967) found that "dream themes are relevant to observable patterns of behavior" (p. 181) and that "dreams were analogous to the kind of suffering the depressed patient experienced in his waking life" (p. 208). These findings are in full accord with Adler's contention that dream themes are directly relevant to the patient's waking life and identified behavioral experience. Dreams are the product of the dreamer's internal world, but they maintain an essential continuity with the waking thought process. In studying typical dreams of psychiatric patients, Ward, Beck, and Roscoe (1961) and Beck and Ward (1961) found dream themes characteristic of the particular disorder manifest in the patient's waking experience. Beck (1967) states: "In the course of the psychotherapy of patients with neurotic-depressive reactions, it was noted that there was a high incidence of dreams with unpleasant content" (p. 170). As treatment progressed and the individual was better able to meet and overcome the day-to-day problems of life, the dream content changed to reflect the waking changes.

Freeman (1981) and Freeman and Boyll (1992) addressed the use of dreams and attendant imagery by integrating both Beckian and Adlerian perspectives.

Doweiko (1982), using a rational emotive (RET) approach, suggested that the therapy could help the patient directly challenge depressive cognitions reflected in the dream. As a result, the depression would not be so powerfully reinforced. Doyle (1984) tested whether dreamers could learn to control their dream content through several skills training sessions using cognitive restructuring, self-instruction techniques, and maintenance of a dream log in which they recorded their dreams on a daily basis. She found that those trained in the restructuring strategies were able to control the dream content in a pleasurable direction. Rosner (1997) suggested that the constructivist approach of helping patients to understand the reality that they construct is applicable to the dream phenomenon and would be a useful approach to cognitive therapy work with dreams. Perris (1998) described the use of dreams in the cognitive therapy of chronic psychiatric patients. She found that dream work was well accepted by the patients and easily integrated into the broader treatment that examined the patient's automatic thoughts and schemas.

WORKING WITH DREAMS

The cognitive view of dreams is that the dream material is idiosyncratic to the dreamer. It is essential that the therapist avoids the pitfall of universal dream symbols (i.e., a certain symbol always has the same meaning). Adler (1927) outlined several common dream themes that he viewed as extensions of the individual's waking cognitions, behavior, and lifestyle. Consequently, dreams of falling *might* represent a loss of status or prestige, while dreams of flying *might* represent activity, ambition, or a sense of looking forward. Dreams about dead people *might* reflect the fact that the dreamer has not "buried" the person or the meaning that that person had for the dreamer and is still under his or her influence.

The therapist must work to understand the dream content and the broader dream themes in the context of the patient's life, experience, and base of knowledge. Since the dream is not fettered by the constraints of the waking state (e.g., attending to necessary or vital circumstances such as watching the road while driving), the dreamer is freer to express a broad range of ideas, utilize magical thinking, and be as creative and unreal as possible. Some dreams may goad the person into action and may presage activities. The dream in this case may then have a predictive value. An example of a marker of positive movement in therapy might be the patient who previously has had dreams of helplessness, crisis, or failure but now begins to have dreams that reflect coping, mastery, and success.

In keeping all possible avenues opened for data collection, the dream can add immeasurably to the therapy work. It should be stressed that not all patients will come in reporting their dreams. The therapist need not suggest or require that patients record and report their dreams but should be prepared to deal with them when offered.

RECORDING AND REPORTING DREAMS

Two reporting techniques are used, the Dream Log (DL) and the Dream Analysis Record (DAR), an adaptation of the Dysfunctional Thought Record (DTR). Both are generally done as homework, although the DAR can be used in the office as part of the session work. The DL involves patients keeping a small notebook near their bed so that they can record dreams, dream fragments, and images soon after waking. They are also asked to record affective and physiological responses. For these latter issues, they are asked to use scaling to identify their level of response on a 0–10 scale (e.g., "woke up scared—8" or "the dream was sad—4").

The DAR (Figure 6.1) asks patients to enter the date that they had the dream in column 1. In column 2 they enter the highlights of the dream. In column 3 they enter their affective reactions and rate the degree of their reactions. In column 4 they enter the restructuring of the image. In column 5 they enter a reassessment of the degree of emotion associated with the dream image.

GUIDELINES FOR USING DREAMS

The following guidelines can assist the clinician in utilizing dreams within the context of CBT.

1. *The dream needs to be understood in thematic rather than symbolic terms.* The particular images and ideas expressed by patients in their dream can be taken at face value. The dreams are not necessarily cognitive transformations that are representations of something or someone else, but stand within the context of the patient's life experience and schema. The search for symbols may, in fact, distract from the effective use of dream work. As the therapist might continue to search for the "true meaning" expressed in the dream symbols, he or she may begin to stray from a basic understanding of the individual. Even Freud would probably have agreed that, at times, a cigar might be a cigar and nothing more.

Date	Dream Recall (Record Dream Ver Batim)	Degree of Emotion (0–100)	Adaptive Restructuring	Rerate Emotion (0–100)

FIGURE 6.1   Dream analysis record.

2. *The thematic content of the dream is idiosyncratic to the dreamer and must be viewed within the context of the dreamer's life.* In maintaining the cognitive continuum from waking to sleep, we are able to view the dream as part of the overall life experience. Dreams are not isolated phenomena and need to be connected to the patient's current concerns. The terms, beliefs, and issues expressed in waking are to be found in the dreams. What a particular dream experience means must be seen in the overall view of life maintained by the patient. The question that the therapist can ask is how this dream material is consistent or inconsistent with the patient's life, experience, life conflicts, successes, or failures.

3. *The specific language and imagery of the dream are important to the meaning.* The words, voice tone, visual images, and quality of language very much influence the affect being expressed. By using the dreamer's words and images, we can better understand his or her dream interest. For example, a dream image of being alone in a large stadium conveys a very different sense from being alone in a small room. Having a lover whisper in your ear differs from having a lover scream insults in your ear.

4. *The affective responses to the dreams can be seen as similar to the dreamer's affective responses in waking situations.* Just as we would help patients connect their thoughts, feelings, and behaviors in the waking state, the dream work does exactly the same thing. Happiness, anxiety, depression, or any of the range of emotional responses would be the same in dreaming or waking situations. The therapist needs to question where and how the emotions are being generated. Similarly, the patient may have no recollection of the dream content or images but still awake with an affective residue. The affective residue responses or residue of the dream can be dealt with as in any waking emotional response.

5. *The particular length of the dream is less important than the content.* Since we dream in images and pictures, a dream image or fragment may be exceptionally brief but yet have tremendous emotional impact. The adage, "A picture is worth one thousand words" applies here. For example, a fragment of an image where the dreamer sees her child lying dead on the street in front of a car can produce a sense of terror that persists well into the following day. Dreams that seem to go on for long periods of time do not necessitate going through each and every small piece for potential meaning. The overall theme, mood, and content should be the focus.

6. *The dream is a product of, and the responsibility of, the dreamer.* The particular material that the dreamer chooses to include in the dream, while possibly being a product of the previous day's experience, still

becomes a function of, and idiosyncratic to, the dreamer. For example, a patient reported a dream of his boss being cruel to him. The affective experience was first fear and then anger that the boss had intruded on his sleep. As the patient spoke about the boss, he became angry that even his time at home was not safe. The therapist reminded the patient that the boss did not intrude on his dream or his leisure time. Instead, it was the patient who carried a mental representation of the boss with him wherever he went. While there may have been reality issues related to the boss, his intrusion on the dream needed to be identified clearly as a product of the dreamer.

7.   *Dream content and images are amenable to the same cognitive restructuring as are automatic thoughts.* Dreams can be reworked to arrange affect shifts, alternative outcomes, or new solutions. When the DAR is used, dreams can be restructured with appropriate disputation and rational challenges to the depressogenic, anxiogenic, or dysfunctional dream material. The patient can then learn to dispute the dysfunctional themes embodied in the dream and thus to change his or her affective response to the dream.

8.   *Dreams can be used when the patient appears "stuck" in therapy.* Practicing the process of adaptive responding on the patient's dreams can assist the patient in building further skills to deal rationally with dysfunctional thinking. When the particular direction or momentum of therapy seems lost, the dream material can be a valuable adjunctive tool providing an arena for practice. Patients often readily accept the use of dreams because they are so personal and such a familiar part of their experiences.

9.   *The dream material and images will reflect the patient's schema.* The patient's schema will also be reflected in the situations and circumstances scripted by the dreamer. Given that there may not be the same censoring of the themes and activities, patients sometimes feel guilty about dreaming of certain activities. Patients who have active schemas regarding the importance of order and rules may have dreams that deal with "propriety," "orderliness," or the "rightness" of actions or words. If their actions in the dreams are not in keeping with their schemas, they may experience dissonance or awake feeling guilty about what they "did" in the dream.

10.   *Dreams need to be dealt with as part of the session agenda setting.* An active dreamer may wish to use the entire therapy hour to discuss several dreams. The therapist needs to be judicious in using dreams in the session so that other important material is not excluded.

11.   *A system and regimen for the collection and logging of the dream material should be encouraged.* The therapist should help patients keep

their dream logs handy, along with a pen or pencil. Given that the dream images may fade fairly quickly, it would be good to capture them while they are most clear. Patients must also be informed that any recollection, no matter how brief, can be useful as a central point for discussion.

12. *The patient should be helped to develop skill at restructuring negative or maladaptive dream images into more functional and adaptive images.* The metaphor that we would offer is that of a pilot in a simulator. When there are repetitive dreams or common, troubling dream themes, the patient can develop and polish a standard restructuring. With dream images that are less frequent, the patient must learn how to respond quickly, just as he or she would to a waking negative cognition.

13. *The patient should try to encapsulate and draw a "moral" from the dream.* The patient can learn to draw a conclusion or moral from the dream. He or she can focus on the overall theme and on what can be encapsulated from the particular dream experience. This new "learning" can then be used in the therapy to further build the patient's coping repertoire.

14. *The dream images, as appropriate, can be used as a shorthand in the therapy to describe far more complex experiences and phenomena.* Often the dream picture or image can be used as a shorthand to identify a pattern of responding or to clarify a course of action.

15. *The collection and analysis of the dream content should be used as a standard homework task.* The collection of dream material, the analysis of the dreams, and the morals gained from the experience can be encapsulated and shared with the therapist. The goal of the homework is not to make the patient dependent on the therapist to intercede and tell him or her the meaning of the dreams, but rather for the patient to learn the skill of understanding and using dream material.

DREAMS AND RELATED IMAGERY

Using dreams in therapy requires the use of associated imagery. The dream restructuring process is, by definition, an exercise in imagery. Since few patients can describe symptoms without describing accompanying images, the image is a ready and accessible entry point for cognitive intervention. Images may be visual, auditory, gustatory, or olfactory. They may utilize an economy of words, but they provide a directness of meaning and a vivid affective experience for the patient. The affect-laden image can often penetrate the depression and isolation of the lonely patient just as the calming image can reduce the arousal of the anxious patient. Beck, Laude, and Bohnert (1974) observed that, with the onset or exacerbation of anxiety, many patients have thoughts or visual fantasies revolving around the theme of danger. The anxiety, they conclude, is a direct result of the visualization of the danger-laden image. Their observations have direct implications for the treatment of anxiety.

The image maker does not always have to be the patient, since the therapist can suggest images and imagining techniques to effectively break through a number of symptoms. Images can be made more powerful and evocative through the inclusion of multisensory elements.

The imaging can become part of the homework assignment on which the patient and therapist decide. The patient can be asked to develop a number of images that help focus on the particular symptoms currently being addressed in treatment.

CASE EXAMPLES

Using the treatment guidelines, the following cases demonstrate the cognitive use of dreams.

Case 1

This process can be seen quite clearly in the case of Stuart, a 27-year-old graduate student who had been procrastinating over completing his dissertation for over a year. The material to be written was laid out on his desk. He had written the introduction, the review of the literature, and the method section and had conducted the research project. He had coded the data and analyzed the results but was unable to complete the results section (appropriate charts and tables) and to write the interpretive prose of the discussion section, in some ways the easiest part of the entire project. His automatic thoughts, both general and specific to the dissertation project, showed that the major schematic themes related to (1) intellectual adequacy, (2) ability to succeed, (3) overwhelming concern about the views of others, (4) demand for personal perfectionism, and (5) low sense of personal worth.

In his automatic thoughts the student tended to minimize his ac-complishments, question his ability to complete the dissertation suc-

cessfully, undercut his confidence that he could earn the doctorate, downplay the relative lack of value of the dissertation to the literature of the field, and emphasize the major flaws in the experimental design and concerns with how the dissertation would be received and reviewed by colleagues.

In addition, his perfectionism demanded that his dissertation be seen as one that would earn a Nobel Prize for content and a Pulitzer Prize for style. He believed that his worth and value as a human being were centered on his productivity. Since he believed that he was worthless, any product of his must be similarly tainted and worthless. As the days grew to weeks and the weeks became months, Stuart had numerous dreams that would cause him to wake several times during the night with anxiety and a "sense of dread." The thought that accompanied the dream, although the exact content of each dream was not always clear, was "I've got to get going. The material is sitting there waiting to be worked on, but I can't work on it." The most common dream themes were of work uncompleted and uncompletable. Several dreams were sexual in nature, and in these the sexual relationships were never consummated. The cognition associated with the dreams was "I can't finish anything." The goals in therapy were to take both a cognitive and a behavioral focus. The cognitive focus was on the thoughts surrounding personal efficacy, personal worth, and ability to succeed. The behavioral focus involved a graded task approach to the completion of the project, activity scheduling, and mastery and pleasure activities. As Stuart actively challenged the various dysfunctional cognitions in the course of therapy with a simultaneous focus on working on the dissertation in small bits, the frequency of the anxiety dreams diminished. As he experienced a growing sense of mastery, he was able to accept his advisor's rule that the dissertation needed only to be good, appropriate, and acceptable. As Stuart was able to see concrete progress, the amount of work produced increased until the dissertation was almost complete. He reported occasional anxiety dreams but overall was able to sleep better. On follow-up at six-month intervals over the next three years, Stuart reported that anxiety dreams were experienced only in those situations where he had procrastinated and not completed required work. The anxiety dream became a signal for him to either organize or increase his efforts. He said that when he was awakened by a fearful dream in the middle of the night, rather than lying awake and ruminating, he would resolve to take concrete and positive action in the morning to address whatever issue existed as a source of anxiety. The anxiety dream in this case became a trigger for success, not simply an aversive stimulus.

Case 2

Alice, a 31-year-old woman, reported the following dream: "I was sitting on the couch when out from the opposite wall came this huge snake. It struck at me with incredible speed, not allowing me to move away. It sank its fangs into my arm. All I could do was look at it and react to the pain and to the fact that it was biting me. I woke up feeling anxious and frightened. It was a scary dream." Alice also reported similar dreams.

In discussing the dream, Alice identified the basic cognitive elements as her helplessness and inability to react when under attack. She was passive in response to being attacked, and her feelings of anxiety seemed strongest when she was placed in a position that required direct action. She was able to see rather quickly that these cognitions paralleled her dysfunctional cognitions in the waking state. She was extremely effective on the job but often felt anxious, even paralyzed, when called upon to be assertive and take direct action. She often felt that the people working in her department took advantage of her because they knew that she would not respond if they came on assertively.

The therapist helped her to restructure the dream experience (and by extension the waking experience) by asking her what she might have done differently in the dream. Her initial response was that she could do very little, that she was at the mercy of the situation. In effect she saw herself as victim to her dream content (cognitions). The therapist emphasized that, since she was the sole producer, director, stage manager, and casting director (after all, she recruited the snake), she could recast or restructure the scene in any way that she wished.

At first, Alice restructured the dream very tentatively by visualizing herself trying to hold something over the snake hole in the wall (a "finger-in-the-dike" response). When the therapist asked her how that would help, she shrugged her shoulders and said, "You're right, that wouldn't work. There is nothing I can do."

Her second idea was to quickly nail some boards over the hole. She then dismissed this as ineffective, saying, "The snake would just knock them away."

With further encouragement and some modeling on the therapist's part, she restructured the scene so that she immediately severed the snake's head. When she protested that she did not have a knife, it was pointed out that the knife could come from the same source as the snake, her imagination. As she restructured the dream scene to one of her taking greater control and asserting herself, there was a rapid affect shift from anxiety to relief. The therapy work consisted of training her in assertiveness, monitoring her anxiety, and challenging the ideas that she did not have a right to respond or react to the demands of others in a negative way.

An alternate technique would be to have Alice revisualize the dream but for the primary purpose of altering the negative elements. The snake could become a Sesame Street character, or the patient could offer the snake a treat or erect a transparent shield. In restructuring the dream, a positive outcome can always be effected (Leurner, 1969). The key element would be to make the automatic thoughts manifest.

Case 3

Pam, a 24-year-old-female graduate student, reported the following dream fragment: "I woke up early one morning. I dreamed that I was at my parent's home. I went downstairs and saw my boyfriend's car parked in my garage. I felt annoyed because he didn't ask for permission or tell me he was going to do it."

The affect associated with the dream was anger and helplessness. The associated information elicited involved an ongoing conflict over her relationship with her boyfriend. She felt that he would often be unaware of her needs or insensitive to her feelings. His demands took precedence. He would often make plans for them as a couple without any consultation or discussion with Pam. She never confronted him, and she experienced anger and depression as a result.

In this brief dream fragment, the basic themes are the patient's loss of control and her subsequent anger. In restructuring the dream during the therapy session, the patient attempted a number of strategies in dealing with the unwanted car. She first tried locking the garage doors, thus forcing the boyfriend to park out in the cold. This *strategy set up a situation where he had to ask to be allowed to park in the garage. Further images included demanding that she be informed of his desire to park, discussing his parking as part of a mutual decision, and even having him park on her demand. As she discussed the various strategies that she might have used in the dream, there was a rather rapid affect shift resulting from the dream restructuring. She experienced a sense of pleasure and satisfaction that helped her to resolve that she would not allow herself to be used any longer. By utilizing the restructured images in her dream, she was able to begin asserting herself in the relationship with her boyfriend.*

The therapist can, of course, utilize imagery and imaginal restructuring as a major tool for both dream-related images and waking images.

SUMMARY

This chapter deals with the use of dreams and images in the context of cognitive-behavioral therapy. While dreams have historically been an important part of the psychotherapeutic process, the therapist trained in cognitive-behavioral therapy is frequently not trained or prepared to work with dreams. The therapist and patient may lose valuable opportunities to tap the richness of imagery offered in dreams.

The cognitive model sees the dreamer as idiosyncratic and the dream as a dramatization of the patient's view of self, world, and future, subject to the same cognitive distortions as the waking state.

The following guidelines can be set for dream work in CBT:

1. The dream needs to be understood in thematic rather than symbolic terms.
2. The thematic content of the dream is idiosyncratic to the dreamer and must be viewed within the context of the dreamer's life.
3. The specific language and imagery of the dream are important to the meaning.
4. The affective responses to the dreams can be seen as similar to the dreamer's affective responses in waking situations.
5. The particular length of the dream is less important than the content.
6. The dream is a product of, and the responsibility of, the dreamer.
7. Dream content and images are amenable to the same cognitive restructuring as are automatic thoughts.

8. Dreams can be used when the patient appears "stuck" in therapy.
9. The dream material and images will reflect the patient's schema.
10. Dreams need to be dealt with as part of the session agenda setting.
11. A system and regimen for the collection and logging of the dream material should be encouraged.
12. The patient should be helped to develop skill at restructuring negative or maladaptive dream images into more functional and adaptive images.
13. The patient should try to encapsulate and draw a "moral" from the dream.
14. The dream images, as appropriate, can be used as a shorthand in the therapy to describe far more complex experiences and phenomena.
15. The collection and analysis of the dream content should be used as a standard homework task.

The cognitive therapist can enrich his or her armamentarium by including dreams and imagery as part of the psychotherapeutic collaborative process. Dreams offer an opportunity for the patient to understand his or her cognitions as played out on the stage of the imagination and to challenge or dispute depressogenic or anxiogenic thoughts, with a resultant positive affect shift. The dream would not then necessarily be the royal road to the unconscious but rather a route toward understanding our own idiosyncratic interpretations of conscious experience.

REFERENCES

Adler, A. (1927). *The practice and theory of individual psychology.* New York: Harcourt, Brace.

Alexander, F., & Selesnick, S. T. (1966). *The history of psychiatry: An evaluation of psychiatric thought and practice from prehistoric times to the present.* New York: Harper & Row.

Beck, A. T. (1967). *Depression: Clinical, experimental, and theoretical aspects.* New York: Harper & Row.

Beck, A. T. (1971). Cognition, affect and psychopathology. *Archives of General Psychiatry, 24,* 495–500.

Beck, A. T., Laude, R., & Bohnert, M. (1974). Ideational components of anxiety neurosis. *Archives of General Psychiatry, 31,* 319–325.

Beck, A. T., & Ward, C. H. (1961). Dreams of depressed patients: Characteristic themes in manifest content. *Archives of General Psychiatry, 5,* 462–467.

Doweiko, H. E. (1982). Neurobiology and dream theory: A rapprochement model. *Individual Psychology: The Journal of Adlerian Theory, Research, and Practice, 38*(1), 55–61.

Doyle, M. C. (1984). Enhancing dream pleasure with the Senoi strategy. *Journal of Clinical Psychology, 40*(2), 467–474.

Ellis, A., & Harper, R. A. (1975). *A new guide to rational living.* Englewood Cliffs, NJ: Prentice Hall.

Erikson, E. (1954). The dream specimen of psychoanalysis. *Journal of the American Psychoanalytic Association, 2*, 5–56.

Fine, R. (1990). *History of psychoanalysis.* Northdale, NJ: Jason Aronson, Inc.

Freeman, A. (1981). The use of dreams and imagery in cognitive therapy. In G. Emery, S. Hollon, & R. Bedrosian (Eds.), *New directions in cognitive therapy.* New York: Guilford Press.

Freeman, A., & Boyll, S. (1992). The use of dreams and the dream metaphor in cognitive behavior therapy. *Psychotherapy in Private Practice, 10*(1–2), 173–192.

Freud, S. (1999). *The interpretation of dreams* (J. Strachey, Ed.). New York: Oxford University Press. (Original work published in 1900)

Leurner, H. (1969). Guided affective imagery (GAI): A method of intensive psychotherapy. *American Journal of Psychotherapy, 23*, 4–22.

Mahoney, M. J. (1974). *Cognitive behavior therapy.* Cambridge, MA: Ballinger.

Perris, H. (1998). Less common therapeutic strategies and techniques in the cognitive psychotherapy of severely disturbed patients. In C. Perris & P. D. McGorry (Eds.), *Cognitive psychotherapy of psychotic and personality disorders.* Chichester, UK: John Wiley & Sons.

Rosner, R. (1997). Cognitive therapy, constructivism, and dreams: A critical review. *Journal of Constructivist Psychology, 10*(3), 249–273.

Shonbar, R. (1968). Confessions of an ex-nondirectivist. In E. Hammer (Ed.), *Use of interpretation in treatment.* New York: Grune & Stratton.

Ward, C. H., Beck, A. T., & Roscoe, E. (1961). Typical dreams: Incidence among psychiatric patients. *Archives of General Psychiatry, 5*, 606–615.

CHAPTER 7

Imagery Rehearsal Therapy for Chronic Posttraumatic Nightmares: A Mind's Eye View

BARRY KRAKOW

INTRODUCTION

Imagery rehearsal therapy (IRT) is a cognitive imagery technique that has recently been established as an effective treatment for chronic nightmares in patients suffering from posttraumatic stress disorder (PTSD) (Krakow et al., 2000c, 2001c). An IRT research program was initiated by Dr. Robert Kellner, vice chairman of the Department of Psychiatry at the University of New Mexico (UNM) School of Medicine in the mid-1980s (Kellner, Singh, & Irogoyen-Rascon, 1991). In the late 1980s, Dr. Joseph Neidhardt teamed with Dr. Kellner to conduct a randomized controlled trial on the treatment of chronic nightmares by comparing IRT to a systematic desensitization approach (Kellner, Neidhardt, Krakow, & Pathak, 1992). I joined their research team near the end of that study because of my growing interest in sleep disorders medicine. At the time, most of the treated patients reported chronic nightmares and mild to moderate levels of anxiety and depression, but few were diagnosed as suffering anxiety or mood disorders, and only a rare patient suffered from PTSD. Based on this early work and a second controlled study (Neidhardt, Krakow, Kellner, & Pathak, 1992), Dr. Neidhardt and I coauthored a book on the treatment of chronic nightmares (Krakow & Neidhardt, 1992).

After Dr. Kellner's death in 1992 and Dr. Neidhardt's departure from the university, I initiated a new sleep research program at UNM that focused on the development of IRT for chronic nightmares in trauma survivors. Our research team approached the program from a sleep disorders medicine perspective because those with chronic nightmares almost invariably suffer from insomnia (Krakow, Tandberg, Scriggins, & Barey, 1995b). By treating nightmares, we expected to help patients to sleep better, and in particular, we were interested in knowing how trauma patients would respond if we decreased their bad dreams and enhanced their sleep. In the course of this work, we learned that IRT worked well in conjunction with other cognitive-behavioral strategies, notably cognitive restructuring (Krakow, Kellner, Neidhardt, Pathak, & Lambert, 1993; Krakow, Kellner, Pathak, & Lambert, 1995a; Krakow, Kellner, Pathak, & Lambert, 1996). We learned and developed these therapeutic approaches with the assistance of Dr. Michael Hollifield, another UNM psychiatrist who has worked extensively with trauma survivors. Therefore, we now use IRT in a group setting, and the therapy lasts from 4 to 10 hours, depending upon the severity of the cases. Based on our results and experiences, we imagine that IRT could serve as a useful tool in the hands of therapists who work with patients suffering from chronic nightmares and PTSD.

THE IMAGERY SYSTEM
AND SLEEP DYNAMIC THERAPY

The human imagery system plays an exquisitely important role in promoting and maintaining mental health. An intact and viable imagery system provides humans with the capacity to dream, daydream, picture solutions to problems, get new ideas, and perhaps most fundamentally, observe and reckon with our thoughts and feelings through an incredibly powerful yet shorthand system of perception. Indeed, the power of the imagery system seems to derive from its innate ability to integrate information, facts, and knowledge about our thoughts and feelings into snapshots or a series of brief pictures worth far more than a thousand words. This remarkable system, so natural and basic to human consciousness, is usually not emphasized in the scientific literature, neither as an integral component of the human mind nor as a target of therapy for individuals with mental health problems. Yet, in traditional behavioral models, we talk about thoughts, feelings, *and images* as three essential components of human behavior (Glasser, 1984).

The human imagery system may have a far greater impact on health than we currently appreciate, and this is readily apparent when the imagery system becomes damaged or deranged, which occurs commonly among trauma patients who develop chronic nightmares (Krakow et al., 2002c). The imagery system of a nightmare sufferer malfunctions in many ways, and numerous models have attempted to explain disturbing dreams. However, most prevailing paradigms relegate bad dreams and nightmares to the category of a symptom occurring within the context of another mental health disorder, usually PTSD, anxiety, or a depressive disorder (American Psychiatric Association, 2000). This perspective seems logical because it has been well documented that disturbing dreams and nightmares often arise following trauma or upon the inception of a mental disorder. Notwithstanding, a question remains: why do disturbing dreams often last for years or decades? Is it because chronic nightmare sufferers have never dealt with the mental health problem that caused the bad dreams in the first place? Or is it possible that nightmares take on a life of their own and become a primary or comorbid disorder requiring distinct treatment?

When we first traveled down a path directly targeting nightmares with cognitive imagery techniques, I observed a mixture of reactions from my two mentors. Dr. Kellner was astonished at the remarkable effectiveness of IRT because it produced such a rapid resolution of a chronic mental health symptom, that is, chronic nightmare disorder (CND). Dr. Neidhardt, on the other hand, was less surprised, because he had thoroughly investigated various dream theories and had trained in the use of numerous dream interpretation techniques for 20 years as a family medicine physician prior to becoming a psychiatrist (Krakow & Neidhardt, 1992; Neidhardt et al., 1992). Thus Dr. Neidhardt had a long-standing interest in the human imagery system and was keenly aware of the potential potency of imagery-based therapies. Still, we had not worked extensively with trauma patients or those with nightmares and other diagnosable mental health comorbidities, although virtually all the nightmare patients we had treated reported elevated levels of anxiety and depression symptoms (Krakow et al., 1995a; Neidhardt et al., 1992; Kellner et al., 1992).

In 1994, our sleep research program was awarded an NIMH grant to conduct a research study to treat nightmares in trauma patients. We were surprised that IRT not only decreased nightmares but also improved sleep and posttraumatic stress symptoms, even though this cognitive imagery technique did not directly target sleep or non-sleep-related PTSD symptoms

(Krakow et al., 2001b, 2000c). Since then, in working with several hundred sexual assault survivors (Krakow et al., 2000b), crime victims (Krakow et al., 2001d), and disaster survivors (Krakow et al., 2002d), we have learned that other pathophysiological elements may also adversely influence the imagery system among trauma survivors.

Briefly, we observed that nearly all nightmare sufferers develop psychophysiological insomnia as a byproduct of their bad dreams (Krakow et al., 2001d). Worse, when these two sleep disorders (nightmares and insomnia) jump into bed together, they have the potential to spawn physiological havoc within the brain in the form of objective sleep fragmentation and mini-awakenings or, technically, arousal or microarousal activity on the electroencephalogram (EEG). Sleep fragmentation appears to destabilize the human upper airway, making it more vulnerable to the development of sleep-disordered breathing (SDB) events (Series, Roy, & Marc, 1994; Meurice, Marc, & Series, 1996). The story now circles back to dreams and imagery, because SDB has the potential to further influence mental health in general and the imagery system in particular, and in our work we have observed epidemic rates of SDB among trauma survivors (Krakow et al., 2002a, 2002b, 2001a, 2001d, 2000a, 2000b). Because SDB causes hundreds of arousals or microarousals at night, the sleeper may suffer increasing awareness of dreams or, in this case, nightmares. Moreover, anecdotal evidence suggests that SDB patients suffer more dreams about drowning or suffocation, which is consistent with a current conceptualization of SDB pathophysiology as *recurrent mini-suffocation episodes.* Last, SDB may cause inordinately severe damage to rapid-eye-movement (REM) sleep, the stage of sleep that many researchers believe is not only related to more active dream processes (we actually dream in all stages of sleep), but that also is necessary for healthy and successful processing of information, memory, and emotions (Hartmann, 1998). Thus the pathophysiological mechanisms of sleep-disordered breathing may worsen both nightmares and insomnia; and, based on our research with trauma survivors, this psychophysiological cycle often continues unabated for years (Krakow et al., 2002a, 2002b).

In our latest efforts to treat this unusual complex of sleep disorders, which we believe to be prevalent in a very high proportion of patients with chronic PTSD, we developed a sleep dynamic therapy program, which uses IRT for nightmares, advanced sleep medicine cognitive-behavioral therapies (CBT) for insomnia, and various and standard sleep medicine physiological treatments for SDB, none of which typically involve sedating medications (Krakow et al., 2002d). We target these sleep disorders one at a time, or in varying sequences, or in combined forms, depending upon the patient's receptivity to the program. Severe PTSD patients usually gravitate toward insomnia or nightmare treatment first, whereas patients with moderate severity levels of sleep disturbance tend to be more receptive to the simultaneous delivery of the full package of therapeutic options. However, anecdotally, I wish to point out that very severe PTSD patients often suffer from severe SDB, which produces such a striking degree of cognitive impairment that it would be easy to confuse this common sleep disorder with vegetative depression or in some cases a dissociative disorder. Nonetheless, in current health care climates, such patients are not likely to find themselves referred to sleep disorder centers for aggressive SDB treatment.

Our two sleep centers operate in Albuquerque, New Mexico. The Sleep and Human Health Institute is a nonprofit, private research center that grew out of our work at the university sleep research program. Maimonides Sleep Arts and Sciences is a clinical and laboratory-based sleep medicine program that specializes in mental health patients with chronic sleep problems. Through both centers, we treat patients with sleep dynamic therapy, and each patient's individualized treatment depends upon the complexity of his or her sleep disturbance and whether he or she is receiving treatment through the research institute or the clinical sleep center.

To date, of the three main components of SDT, we have organized the IRT component of the program into a formal teaching manual, *Turning Nightmares Into Dreams*, which is a 4-hour CD series accompanied by a 100-page treatment workbook (Krakow, 2002). The manual consists of 20 sections, each of which includes, on average, 10 to 30 minutes of instruction and a companion section in the workbook consisting of exercises and key points to train oneself in the use of IRT. The manual is designed for either patients or therapists, although we believe the program is best administered by a therapist unless the trauma patient has had extensive and successful psychotherapy in the past. Patients with mild PTSD or less severe psychiatric distress could also manage the program without supervision, but the program contains several cautionary instructions at key points to remind the user to work with a therapist if difficulties arise. The audio series and workbook are available through our website *www.nightmaretreatment.com*, and in the future we hope to develop an online version of the IRT program for patients to work on directly over the Web, while receiving additional support from our center or with their local therapists.

The remainder of this chapter will describe key technical elements of IRT that, in our experience, produce the best outcomes and for which space is often not sufficient to detail in a journal article. I will also attempt to dispel two common misconceptions about this cognitive imagery technique. Then

I will provide an overview of salient treatment research results, and finally, I will mention areas of interest for future clinical applications and research directions involving IRT use.

THE BASIC ELEMENTS OF IRT

Change Two Nightmares and Call Me in a Week

I believe it is important and useful to recognize that IRT has been around forever. I cannot think of a single thing about this cognitive imagery approach that could be perceived as new, and I am convinced that many adults without any sort of health care background have known the technique since childhood. My sense of this derives from what I learned at numerous social gatherings and scientific meetings during the past decade, because virtually everyone has had a nightmare or two and tends to be curious about them. I have met many people who reported frequent bad dreams, which was not surprising, because the prevalence of chronic nightmare disorder probably ranges between 4% and 8% in the general population (Neilsen & Zadra, 2000). Among this group, however, most could not imagine the existence of a "treatment" for bad dreams. On the other hand, I met many adults who had suffered frequent nightmares in childhood, and most were able to provide an explanation for why they no longer suffered from disturbing dreams. At a rate exceeding 90% in this ongoing straw poll, I have heard the same explanation with a hundred minor variations about how "my father or mother" (or fill in the blank) "told me to change my dream by" (fill in the blank), and "then practice the new dream by" (fill in the blank). In other words, it seems likely that numerous variations of what is currently dubbed IRT have probably been practiced well before the advent of the scientific literature.

We currently use Neidhardt's variation to "change the nightmare any way you wish" (Krakow & Neidhardt, 1992; Neidhardt et al., 1992), but we no longer suggest that the patient write down the old nightmare unless such a process is helpful in learning the technique. The full instructions involve the following steps: (1) select a disturbing dream, preferably one of lesser intensity and not a reenactment of a trauma; (2) change this nightmare any way you wish; (3) rehearse this new dream a few minutes each day at a time of your choosing; and (4) continue these instructions every day and consider working with another nightmare to change it into a new dream every 3 to 7 days, such that you *only rehearse one or two new dreams each week* (Krakow et al., 1995a).

Selecting a Nightmare

How patients select their nightmares for IRT will often present clues as to how they will embrace or avoid IRT and whether or not they view it as a credible therapy. Using a "crawl before you walk" metaphor, we explain that IRT has potential efficacy for all types of nightmares, but it is important to learn the technique first on disturbing dreams of lesser emotional intensity. Our goal is to trigger minimal or no emotional response, because our objective is *not* to expose patients to traumatic content. Instead, we want them to select this bad dream so that they have material with which they will learn IRT. A nightmare replay of a trauma therefore is discouraged during first efforts, even though patients are instructed to work on these sorts of dreams once they gain confidence in the method. Some patients, for reasons that we do not understand, will still select an overwhelming replay-type nightmare for the first attempt at IRT. And they often, but not always, report that IRT does not work, doesn't feel right, or simply cannot be used. Even though they received clear and repeated instructions that more intense nightmares should be worked on only *after* the technique has been practiced several times, we have observed that these particular types of trauma patients tend to have more severe PTSD, and they usually suffer from other symptoms, such as dissociation or cognitive deficits in attention, concentration, and memory, all of which may make it difficult for them to digest the principles behind IRT, including the basic instructions. As a footnote, many of these individuals appear to suffer from severe SDB and have marked degrees of sleep fragmentation and hypoxia, leading to fairly pronounced cognitive impairment that may thwart many of their attempts to improve their mental health.

In contrast, patients who select a less threatening nightmare and who find it relatively easy to imagine a changed version almost invariably find the technique palatable. In more than half of all patients with whom we have worked, it seems apparent in about 15 to 30 seconds that the instruction "to change the nightmare" is a welcome idea that they had probably wondered about on their own. These individuals are able to begin writing down a new dream immediately to use in the rehearsal process, almost as if permission to change their dreams had finally been granted.

Changing the Nightmare

Changing the dream often meets with mild resistance in a minority of patients, but only rarely do nightmare patients resist by declaring that changing the dream "can't be done because that's what happened to me" or "that was my dream, how can I change it?" Changes take many forms; we are not aware of any particular change schema that is more powerful than others, although we suspect that Neidhardt's model (Neidhardt et al., 1992; Krakow & Neidhardt, 1992) to "change it any way" is more powerful than to narrow the scope by suggesting, "change it to something positive or triumphal." We speculate that this broader instruction leaves open a psychodynamic window through which patients may intuitively glimpse multilayered solutions to other emotional conflicts in addition to, or arguably as part of, their nightmare resolution. Such a process is not dissimilar to the "peeling away layers of onion skin" metaphor used to describe dream interpretation techniques, but now the opportunity is taken advantage of in the waking state and under a semblance of greater control. Some people change minutiae in the dream, while others develop an entirely new story. Therefore, notwithstanding the above-mentioned psychodynamic speculation, we would also not be surprised if a major active ingredient of IRT were shown to be the ability to reconnect with the natural, human capacity to change imagery in the mind's eye, beyond any specific changes of content within the new dreams.

Rehearsing the Nightmare

The most important instruction to give prior to rehearsing the dream, such as in a group therapy setting, is to remind the patients that "we will now rehearse the new dream only, *not* the nightmare." In other words, we continue to avoid exposure. Instead, we encourage patients to reinvigorate their natural imagery capacity. This session can last 5 to 15 minutes, depending upon the comfort level of the group with their imagery capacity. Rarely have we seen a patient stop the rehearsal because of unpleasant images, but we caution them about this possibility, and we provide them with some imagery training the week before initiating IRT so that they are prepared to intervene if unpleasant images arise.

Practice

Patients are informed that they are learning how to activate their imagery system in a specific way to take control of their nightmares. Therefore, the early emphasis should be on understanding what it means to activate the imagery system and on gaining some control and comfort with that process.

In time, more nightmares can be targeted, if necessary, but each and every nightmare does not have to be treated, because IRT jumpstarts a natural human healing system that was previously dormant. In other words, working on just a few bad dreams and turning them into new dreams will have a ripple effect on other nightmares. And, in the best-case scenario, the new emphasis and interest on imagery will lead to a natural incorporation of these ideas into one's consciousness, so that IRT processes might suddenly appear in the middle of the night while dreaming or during the day while trying to solve a problem. Thus the actual amount of time that needs to be spent working on any particular nightmare is variable and unpredictable, and early in treatment, obsessing about a particular bad dream may prove counterproductive. Then again, we know of some patients who enjoyed and benefited from working on just one or two new dreams by constantly changing them for several months before considering any other nightmares, if any nightmares persisted. Again, we reiterate that the most important step is to learn the technique and gain control and comfort with it, and this may explain why some people choose a path to initially work with fewer new dreams.

COGNITIVE RESTRUCTURING AND IRT

IRT can be taught to mild-severity nightmare patients in less than 30 minutes, but we learned early on that among those with increasing severity of nightmares and psychiatric distress, cognitive restructuring was required, mostly to enhance the credibility of the technique for those mental health patients willing to pursue this form of therapy.

Several barriers had to be addressed in working with trauma survivors, the most salient of which were the following: (1) because most trauma survivors with chronic nightmares had been inculcated with the belief that their nightmares were secondary to their PTSD, they believed that the only way to eradicate them would be through treatments directed at this vexing mental health disorder; (2) because of the first barrier, most trauma survivors could not easily imagine that bad dreams reflect a learned behavior or a habitual derangement of the human imagery system; (3) because of the widely held belief among patients *and* therapists that nightmares represent unfinished business, most nightmare sufferers harbor fears about symptom substitution if the nightmares were to decrease; (4) because trauma survivors have grown accustomed to having nightmares, they appear to have developed a "nightmare sufferer identity," which may provoke feelings of insecurity or confusion in response to the idea of change (paradoxically, having to consider a life without bad dreams might be threatening); and, (5) because of the common confusion or ignorance about the human mind's natural capacity for imagery and its relationship to thoughts and feelings, a credibility gap has to be overcome for the patient to become sufficiently motivated to pursue this form of treatment.

Nightmares as a Primary or Secondary Phenomenon of PTSD

One would think that when a trauma patient reports having had various psychotherapies for PTSD and having tried various medications for it as well, yet still suffers from nightmares, then it ought to be a straightforward transition to suggest that PTSD may not be the primary agent currently causing the bad dreams, particularly when the PTSD has improved with psychotherapy or medication but the nightmares have not. This has not been the case. Most nightmare patients start out with a number of concerns about treating their bad dreams, chief of which is: "Will I have to talk about my traumatic experiences or my nightmares?" They routinely expect to be asked to recount the vivid and horrific details of their nightmares, which are sometimes more grisly than their actual traumatic events. Even though they are informed several times *before* group treatment that we do neither of these things, they remain suspicious until we demonstrate our approach during the first treatment session.

A fast way to demonstrate to them that we are interested in their sleep, not their trauma (without discounting their trauma or PTSD), is to start with insomnia treatment instead of nightmare treatment, because it is easier for them to conceive how sleep might get better without psychotherapy or sleeping pills. When we start with nightmare treatment, though, another user-friendly approach is to show the trauma patient how nightmares cause insomnia. This approach does not detach the nightmares from PTSD, but it creates a new and interesting hypothesis in the mind of the trauma survivor in which the promise of nightmare treatment might lead to better sleep. The intention of this approach is to lead patients toward a sleep medicine perspective in which we do *not* ask them to discount or ignore their traumatic experiences or their PTSD, but rather we ask them to spend time working on their sleep problems (nightmares or insomnia or both), regardless of whatever turns out to be their cause. This approach begins the process of teaching the patient about the possibility that the nightmares may have taken on a life of their own.

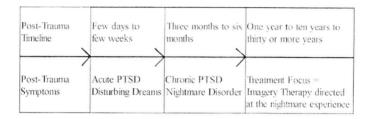

Post-Trauma Timeline	Few days to few weeks	Three months to six months	One year to ten years to thirty or more years
Post-Trauma Symptoms	Acute PTSD Disturbing Dreams	Chronic PTSD Nightmare Disorder	Treatment Focus = Imagery Therapy directed at the nightmare experience

FIGURE 7.1

Trauma-vs.-Habit Paradigm

A sleep medicine perspective segues into a simple chalk talk in which each member of the group is asked to rate by percentage the impact of trauma on the nightmares versus the impact of habit or learned behaviors. Using a 100% maximum, we ask them to give two numbers, one for each column on the board. Depending upon the group, this exercise may done early on if it is clear that some group members already sense that a habit component causes a part of their disturbing dreams. If the group has more severe PTSD or if they are perplexed by a nontechnical discussion of Pavlov's dogs, then the chalk talk may be deferred for another hour, so that more discussion can be developed about how certain sleep or perhaps other psychological habits can be learned.

During the remainder of the session or subsequent sessions, the trauma-vs.-habit paradigm is revisited, and usually 70% to 80% of patients will remark that it now seems plausible that habit might be more salient than trauma as the causative agent of their current problem with disturbing dreams. To assist the patient in making this cognitive shift, we draw a timeline on a board, which starts with a hypothetical assault and then runs for as many number of years as the nightmares have occurred (Figure 7.1). On the timeline, we show that nightmares and insomnia are very common in the first few weeks after the traumatic exposure but that the majority of traumatized individuals recover without developing chronic PTSD, nightmares, or insomnia. Instead, approximately 3 to 6 months after traumatic events, most people report fewer symptoms. The question is then posed, "Why 20 years later (at the far end of the timeline) would you still have nightmares? Is it because of the thing that happened 20 years ago, or is it possible that all during the intervening years, you learned how to keep having nightmares for various reasons, including you had so many to begin with, your mind just became accustomed to having them?"

Symptom Substitution

Symptom substitution is a concern because if nightmares were really all about trauma, then getting rid of them without resolving all the trauma issues would naturally lead to worse problems. We know this belief is strongly held, because we ask each member to predict what happens to anxiety, depression, somatization, and hostility levels once nightmares are reduced. The specific example is described as "What if we could wave a magic wand that miraculously took away your nightmares without affecting any other part of your mind or body?" The question that follows is "What would happen to your anxiety levels, your depression, and so on?" In these discussions, about 80% of participants report that their distress levels should go *up* or stay the same. Rarely do individuals hold a strong conviction that distress levels should go down, unless they entered the program convinced that chronic nightmares are mostly learned behaviors. Once we show them the data that anxiety almost always goes down and that other symptoms often go down when nightmares are decreased (Krakow et al., 1995a, 2001c, 2002d), we have not only helped patients allay their fears about symptom substitution, but we also have given them more insight into how the nightmares might have taken on a life of their own independent of PTSD. We also mention that we do not know of a single nightmare patient who reported feeling worse by decreasing their disturbing dreams. At this juncture, the group is open to the discussion that the nightmare habit constitutes a form of "retraumatization" that clearly serves no useful purpose. In turn, this conceptualization allows for patients to further question the validity of the "unfinished business" theory of traumatic nightmares as the only way to understand disturbing dreams.

Nightmare Sufferer Identity

Nightmare sufferer identity is one of the most fascinating aspects of working with individuals who suffer from chronic bad dreams. In the simplest paradigm, sufferers are resistant to change because they have spent so many years identifying with the problem of nightmares that the thought of going without them is unnerving. On a deeper, arguably psychodynamic level, nightmare patients may find themselves caught up in a "victim paradigm" in which their trauma is one of the major defining experiences in their life, or *the* major experience. Therefore, the nightmares appear to serve this paradigm by providing reminders of the traumatic experience. However, the manner in which disturbing dreams serve as reminders is a little fuzzy, because in our work, and contrary to what seems to be widely expressed in the scientific literature, most trauma survivors do not actually suffer from a consistent spate of reenactment or replay dreams of their trauma (Kramer, Schoen, & Kinney, 1987); instead, the majority may report thematically related dreams of the trauma but not the trauma itself.

As a side note from our experience, those who report frequent replay types of trauma dreams or *only* replay dreams almost always have the greatest severity of PTSD, the least capacity to undergo or retain knowledge from psychotherapy or CBT, and the most severely damaged, malfunctioning, or even nonexistent imagery system except for nightmares. Interestingly, in our population of trauma survivors, these individuals often suffer extremely complex sleep disorders with very severe insomnia and sleep-disordered breathing problems. These individuals are not ideal candidates for IRT because they really are unstable in multiple dimensions of mental health. IRT may be attempted, but it would require extremely close supervision.

Regardless of the actual content of the dreams, nightmares inflict upon the individual the sensation that he or she is being assaulted again, which further entrenches the nightmare sufferer identity; and worse, because the attack comes during sleep, the sensation is amplified by the belief that disturbing dreams come from the unconscious mind and are therefore uncontrollable. This goes to the heart of the identification problem. Because of widespread historical and cultural beliefs that nightmares can only spring from unconscious, deep-seated, internal conflicts or emotional turmoil, and dreams in general are uncontrollable, nightmares must be the *most* uncontrollable (Lansky & Bley, 1995). The nightmare patient often needs time to reevaluate these beliefs. Patients with a history of relatively successful therapy for PTSD or knowledge about conditioning theories may find it easy to rethink this paradigm of the unconscious, and they certainly do so once they begin to see how the activation of their imagery system dissipates nightmares. Patients with greater "investment" in the nightmare sufferer identity, those who might have had limited access to psychotherapy, or those whose therapy might have cemented narrow beliefs about how nightmares operate, always need more time to digest an IRT approach. So, we ask them, "Are you ready to let go of your nightmares?"

Discussion on this theme is important because it may help bring out whatever attachments individuals might have developed about their disturbing dreams. We explain that it is natural, if not the human condition, to become enveloped in one's own experience in such a way as to believe that *what we experience is who we are*. Developing a nightmare condition, regardless of whether it is *trauma-induced* or *habit-sustained*, usually means suffering many years from disturbing dreams, and therefore it is logical to imagine that bad dreams would seem to stick like glue. The most useful way to help patients overcome the nightmare identity problem is to achieve early results with IRT, which begins by helping them develop a strong interest in and understanding of the human imagery system and its capacities.

Imagery Capacity

Nightmare patients with whom we have worked seem to spend a disproportionate amount of time and energy in the realm of verbal thought; as a consequence, they seem to spend less time engaged with their feelings and their imagery. We present this concept to the group by suggesting that each person has thoughts, feelings, and images, which require a proper balance to enhance mental health. In our early work with nightmare patients with past trauma (and in our subsequent work with insomnia patients), we were struck by how much these patients resonated with this paradigm about cognitive balance (or imbalance). Moreover, they readily appreciated that traumatic exposure and a constant refrain of nightmares would reasonably explain why and how someone might learn to avoid imagery in general for fear of what might arise at any time. This paradigm is surprisingly nonthreatening because it builds the person's confidence, normalizing the person's instinct for attempting to avoid something unpleasant and showing how such a process can infect one's overall imagery capacity.

Next, we draw another timeline to discuss the natural course of nightmares, based on widely discussed ideas from the field of dream research (Figure 7.2). We refer to this schematic as either the metamorphosis process of nightmares or how nightmare sufferers spontaneously recover. The discussion deals with how the imagery mechanism is in constant flux both in the form of waking and of dream images, similar to the analogy that the "only constant

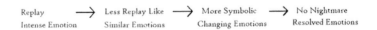

FIGURE 7.2

is change." Nightmares seek to change, and close inspection of disturbing dreams about trauma almost invariably demonstrates various alterations in detail or changes in the big picture, despite the protestations of certain fixated patients whose only perception about their dreams appears to be that the nightmares are always the same, identical, or traumatic replays. Notwithstanding the serious and severe difficulties experienced by this entrenched group, which as I've stated may not find IRT interesting or useful, the idea that nightmares have a natural tendency to change usually sparks a great deal of interest in the group. We explain that most people with nightmares following trauma go on to have no nightmares, and one explanation for this shift is that during a few weeks' to a few months' time, their dreams gradually keep changing as if the dreams themselves were working out some aspect of the emotional turmoil generated by the trauma (Barrett, 1996). Indeed, many anecdotal reports indicate that among traumatized individuals whose dream experiences transform over time, there is less susceptibility to developing chronic PTSD (Rothbaum & Mellman, 2001). The upshot, then, is that it may be natural for the nightmares to come and then gradually change into something less problematic.

We explain to nightmare patients that this capacity for one's imagery to change naturally is something they have always possessed and in fact still employ from time to time in their daily life, but that they may not be noticing this system as much of late because of their general fears about images and specific fears about bad dreams. Sometimes a simple metaphor (a needle on a turntable keeps skipping back to an earlier groove) helps the patient consider an informative imagery concept such as "nightmares as a broken record." We use this image because many nightmare sufferers have spontaneously used it to express their feelings about their disturbing dreams. We also believe that it helps them consider their disturbing dreams as learned behaviors triggered by trauma but sustained by a malfunctioning imagery system that has lost its natural self-corrective capacity, which may be remedied by "lifting the needle off the turntable."

MISCONCEPTIONS ABOUT IRT

There are two main misconceptions about IRT that usually crop up either from the patient's perspective or from a therapist learning about IRT.

Therapist's Perception of IRT as Exposure Therapy

IRT is not exposure therapy as I understand it, although some aspect of exposure certainly may be embedded within it. Patients using IRT are neither instructed to work with nightmares nor to conduct dream rehearsal on them. They are discouraged from spending any more than a few moments or seconds on changing the nightmare into a new dream, after which their energy is to be directed toward rehearsal of the new dream. In the course of our group programs, when individuals attempt to talk about their traumatic event, we interrupt them by explaining that the focus of our program is to "help someone sleep better by decreasing their disturbing dreams or nightmares." And, in our experience, talking about traumatic events without doing so in the context of a formal and properly administered exposure therapy program (Ballenger et al., 2000) may trigger more disturbing dreams in the one doing the talking or among those who must listen.

Undoubtedly, it could be argued that the individual who practices IRT is really going through a much more elaborate process in his or her mind's eye than we are describing here, and this may include spending more time with the old nightmare and becoming desensitized to it. That is entirely plausible and probably happens in some cases. However, when we asked people to record how they used IRT every day for three consecutive weeks, only a rare individual reported that she or he was spending time thinking about or working on the old nightmare in any way (Krakow et al., 2000c). More importantly, from these data and other subsequent work with IRT, we have observed that most patients spend only a few minutes each day or every other day, if that, on the entire process. That is, once they gain comfort with the concept of changing a nightmare and find it relatively easy to do so, which normally takes a few days to a few weeks, most people adopt IRT as a mental skill that requires a marginal investment in time. Again, in contrast to psychodynamic therapy and possibly exposure therapy, few patients have reported the occurrence of an intense emotional process when using IRT. In our experience, few patients report that practicing the new images somehow invoked an abreaction and/or cathartic experience, although many reported an "aha" experience while using IRT.

Patient's Perceptions of Using IRT on Every Nightmare

From the beginning, we wondered how IRT could produce such a strong ripple effect in an individual reporting 100 nightmares per month, yet who only worked on one or two new dreams each week. As mentioned, the data have persuaded us that IRT is a naturally occurring process within the human mind, and that once the corrupted "software" that damaged this innate operating system is discarded, the original system on the "hard drive" can function normally again. As this process unfolds, then, it is the readoption of one's imagery capacity that may explain in part how or why patients do not need to work on each and every bad dream they have experienced. Fairly severe patients with deeply entrenched PTSD and other psychiatric disturbances often concatenate that each and every nightmare requires therapy, and this again shows why these patients may not be suitable candidates for IRT, because in our experience, trying to attempt IRT on every nightmare would be like trying to give up sweets while working in a candy shop. For similar reasons, we were also persuaded to eliminate the regular recording of nightmares in IRT, because it clearly had the potential to worsen the problem among more severe cases. Since 1992, we adopted the approach that the patient would be asked to write down only one nightmare for the purpose of learning the technique, but if the patient elected to forego this step and simply complete the entire process mentally, then we supported him or her in that approach. Ultimately, it appears that the proper dose of IRT is usually small, because imagery by its nature is very powerful, whether elicited in the form of a therapeutic behavior or experienced in the form of a threatening nightmare.

RESULTS

We know from early work that IRT is highly effective among chronic nightmare sufferers who do not apparently experience major psychiatric distress or disorders. The treatment is well received and has proven effective in arguably 90% of cases or greater in which the patient attempted the technique for at least a few weeks (Krakow et al., 1995a; Neidhardt et al., 1992; Kellner et al., 1992). In trauma survivors, using a rigorous, intent-to-treat analysis (a conservative approach in which all participants' data are used regardless of whether they finished the study), the rate of success is much lower because in our largest study more than one third of sexual assault survivors dropped out of the program very early in treatment or before even initiating treatment (Krakow et al., 2001b). Thus IRT or the specter of IRT does not resonate well with certain trauma survivors, so its overall cost-effectiveness must be considered in light of who will prove motivated to consider and try out this therapeutic paradigm. Nonetheless, among those trauma survivors who actually use IRT for some period of time, we again can safely state that 90% or greater will experience some improvement in their disturbing dreams and nightmares, usually of a moderate to large degree.

It is equally important to note that few patients reported a complete cure for their nightmares. However, the degree of nightmare reduction was substantial enough in most patients that they were largely pleased with their results compared to their previous and usually long history (decades in most cases) of chronic nightmares. Imagine, if you will, how it might feel to experience disturbing dreams several times a week for several years, and then following IRT, you only suffer them a few times a month or less. This was the average experience for many of the trauma survivors we treated (Krakow et al., 2000c, 2001b), and although nightmares a few times per month could still be considered a chronic nightmare disorder, most of the patients reported these results as moderate to large-scale improvements despite these residual disturbing dreams.

Thus we doubt that IRT is a cure-all for nightmares among trauma survivors, even though it has a high therapeutic potency. The reasons that it may not cure all nightmares are myriad, and might include persistent nightmares due to PTSD effects, physiological predisposition to disturbing dreams, medication side effects (Pagel & Helfter, 2003), and possibly sleep-disordered breathing in certain trauma survivors (Krakow et al., 2001a, 2001d).

One other outcome that must be mentioned was that IRT resulted in decreased symptoms of PTSD in our largest controlled study in which sexual assault survivors received about 7 hours of group instruction (Krakow et al., 2001b). PTSD improvements were as large as in recent studies using psychotropic medications (Davidson, Rothbaum, van der Kolk, Sikes, & Farfel, 2001), and IRT has rare side effects. Our explanation for this is as follows. First and foremost, when nightmares are decreased, most trauma patients reported sleeping better. Therefore, enhanced sleep likely contributes in some way to enhanced daytime functioning and decreased symptoms. Specifically, successful patients reported decreases in insomnia symptoms, which in and of itself leads to decreases in overall frustration about sleep. So, by looking at chronic nightmare disorder as a sleep disorder and aggressively treating this sleep disorder, we expected some improvement in PTSD, because nightmares and insomnia are two major criteria for this mental health disorder.

In addition, we have also speculated whether imagery capacity enhancement yields supplemental outcomes beyond that which was organized into the therapeutic paradigm. For example, the rapid self-efficacy of the imagery technique may carry over into the manner in which PTSD patients handle other symptoms. Many IRT patients have reported that the use of the technique led them to alter daytime behaviors in positive ways, and they reported that imagery-based manipulations facilitated these new behaviors. Nevertheless, we could not demonstrate an association between those who reported these extratherapeutic uses of IRT during the daytime and PTSD improvement. Thus this theory remains speculative and awaits additional research.

FUTURE CLINICAL APPLICATIONS
AND RESEARCH DIRECTIONS

It would seem worthwhile to tease apart the core elements of IRT, since this may also help us understand how it operates naturally within the human mind. Simplistically, we imagine that it works because the mind has an innate or perhaps internal capacity to work with imagery and to change it at will, which in turn elicits a powerful influence on one's thoughts and feelings. Surely, various media, including television and advertising, have successfully made use of this concept through the use of external imagery, which regrettably may have contributed to some confusion about how to access or control our imagery through internal means.

Regardless of how IRT works, our future programs will examine how the combination of nightmare treatment, insomnia treatment, and physiological sleep breathing treatments affects PTSD. We will be particularly interested in comparing our sleep dynamic therapy (SDT) approach with state-of-the-art exposure therapy, and we would like to investigate whether a trial of combined SDT and exposure therapy maximizes therapeutic outcomes in trauma survivors. Clinically, we speculate that a sizable number of patients with refractory PTSD will be found to suffer complex sleep disorders that ought to improve with SDT but that may respond marginally to standard PTSD treatment, such as exposure or medications. I would further speculate that PTSD patients who respond very well to exposure or other therapies probably have less severe or less entrenched sleep disorder components to their posttraumatic stress symptoms.

CONCLUSIONS

IRT is a brief, relatively nonthreatening approach to the problem of chronic nightmares. It can be administered easily to individuals or groups, and it appears to have a strong impact on that component of disturbing dreams that results from conditioning influences or other learned behaviors. The exact mechanism of how it works remains unclear but will probably involve various active ingredients, chief of which, we believe, is the remarkable and natural healing power of the human imagery system.

REFERENCES

American Psychiatric Association. (2000). *Diagnostic and statistical manual of mental disorders* (DSM-IV-TR) (4th ed.). Washington, DC: American Psychiatric Association.

Ballenger, J. C., Davidson, J. R., Lecrubier, Y., Nutt, D. J., Foa, E. B., Kessler, R. C., et al. (2000). Consensus statement on posttraumatic stress disorder from the International Consensus Group on Depression and Anxiety. *Journal of Clinical Psychiatry, 61*, Suppl 5, 60–66.

Barrett, D. (Ed.). (1966). *Trauma and dreams*. Cambridge: Harvard University Press.

Davidson, J. R., Rothbaum, B. O., van der Kolk, B. A., Sikes, C. R., & Farfel, G. M. (2001). Multicenter, double-blind comparison of sertraline and placebo in the treatment of posttraumatic stress disorder. *Archives of General Psychiatry, 58*, 485–492.

Glasser, W. (1984). *Control theory: A new explanation of how we control our lives*. New York: Harper & Row.

Hartmann, E. (1998). Nightmare after trauma as paradigm for all dreams: A new approach to the nature and functions of dreaming. *Psychiatry, 61*, 223–238.

Kellner, R., Neidhardt, J., Krakow, B., & Pathak, D. (1992). Changes in chronic nightmares after one session of desensitization or rehearsal instructions. *American Journal of Psychiatry, 149*, 659–663.

Kellner, R., Singh, G., & Irogoyen-Rascon, F. (1991). Rehearsal in the treatment of recurring nightmares in post-traumatic stress disorders and panic disorder: Case histories. *Annals of Clinical Psychiatry, 3*, 67–71.

Krakow, B. (2002). *Turning nightmares into dreams* (J. K. Krakow, Ed.). Albuquerque, NM: The New Sleepy Times.

Krakow, B., Artar, A., Warner, T. D., Melendrez, D., Johnston, L., Hollifield, M., et al. (2000a). Sleep disorder, depression, and suicidality in female sexual assault survivors. *Crisis, 21*, 163–170.

Krakow, B., Germain, A., Tandberg, D., Koss, M., Schrader, R., Hollifield, M., et al. (2000b). Sleep breathing and sleep movement disorders masquerading as insomnia in sexual-assault survivors. *Comprehensive Psychiatry, 41*, 49–56.

Krakow, B., Germain, A., Warner, T. D., Schrader, R., Koss, M., Hollifield, M., et al. (2001a). The relationship of sleep quality and posttraumatic stress to potential sleep disorders in sexual assault survivors with nightmares, insomnia, and PTSD. *Journal of Traumatic Stress, 14*, 647–665.

Krakow, B., Hollifield, M., Johnston, L., Koss, M., Schrader, R., Warner, T. D., et al. (2001b). Imagery rehearsal therapy for chronic nightmares in sexual assault survivors with posttraumatic stress disorder: A randomized controlled trial. *JAMA, 286*, 537–545.

Krakow, B., Hollifield, M., Schrader, R., Koss, M., Tandberg, D., Lauriello, J., et al. (2000c). A controlled study of imagery rehearsal for chronic nightmares in sexual assault survivors with PTSD: A preliminary report. *Journal of Traumatic Stress, 13*, 589–609.

Krakow, B., Johnston, L., Melendrez, D., Hollifield, M., Warner, T. D., Chavez-Kennedy, D., et al. (2001c). An open-label trial of evidence-based cognitive behavior therapy for nightmares and insomnia in crime victims with PTSD. *American Journal of Psychiatry, 158*, 2043–2047.

Krakow, B., Kellner, R., Neidhardt, J., Pathak, D., & Lambert, L. (1993). Imagery rehearsal treatment of chronic nightmares: With a thirty month follow-up. *Journal of Behavior Therapy and Experimental Psychiatry, 24*, 325–330.

Krakow, B., Kellner, R., Pathak, D., & Lambert, L. (1995a). Imagery rehearsal treatment for chronic nightmares. *Behavior Research and Therapy, 33*, 837–843.

Krakow, B., Kellner, R., Pathak, D., & Lambert, L. (1996). Long term reductions in nightmares treated with imagery rehearsal. *Behavioural and Cognitive Psychotherapy, 24,* 135–148.

Krakow, B. J., Melendrez, D. C., Johnston, L. G., Clark, J. O., Santana, E. M., Warner, T. D., et al. (2002d). Sleep dynamic therapy for Cerro Grande fire evacuees with posttraumatic stress symptoms: A preliminary report. *Journal of Psychiatry, 63,* 673–684.

Krakow, B., Melendrez, D., Johnston, L., Warner, T. D., Clark, J. O., Pacheco, M., et al. (2002a). Sleep-disordered breathing, psychiatric distress, and quality of life impairment in sexual assault survivors. *Journal of Nervous and Mental Disorders, 190,* 442–452.

Krakow, B., Melendrez, D., Pedersen, B., Johnston, L., Hollifield, M., Germain, A., et al. (2001d). Complex insomnia: Insomnia and sleep-disordered breathing in a consecutive series of crime victims with nightmares and PTSD. *Biological Psychiatry, 49,* 948–953.

Krakow, B., Melendrez, D., Warner, T. D., Dorin, R., Harper, R., & Hollifield, M. (2002b). To breathe, perchance to sleep: Sleep-disordered breathing and chronic insomnia among trauma survivors. *Sleep and Breathing, 6,* 189–202.

Krakow, B., & Neidhardt, J. (1992). *Conquering bad dreams and nightmares: A guide to understanding, interpretation, and cure.* New York: Berkley Books.

Krakow, B., Schrader, R., Tandberg, D., Hollifield, M., Koss, M. P., Yau, C. L., et al. (2002c). Nightmare frequency in sexual assault survivors with PTSD. *Journal of Anxiety Disorders, 16,* 175–190.

Krakow, B., Tandberg, D., Scriggins, L., & Barey, M. (1995b). A controlled comparison of self-rated sleep complaints in acute and chronic nightmare sufferers. *Journal of Nervous and Mental Disorders, 183,* 623–627.

Kramer, M., Schoen, L. S., & Kinney, L. (1987). Nightmares in Vietnam veterans. *Journal of the American Academy of Psychoanalysis, 15,* 67–81.

Lansky, M., & Bley, C. (1995). *Posttraumatic nightmares: Psychodynamic explorations.* Hillsdale, NJ: Analytic Press.

Meurice, J. C., Marc, I., & Series, F. (1996). Effects of naloxone on upper airway collapsibility in normal sleeping subjects. *Thorax, 51,* 851–852.

Neidhardt, E. J., Krakow, B., Kellner, R., & Pathak, D. (1992). The beneficial effects of one treatment session and recording of nightmares on chronic nightmare sufferers. *Sleep, 15,* 470–473.

Neilsen, T., & Zadra, A. (2000). Dreaming disorders. In M. Kryger, T. Roth, & W. Dement (Eds.), *Principles and practices of sleep medicine* (3rd ed., pp. 753–771). Philadelphia: WB Saunders.

Pagel, J. F., & Helfter, P. (2003). Drug induced nightmares: An etiology based review. *Human Psychopharmacology, 18,* 59–67.

Rothbaum, B. O., & Mellman, T. A. (2001). Dreams and exposure therapy in PTSD. *Journal of Traumatic Stress, 14,* 481–490.

Series, F., Roy, N., & Marc, I. (1994). Effects of sleep deprivation and sleep fragmentation on upper airway collapsibility in normal subjects. *American Journal of Respiratory and Critical Care Medicine, 150,* 481–485.

PART III

Constructivist Approaches

CHAPTER 8

The "Royal Road" Becomes a Shrewd Shortcut: The Use of Dreams in Focused Treatment

DEIRDRE BARRETT

Since the publication of Freud's *The Interpretation of Dreams* (1900/1965), scientific knowledge about dreams has expanded rapidly. We've learned that dreams don't arise only in conflict, but rather they happen four to six times a night during each REM sleep period. Even Freud acknowledged, after studying the combat dreams of World War I, that they are not always wish fulfillment. Similarly, Hall and van de Castle's (1966) extensive content studies found that the average dream's emotional tone is negative—representing our fears and disappointments more than our desires.

Freud elicited chains of associations that went far afield from the patient's dream because he was interested in an open-ended exploration of the dreamer's entire history. Contemporary therapists stay closer to what Freud called the "manifest content"—that is, the actual dream. They are likelier to ask, "Is there someone in your waking life who speaks in the demeaning manner in which that dream character did?" or "Is there anything you've been feeling helpless about like in the situation in the dream?" In symptom-focused therapy, a dream-oriented therapist often simply asks, "Have you had any dream related to . . . ?" If a patient offers a dream, it may be either overtly about the symptom or something subjectively felt to be related to it—in either case more relevant than Freud's open-ended inquiries.

Among the elements of Freud's dream theory that have endured modern scrutiny are his observations on the cognitive content of dreams: the "visual representation" of concepts in ways that may resemble puns, the "condensa-tion" of multiple people or places into one dream character or setting, and the predominance of emotion over logic. These characterizations are still considered accurate by most dream psychologists, although most have dropped the disguise hypothesis in favor of physiological explanations for distinctive characteristics of this state of consciousness. The idea that dreams reveal the "unconscious" is still utilized in psychodynamic dream work. However, traditional analysts saw dreams as analogous to speakers using a secret code to hide their content from a censor, whereas the modern metaphor is closer to dreaming as a mime whose natural modes of expression are image, movement, and emotion. Interpreting dreams is still judged useful—not because sleep has introduced an intentional disguise but in the same manner that a verbal interpretation can illuminate visual art.

The emphasis is no longer exclusively on interpretation, however; the emotional and visual modes of experiencing are also valued for their own inherent expressive and motivational potential. Dreams are viewed as power-ful metaphors that may get at issues quicker than a patient might otherwise know how to articulate—a shortcut to parts of our psyche of which we are not normally conscious.

Dream techniques developed in this modern psychodynamic tradition have great relevance for cognitive-behavioral and other short-term, symptom-focused approaches. As psychodynamic theory focuses more on "ego func-tion" and cognitive-behavioral therapy on "latent cognitions" and the role of imagery, the two are converging. Beck's (1971) paper presaged this conver-gence:

> In his waking experience, an individual may conceptualize a situation in a variety of ways. He is most aware of the realistic conceptualization; however, the unrealistic one, based on more primitive cognitive patterns, may be a greater influence on both his waking emotions and his dreams, in which it emerges dramatically. (p. 6)

I want to illustrate how modern dream work may be a relevant shortcut for getting at these unrealistic cognitive patterns with examples from specific treatment areas: bereavement, depression, trauma, cross-cultural counseling, and behavioral medicine.

BEREAVEMENT

In my study (Barrett, 1992) of dreams of the bereaved, I found that dreams passed through stages that mirrored waking struggles with loss—but often expressed them more dramatically. For most of the subjects, dreams began with "back to life" dreams in which there was a denial or reversal of the death, often followed by a new loss. The middle grieving period was characterized by pleasant dreams that linked the deceased to the dreamer's waking life as they returned and gave advice to the dreamer. Finally, many subjects had "leave-taking" dreams of a final chance to say goodbye. The dreams appeared to provide a window to where the dreamer was in terms of denial, anger, guilt, or acceptance. For example, one young woman who had cared for her grandmother through a terminal illness reported the following three dreams after the grandmother's death:

> My grandmother came to me at school and told me she didn't die of cancer, she was poisoned. She told me to tell the police. I told a friend Sam who was supportive of me while I was taking care of her; we went to the police and they didn't believe us.
>
> I have a recurring dream that my grandmother calls me at my house while my mother, sister, and I are preparing dinner. I answer the phone and she says "Hi. It's me." I said "Hi grandma." She asks "How are you?" Then I want my mother to talk to her and she says, "No, I called you." When my mother comes to the phone, my grandmother hangs up. My mother replies, "Stop saying it's grandma, she's not there."
>
> Another recurring dream I have is that my grandmother visits me in a hotel. I say, "Oh you've come back to me," and she says, "Yes, we are going to try it again and see if I live this time." Suddenly she collapses on the bathroom floor. I try to revive her, but I can't. I am panic-stricken and scream, "You can't die, I have to do it right this time." (p. 102)

The young woman reported these dreams early in a course of bereavement counseling. This initiated a discussion of feelings that she had let her grandmother down, that her perceived task had been to keep her alive—even though, logically, she knew her grandmother's condition had been terminal. Two and a half months later, she reported a dream that at least signaled—and perhaps even helped to bring about—the end of the incapacitating stage of her grief:

> I had a lucid dream about my grandmother that was probably the best dream I have ever had. In this dream I was little, about five or six years old, and I was in the bathroom at my grandmother's house. She was giving me a bath in this big

claw-footed tub. The old steam radiator was turned on, making it very cozy. I knew that I was dreaming and that I was getting to see my grandmother well again. After the bath, she lifted me out onto the spiral cotton rug and dried me with the blue towel. When that was done, she said she had to leave now; this seemed to mean for heaven. I said, "Goodbye, grandma. I love you." She said, "I love you too Mary." I woke up feeling wonderful. She had been delirious in the last months of her life, so I'd never really gotten to say goodbye. (p. 103)

Through these dreams and discussions of them, this young woman was able to access her less logical beliefs about her grandmother's death, to recognize and modify irrational guilt, and to gain access to comforting memories.

DEPRESSION

Aaron Beck and his colleagues (Beck & Hurvich, 1959; Beck & Ward, 1961) studied dreams of depressed patients and found them to contain frequent themes of frustration and passivity. Cartwright (1996) followed this up in a series of studies of dreams during and after divorce. She found that subjects who were coping well with divorce and not clinically depressed were much likelier to be dreaming about their ex-spouse directly and especially in ways that acknowledged the separation. Cartwright followed the depressed divorced group and observed that those who remained depressed after one year were still not dreaming about former spouses and the divorce—or they were now having repetitive angry or sad, stuck dreams such as the following two examples:

We're in a restaurant like a pharmacy. My husband wants a lager, warmed. But they don't have this, so he turns to me and says, "I'm divorcing you. Leaving you," and got up and walked out. I was stunned and embarrassed. (pp. 182–183)

My ex-husband told me to go to the hospital for a problem. It turned out I didn't have a problem. He was just giving me a hard time. (p. 183)

Subjects coming out of depression had more varied dreams about their former spouses, such as the following:

We were playing a memory game, going from room to room in a house we bought back in 1977. My former wife was not playing but went to take a nap and we had to turn on the light briefly to remember what you could see in each room. She said, "Give me a break." (p. 184)

The nondepressed group often showed more signs of mastery over what began as unpleasant themes:

> I was invited to dinner by a friend and she said, "Sorry Pat (my ex) is not coming, so no dinner." So I went home to bake a cake for myself. (p. 184)

Cartwright (1996) pointed out that it is impossible to know to what extent the dreams incorporating divorce helped dreamers recover from depression and to what extent they merely reflected that recovery. However, she concluded that dreams at least delineated who was at risk for prolonged depression after divorce.

TRAUMA

In simple one-time trauma, immediate dreams often provide a window into less verbal aspects of a person's attributions about a catastrophic event. An example from Alan Siegel's (1996) study of dreams of survivors of the Oakland and Berkeley firestorm illustrates this:

> *The Fire Seed*
>
> What I recall is an absolutely terrifying nightmare in which the fire had developed an organic consciousness. It was the embodiment of evil. It hid itself very well up on the hill in a pile of brush where it waited for all the fire department to leave. Then it came back to get the houses it had missed. Somehow it had marked these houses with a fire seed and all it had to do was pass by the fire seeds for the house to ignite. I woke up screaming because I saw our "fire seed" begin to swell. In the dream, I was alone in the house. (p. 162)

In this dream one can also see fear of recurrence and what is often called "survivor guilt."

For war-related posttraumatic stress disorder (PTSD), dreams can be an excellent way to explore the impact of combat experiences, since many veterans do not easily talk about these experiences, especially to outsiders. In a study by van der Kolk and colleagues (1984), Vietnam veterans who were most likely to develop posttraumatic nightmares were the youngest and those who had lost close friends. They described a combination of direct fear and survivor guilt much like the fire survivor above. The following recurring dream was typical:

> They tag the body and put the body in a green plastic bag which is tagged again. You go in; they unzip the bag and they ask, "Do you know who this is?" and one

after the other I recognize guys. (So far it's exactly the way it really was.) I identify a couple guys and in my nightmare—I identify myself! At that point, I start to run and can't stop running until I wake up. (Kolk et al., 1984, p. 189)

Jungian analyst Wilmer (1996) found similar issues reflected in dreams collected from a more disturbed inpatient sample of Vietnam veterans. However, in addition to direct fear and irrational survivor guilt, Wilmer found that real guilt was an important component of many nightmares. Veterans in his study also reported nightmares about violent acts that they and their comrades had committed. Two of the dreams from his sample were as follows:

Just out of Chu Lai in a helicopter, a Vietnamese interpreter was trying to get the North Vietnamese prisoners to talk. He told them in Vietnamese to talk or we would throw him out. This was done by all of us. Still, all in all, it was something that was inhuman. He wouldn't talk. I don't know how high we were, but they kicked him out of the helicopter. He hit the ground. We were high enough to where I didn't even look back to see, but when we went down I saw he was literally split into four pieces. (Wilmer, 1996, p. 93)

I am on patrol through a village, and this little kid five or six years old starts running toward us hollering, "GI, GI!," and holding up his hands. He has a grenade with the pin pulled in his hand. I shoot him before he gets to us. I had to. He has more than one grenade strapped to his chest. He just blows up. There's nothing left of him. (p. 91)

One hears these dreams and knows that it is not solely these two soldiers' own fears that are the most tormenting part of their PTSD but also the knowledge of violating their own moral code. Wilmer (1996) indicated that conversations about guilt were much easier in the context of a dream than when attempted in terms of veterans' waking history. It is unfortunate how often in Veterans administration systems nightmares are attended to only as symptoms that increase or decrease with medication; they are not examined for clues about exactly what is haunting a particular patient.

In instances of repetitive childhood trauma, the resultant symptoms are often dissociative rather than those of classic PTSD. In dissociative disorders, dreams can also be useful in understanding the structure of a fragmented personality. I did a survey (Barrett, 1996) of therapists working with dissociative disorders that examined how fragmentation showed up in their patients' dreams. They reported that dreams contained much dissociative imagery such as being "twins" or having multiple images appear when the dreamer's photo was taken. Memories normally only accessible to one "alter" personality might be dreamed by the "host"; alter personalities also showed up as dream characters. In many of these instances, the therapist described patients as being able to better understand something about their dissociation as a result of discussing the dream—they were more in touch with childlike parts of themselves or realized their tendency to "go away" in the face of distress.

CROSS-CULTURAL CONSIDERATIONS

Different cultures have diverse beliefs about dreaming that may interact with psychotherapy in which dreams are utilized. For instance, most of the South American Hispanic cultures emphasize dreaming as predicting the future. Native American peoples believe that dreams are communications with one's ancestors. Polynesians describe dreams as produced by conditions of the earth—impending floods, volcanic activity, and droughts—rather than by individual issues of the dreamer.

I had the opportunity to observe Arabic beliefs about dreams while working in Kuwait shortly after the Gulf War. Kuwaitis have a dream tradition shared with all of Islam. In Moslem tradition, Muhammad received his notice that he was "the greatest of all prophets" in a dream, which he recorded as his 65-page *Nocturnal Journey*. The split of Islam into the conflicting factions of Sunni and Shi'ite was based partly on another dream of Mohammed which the Sunnis used to justify their rights as his successors. Popular Arabic traditions have long emphasized the potential of dreams to foretell the future and deliver messages from higher powers.

While in Kuwait, I heard dreams related to the Iraqi occupation. Although in many ways these were classic PTSD nightmares, they interacted with the cultural beliefs. One dreamer had a brother who had fought in the resistance and then disappeared. She had the following recurring nightmare:

> We are at home and the Iraqis come to the house. They break the windows and storm in, searching everywhere, and demand to know where he [the brother] is. My two little children are crying. One soldier is pointing his gun at each of our heads one by one, saying he will shoot us if we do not tell where he is hiding; we do not know. The soldier pulls the trigger and shoots my son, then my daughter. I wake up screaming. In real life, they came into the house almost like this, and did hold a gun to everyone's head while they asked about my brother. But they never shot anyone, they finally left. My brother has never come home. I think they found him and shot him, but my mother believes he is a POW in Iraq. (Barrett & Behbehani, 1995, p. 7)

Other Kuwaitis had nightmares that were more metaphoric representations of the occupation. Some also showed an evolution of mastery in their dreams such as Cartwright (1996) described with her recovering divorcees. For example, one young Kuwaiti woman had a recurring nightmare throughout the occupation in which she was riding in the elevator of a high-rise building along with many people. The elevator cord would break, plunging the elevator several floors and then dangling by a thread, with the terrified passengers not knowing how they could get off before the cord would break and plunge them to their deaths. The dreamer would wake in terror at this point. After the liberation, changes occurred with each repetition of the dream, with the most recent repetition ending in rescuers coming to help people climb to safety through a door in the top of the elevator.

It is interesting that, while the dreams are very similar to Western ones after trauma, the Arabic cultural beliefs lead to a different reception. Those having nightmares about the Iraqis invading thought this indicated a future occurrence. Unlike cultures that have a tradition of dreams as precognitive, the Arabic one has virtually *no* situation in which the dream may be related to the past. For Kuwaitis who were open to input from Western science, it was reassuring to hear that people around the world often have repetitive dreams after trauma. On the other hand, during the occupation, Kuwaitis who dreamed of Iraqis being driven out were much more comforted by those dreams than are Westerners subscribing to Freud's "wish fulfillment" hypothesis.

BEHAVIORAL MEDICINE

In behavioral medicine, dreams can be useful for discerning attitudes about physical symptoms. Inquiring, "Have you had any dreams about your pain?" (or whatever the symptom) may illuminate whether patients view it as a shameful stigma or a badge of courage. If they have dreamed of their affliction as a science fiction monster or a medieval torture device, then you have a more vivid image to use in pain control imagery than they might generate when awake.

Occasionally, dreams become the central focus for short-term behavioral medicine treatment. One example is that of a 36-year-old man who came for treatment of insomnia of two months' duration (Barrett, 1995). He reported a dream in which he saw a boy sleeping in a bed with soft morning light shining in through translucent curtains. Despite the peaceful images of the scene, the dreamer felt a sense of dread. An old-fashioned alarm clock went off, ringing loudly, but the boy did not stir. A woman appeared at the door of the room and called to the boy, who still did not move. The dream ended abruptly with the patient knowing that the boy was dead. The dreamer recalled that there had been a time around age six when he feared bedtime because he might die in his sleep as he'd heard of people doing. Talking about this long-ago fear and being able to rationally reevaluate its high improbability led to some improvement of his insomnia. In the next session, he reported another dream of a little boy in a room—this time not in bed but rather sitting against a wall crying. The dreamer knew the boy was sobbing out of terrible aloneness. This dream triggered more associations to his childhood concept of death as ultimate aloneness—not so much a cessation of consciousness but "they put you in the ground and you stay there forever." Once explicitly aware of his sleep-death-aloneness equation, he discussed how several work and relationship changes had left him more lonely in the last couple of months. His insomnia disappeared as he made more effort to reconnect socially. We spoke in a psychodynamic context, but it would be just as easy to explain the same process in cognitive-behavioral terms.

Dreams may even contain valuable information about physical conditions. Sacks (1966) relates that one patient dreamed of being a living statue shortly before she developed an organic catatonia, and another dreamed of complete incoordination only hours before a neuropathy of this type began to manifest. An elderly man had a series of dreams in which he was either moving in slow motion or was unable to stop some movement; they began months before he exhibited these symptoms with the onset of Parkinson's disease. Sacks believes that, in all of these cases, the disease "was already affecting neural function and the unconscious mind, the dreaming mind, was more sensitive to this than the waking mind" (1996, p. 214).

I have reported elsewhere (Barrett, 2001) on several cases in which patients who had undiagnosed cancers dreamed of them. Some of these dream images were metaphoric—a black panther digging its claw into the patient's back at the exact point where a melanoma was already visible but had not yet raised alarm. Other messages were as clear as a patient being told by a dream character, "You should get checked for cancer—*now*!" It is reasonable to assume that the cancers—already visible in some cases and potentially pressing on nerves in others—had been sensed by the dreamers even though their waking conceptualization was of themselves as healthy.

In an experiment of mine on training students to incubate dreams for objective problem solving (Barrett, 2001), a few chose medical problems. These proved to have a higher rate of dreamed solutions—as rated by both the dreamer and blind judges—than did other kinds of objective problems such as academic ones. For example, one young woman was being worked up by her physician for amenorrhea and incubated a dream on what was causing this. She dreamed of exercising and exercising. Her excessive activity did indeed turn out to be the cause of her missed periods—a concept she probably had all along but the dream highlighted it enough for her to report it to her doctor.

CONCLUSION

I hope the preceding examples give a practical sense of how dreams can be useful for short-term symptom-focused treatments from many perspectives— including cognitive-behavioral. Most of the examples emphasize their diagnostic use in understanding unrealistic beliefs. However, some therapists utilize dreams more actively to attempt change. Cartwright (1966) experimented with her depressed divorcees, suggesting to those having repetitive dreams that they invent "dream" outcomes they liked better. Some of them had nighttime dreams that incorporated this exercise. She observed that the dream changes seemed to carry over into a daytime sense of mastery.

Zadra (1996) did more systematic dream interventions with patients having recurring nightmares, many trauma-related. He trained them to become "lucid"—that is, aware they were dreaming while they were dreaming—and suggested that they could choose to stop the dream and wake or alter the outcome in any way they chose. He found this reduced nightmares and also improved their psychological functioning when awake. More recently, Krakow (2000) ran groups for sexual assault survivors suffering from PTSD nightmares. He trained them in imagery rehearsal techniques to alter the content in the dream for enhanced mastery. He found that this reduced both their nightmare frequency and also their other PTSD symptoms.

Whether used in this active manner or simply to gather information, dreams are frequently the shortest route to what Beck called the "unrealistic . . . primitive cognitive patterns" (Beck, 1971, p. 6) that he pointed out could be the strongest determinant of emotions.

REFERENCES

Barrett, D. (1992). Through a glass darkly: Images of the dead in dreams. *Omega: Journal of Death and Dying, 24,* 97–108.
Barrett, D. (1995). Using hypnosis to work with dreams. *Self and Society, 23,* 25–30.
Barrett, D. (1996). Dreams in multiple personality disorder. In D. Barrett (Ed.), *Trauma and dreams* (pp. 68–81). Cambridge, MA: Harvard University Press.

Barrett, D. (2001). *The committee of sleep: How artists, scientists, and athletes use their dreams for creative problem solving—and how you can, too.* New York: Crowne/Random House.

Barrett, D., & Behbehani, J. (1995). *Post-traumatic nightmares in Kuwait following the Iraqi invasion.* Paper presented at the Twelfth International Conference of the Association for the Study of Dreams, New York, NY.

Beck, A. (1971). Cognitive patterns in dreams and daydreams. In J. H. Masserman (Ed.), *Dream dynamics: Science and psychoanalysis, Vol 19. Scientific proceedings of the American Academy of Psychoanalysis* (pp. 2–7). New York: Grune & Stratton.

Beck, A., & Hurvich, M. (1959). Psychological correlates of depression. 1. Frequency of "masochistic" dream content in a private practice sample. *Psychosomatic Medicine, 21,* 50–55.

Beck, A., & Ward, C. (1961). Dreams of depressed patients: Characteristic themes in manifest content. *Archives of General Psychiatry, 5,* 462–467.

Cartwright, R. (1996). Dreams and adaptation to divorce. In D. Barrett (Ed.), *Trauma and dreams* (pp. 179–185). Cambridge, MA: Harvard University Press.

Freud, S. (1965). *The interpretation of dreams* (J. Strachey, Trans.). New York: Avon Books. (Original work published in 1900)

Hall, C., & van de Castle, R. (1966). *The content analysis of dreams.* New York: Appleton-Century-Crofts.

Krakow, B. (2000).*The impact of nightmare treatment on posttraumatic stress disorder.* Paper presented at the Seventeenth International Conference of the Association for the Study of Dreams, Washington, DC.

Sacks, O. (1996). Neurological dreams. In D. Barrett (Ed.), *Trauma and dreams* (pp. 212–216). Cambridge, MA: Harvard University Press.

Siegel, A. (1996). Dreams of firestorm survivors. In D. Barrett (Ed.), *Trauma and dreams* (pp. 159–176). Cambridge, MA: Harvard University Press.

van der Kolk, B., Blitz, R., Burr, W., Sherry, S., & Hartmann, E. (1984). Nightmares and trauma: A comparison of veterans. *American Journal of Psychiatry, 141,* 187–190.

Wilmer, H. (1996). The healing nightmare: War dreams of Vietnam veterans. In D. Barrett (Ed.), *Trauma and dreams* (pp. 85–99). Cambridge, MA: Harvard University Press.

Zadra, A. (1996). The recurring dream. In D. Barrett (Ed.), *Trauma and dreams* (pp. 231–247). Cambridge, MA: Harvard University Press.

CHAPTER 9

From Reactive to Proactive Dreaming

ÓSCAR F. GONÇALVES
JOÃO G. BARBOSA

The ancient Greco-Egyptian deity Serapis was the god of dreams. Serapis lived in a temple, the Serapeum, where people could go to have dreams induced. Particularly in the Greco-Roman traditions, this primitive form of dream work was associated with healing and fertility. Since those early times, dreams have been linked to the idea of revelation, cure, and spiritual healing. Thus it should come as no surprise that the earliest formulations of psychotherapy—the "scientific" spiritual healing of the 20th century—were closely connected with dream work and the interpretation of dreams.

The birth date of psychotherapy is often identified with Sigmund Freud's publication of his seminal work, *The Interpretation of Dreams* (Freud, 1900/1966). It is in this work that Freud, using the dream as "royal road" to knowledge of the unconscious, offers a theory of mind that constitutes the central theoretical foundation of psychoanalysis. Freud believed, at that time, that dreams were essentially safety valves for unconscious wishes and that through dreams the person was fulfilling primitive desires. The central task of the psychoanalyst was one of helping the analysand decode the analogical and metaphorical language of dreams by means of psychoanalytic interpretation. Interestingly, dreams continued to be regarded as revealing messages, this time not from gods but from within the person. Since Freud, most of the psychodynamic approaches that have been developed tend to use dreams as the "royal road" for the understanding of psychological functioning. Such was indeed the case with the formulations of Jung (1974) and Adler (1936).

Other therapeutic approaches, such as gestalt (Perls, 1969) and experiential therapies (Gendlin, 1969), offered alternative theories of dreams and specific strategies for dream work. Contrary to the psychodynamic therapists, dreams in these approaches were used not as a way of decoding the hidden language of the unconscious but rather as a way of expanding the clients' experience.

In a manner similar to Freud, the early formulations of cognitive therapy came from studies of dreams. In 1959, while Aaron T. Beck was practicing psychoanalysis, he received his first research grant to study dreams (Weishaar, 1993). Beck's research on dreams was instrumental for his early formulations of a cognitive approach to depression. This involved identifying the roots of depressive ideation (Beck & Ward, 1961). From this research program, Beck developed the idea that dreams are highly correlated with the themes of waking life and that both could represent important tools for the study of psychopathology. As Rosner (1997) has recently described, Beck moved dream work from the latent to the manifest level of analysis and shifted his orientation from motivational to cognitive. Other cognitively oriented therapists have suggested using dreams as thematic expressions of the patient's cognitions and not as symbolic expressions to be interpreted or decoded (Freeman, 1981; Freeman & Boyll, 1992; Freeman & White, this volume).

In sum, dream work has been closely connected with the evolution of the psychotherapeutic movement. In the psychodynamic tradition, dreams were seen as symbolic expressions of the unconscious, and the task for the therapist was to decode them through psychoanalytic interpretation. In the experiential tradition, dream work was seen as a way of uncovering and expressing emotions and thus enriching clients' life experience. Finally, early cognitive therapists suggested that dreams offered important expressions of clients' ideational mechanisms that could be used to uncover certain thematic thoughts and could also be used as tools for cognitive restructuring. That is, dreams could be changed in the very same way that we change thought processes. For all these approaches, dream work has been conceptualized as a reactive process in which a dream is used to reveal some unconscious, cognitive, and emotional processes. In what follows we will be describing a cognitive-narrative approach in which dream work is presented as an essentially proactive process in which the therapeutic dyad uses dreams as a way of expanding the client's personal narrative.

A COGNITIVE-NARRATIVE APPROACH
TO DREAM WORK

In her cognitive experiential approach to dream work in psychotherapy, Clara Hill (1996) states that the language of dreaming makes use of two essentially human characteristics: our tendencies to use metaphors and to be inveterate storytellers. In fact, metaphors are the central way of condensing meaning, and the abundant metaphors in dreams can be understood as part of the ongoing construction of meaning (see Gonçalves & Craine, 1990). Additionally, we make meaning out of organizing this experience in terms of narrative (Gonçalves, 1994, 1995a, 1995b). Hill concludes that, given this reliance on narrative and metaphorical processes, dreams are ways of making sense of what happens to us in waking life and to assimilate those experiences. In sum, what Clara Hill seems to be suggesting is that the narratives found in dreams are not different from the narrative patterns of waking life. During dreams, as in waking life, individuals are in a constant process of assimilating the variety and multiplicity of their experiences through the organization of their personal metaphors and narratives.

Seligman and Yellen (1987) developed a curious proposal that predates but is similar to Hill's. They based their formulation on Molinari and Foulkes's (1969) research showing that the REM (rapid eye movements) stage of sleep is composed of two subphases: periodic *bursts* of REM alternating with REM *quiescence.* Apparently, during the bursts, the individual is overwhelmed by visual and sensory stimulation, while in the quiescent period the individual describes more of an intellectual meaning-like experience. The authors suggest, based on this research, that dreams come from the individual's attempt to integrate in a coherent narrative plot the multiplicity and mostly random nature of sensory and emotional stimuli. Seligman and Yellen positioned their proposal within the framework of the improvisationist theory of dreaming as formulated by Hobson and McCarley (1977), stating that "there is internally generated sensory information from the pontine brainstem which periodically rises up into the forebrain where it is integrated with higher perceptual, conceptual, and emotional information" (Seligman & Yellen, 1987, p. 5).

In sum, both Hill's and Seligman and Yellen's theories attribute to the dreamer the role of a storyteller who attempts to construct a coherent narrative out of the bursts of sensory and emotional stimulation experienced during both awake and dream stages. Like any improvisationist, the dreamer is a narrator attempting to bring a coherent plot of meaning out of the diversity of experience. This metaphor of the individual as a narrator brings us to the constructivist and narrative formulations of cognitive therapy (Gonçalves, 1997a, 1997b).

Rosner (1997) has suggested that constructivist psychology has the potential to be "stronger and more comprehensive" in providing theoretical and clinical foundations for understanding dreams clinically. Rosner bases this statement on the following idea:

> Constructivists, and particularly narrative and developmental constructivists [. . .], are further interested in understanding and manipulating those nonconscious, core-organizing principles and processes through which individuals make meaning. The narrativists, for example, view the inherent need to create a coherent *narrative* through which to understand and integrate experience. . . . (p. 263)

According to the cognitive-narrative perspective, human beings actively construct their knowledge by organizing their experience in terms of narratives. The narrative constitutes a way of introducing some kind of order in the face of the chaotic nature of experience (Gonçalves, Korman, & Angus, 2000). Research on the use of narrative in psychotherapy shows that different narrative modes seem to be associated with distinct therapeutic results, with good outcome being associated with increasing levels of coherence, internality, and reflexivity (Angus & Hardtke, 1994; Pennebaker, 1993). This was found to be true for both waking and dream narratives (Luborsky, Barber, & Diguer, 1992).

Cognitive-narrative psychotherapy is a therapeutic methodology aimed at helping clients come up with a multiplicity of narrative contents, explore the variety of narrative modes (a progressive direction from more external to more internal and reflexive), and come up with alternative ways of construing coherence out of their narratives (Gonçalves, 1995a, 1998). The therapeutic process encompasses five phases: (1) recalling narratives; (2) objectifying narratives; (3) subjectifying narratives; (4) metaphorizing narratives; and (5) projecting narratives.

In the first stage, recalling narratives, clients develop a recalling attitude, learning how to use past and daily experiences as important tools for meaning making. The second phase, objectifying narratives, helps clients expand the sensory dimensions of their narratives (e.g., visual, auditory, olfactory, gustatory, kinesthetic). The third stage consists of subjectifying narratives. In this stage, clients are helped in exploring the multiplicity of emotions and thoughts that can be constructed for each narrative. Meaning making is the central objective of the fourth phase of the therapeutic process and involves metaphorizing narratives. Metaphors are seen as ideal meaning-making symbols that are isomorphic with the content of the narrative. The objective is therefore to help clients to develop multiple meanings out of every narrative. The final stage—projecting narratives—aims to help clients in the development of alternative, meaningful metaphors and to test these meanings through the projection of the new narratives. The final objective is to direct the client into forthcoming life narratives, bringing with it a sense of acting and authorship.

Cognitive narrative psychotherapy makes three central assumptions about dreams (see Gonçalves, Korman, & Angus, 2000, for a more detailed presentation):

1. During the dream state (not unlike the waking state), the individual experiences a chaotic multitude of sensory stimulation, emotional states, and cognitive processes. These stimulations emerge randomly as the residue of waking life experience.
2. In face of this continuous stimulation, the individual faces the task of organizing this random and chaotic experience into a coherent meaningful process.
3. Finally, the construction of coherence implies the need to actively impose a narrative order.

Based on these three assumptions, we have derived an application of cognitive-narrative therapy to dream work in order to:

1. expand the complexity of the dreamers' sensorial, emotional, and cognitive experience;
2. allow for the possibility of the emergence of a more coherent and meaningful dream narrative; and
3. provide room for the proactive induction of more complex, coherent, and diverse dreams.

In the following section we will present a cognitive-narrative manual for dream work, illustrating each phase of the dream work process.

THE COGNITIVE-NARRATIVE USE OF DREAMS: A MANUAL

The following guidelines are intended to be used to facilitate dream work in psychotherapy. The central objective of the manual is to help the client use the dream in order to (1) recall the dream for use in the therapeutic session;

(2) increase the level of dream experience by the narrative elaboration of different sensory dimensions; (3) increase the level of dream experience by the narrative elaboration of different emotional dimensions; (4) increase the level of dream experience by the narrative elaboration of different cognitive dimensions; (5) derive multiple meanings from the dream experience; and (6) proactively construct alternative dreams and enhance these dreams in waking life. In order to accomplish these objectives, the client and therapist deal with the dream using the six phases of cognitive-narrative psychotherapy: recalling, objectifying, emotionally subjectifying, cognitive subjectifying, metaphorizing, and projecting.

Introducing the Dream Work

Objective.   The process begins by having the therapist present the therapeutic objectives of the dream work. In the first stage the client is told that the objective of the dream work is to increase the level and complexity of dream experience, to better understand the dream, to make connections between the dream and other issues of wakening life, and to proactively create alternative dreams. At this stage the therapist informs the client about the methodology to be used.

Method.   The following sequence is suggested:

1. Present in simple language the objectives of dream work (e.g., "The objective of our work today is to expand the experience and understanding of your dream, to connect the dream with wakening life, and to rehearse and experience alternative dreams.")
2. Describe the therapeutic sequence (e.g., "We'll begin by recalling the different parts of the dream; then we'll be exploring in detail the sensory, emotional, and cognitive experiences of the dream; next we'll move into constructing some meanings out of the dream; finally we'll explore alternative dreams").

Stage One—Recalling the Dream

Objective.   The recall phase has as its most central objective to allow the client to piece together the dream fragments in order to pursue further clinical work.

Method. This phase follows a three-stage sequence:

1. The therapist prompts the client to elaborate on the dream narrative in a coherent way. The therapists asks open questions, such as: "Please, tell me about what happened. Where did it all take place? Where were you? Who was there? How did it all begin? What did you think? What did you do? What did all the others do? How did it all end?"
2. The client is asked to identify different sections or "chapters" in his or her dream narrative (e.g., "Can you identify or divide your dream into different parts?").
3. Finally, the client is invited to select any part of the dream that he or she wants to pursue further (e.g., "Which part or parts of your dream would you like to pursue further?").

Stage Two—Objectifying the Dream

Objective. The objective of this phase is to increase the level of experience by having the client elaborate on the different sensory dimensions of the dream. Here the client is invited to explore the sights, sounds, smells, tastes, and physical sensations present in the dream.

Method. The following sequence is suggested:

1. Ask open-ended questions about the visual dimensions of the dream (e.g., "What are you seeing as you describe this dream? Tell me about the scenario, the different colors, shades, etc.").
2. Ask open-ended questions about the auditory dimensions of the dream (e.g., "As you describe the episode, which different sounds are you noticing?").
3. Ask open-ended questions about the olfactory dimensions of the dream (e.g., "Tell me now about any smells that you recollect from this experience").
4. Ask open-ended questions about the taste dimensions of the experience (e.g., "What different tastes can you identify in this dream?").
5. Finally, ask open-ended questions about the physical sensations experienced in the dream (e.g., "What are you experiencing in your body as we recall this dream?").

Stage Three—Emotionally Subjectifying the Dream

Objective. The attention of the therapeutic dyad now moves to the internal and emotional side of the experience. This involves an effort to increase the level of dream experience by elaborating on its emotional dimensions.

Method. The client is instructed to go through the different dream scenes and explore the emotions associated with the dream using a three-step process:

1. Emotional activation (e.g., "What are you experiencing physically?").
2. Emotional focusing (e.g., "I would like you to please exaggerate the physical experience")
3. Emotional symbolizing (e.g., "Please identify the emotions associated with the physical experience")

Stage Four—Cognitively Subjectifying the Dream

Objective. Following the emotional subjectification, the client is invited to keep increasing the complexity of the dream experience. This is done by turning the focus of therapeutic work to the narrative elaboration of the different thoughts and cognitions associated with the experience.

Method. The client is instructed to go through the following sequence:

1. Identify any specific thought associated with the experience (e.g., "Tell me now about all the thoughts that come to your mind that are associated with those feelings").
2. Have clients free-associate on those thoughts (e.g., "Try to find the thought that is associated with the first one").

Stage Five—Metaphorizing the Dream

Objective. The metaphorizing phase is the part of dream work where the client is invited to explore the different meanings associated with the dream and the link between these meanings and other thoughts in waking life.

Method. The following process is suggested:

1. Invite clients to come up with a "title" (i.e., metaphor) that in their view ideally encapsulates the central meaning of the dream (e.g., "In the same way as directors and writers choose titles to summarize the core meaning of their work, I would invite you now to come up with a title that metaphorically condenses the meaning of the episode that we have been going through").

2. Once clients have selected a title, the therapist should help elaborate on the meaning constructed (e.g., "Tell me a little bit more about the relationship between the dream and the title you've just chosen").

3. The therapist should encourage clients to construct a range of meanings, exploring the episode from others' perspectives (e.g., "I'm now inviting you to assume a different point of view, a different perspective. It could be from a different character in your episode or it could be from any significant outside observer. What different titles would these people come up with?").

4. The clients are asked again to identify connections between the dream and themes in their waking life (e.g., "What connections can you make between this dream and your waking life?").

Stage Six—Projecting the Dream

Objective. The projecting phase tries to help the client develop a dream that he or she would like to see enhanced as an alternative to the original dream.

Method. The client is invited to follow this sequence:

1. Invite the client to come up with an alternative metaphoric title to the dream to be projected (e.g., "What would be a possible alternative dream? What title might encapsulate the central meaning of the dream? Please, tell me about the general narrative of the dream").

2. Invite the client to identify the different thoughts associated with the dream (e.g., "What thoughts can you identify?").

3. Invite the client to identify the different emotions associated with the dream (e.g., "What emotions can you identify?").

4. Invite the client to identify the different sensations associated with the dream (e.g., "What do you see, smell, hear, taste, or feel physically?").

5. Invite the client to determine the implications of this dream in waking life (e.g., "What are the implications of this dream in your waking life?").

6. Invite the client to determine what he/she could do to project the alternative dream in waking life (e.g., "What could you do to enhance this dream in your awakening life?").

CONCLUSION

One third of our life passes while we are sleeping. A significant part of this sleep is occupied by dreaming. Dreaming is a feature of both our biological and psychological condition, by which we make sense of what goes on in our life during sleep. Therefore, ignoring dreams is to neglect a significant part of our life.

As Hobson (1988) has suggested, during REM sleep there is an interplay between two complementary processes: (1) the brain stem activates brain functioning by generating a chaotic process of stimulation; and (2) the forebrain tries its best to bring a synthetic sense of coherence to this stimulation by introducing a narrative order. The process is not at all different from what takes place in waking, with the single difference that most of the sensory input and motor output of waking life are not involved.

The task of the dreamer is to experience the diversity of sensorial, emotional, and cognitive experiences while simultaneously struggling to integrate them into a coherent narrative and plot. The absence of waking contextual constraints allows the possibility for an unlimited creativity (e.g., hallucination qualities; intense emotionality). Also, the lack of some fundamental external constraints creates obstacles for the dreamer as he or she attempts to come up with a coherent narrative (e.g., distortions of time, place, and persons; delusional qualities).

The cognitive-narrative approach to dream work tries to build on the strengths and overcome the weaknesses of the dream experience by (1) building on the dreamer's creativity by expanding the level of sensorial, emotional, and cognitive experiencing; and (2) helping the dreamer construct meaningful possibilities of coherence for the dream narrative. Thus, rather than propose a retroactive and interpretative approach to dream work, we suggest a proactive methodology to enhance the qualities of both dreaming and waking experience. As Hobson (1988) aptly reminded us:

> All subjective experience, including dreaming, tends to be organized by the linguistic faculty of our brain-minds as a narrative-scenario. And we are so intensely involved—and in such peculiar ways—in these story-films that we tend to adopt an interpretative literary stance when reacting to our dreams. But just as literature and film—regardless of their content—may be profitably regarded as particular forms

of expression, so may dreams also be profitably viewed as particular forms of mental experience. (pp. 203–204)

REFERENCES

Adler, A. (1936). On the interpretation of dreams. *International Journal of Individual Psychology, 2*, 3–16.

Angus, L. E., & Hardtke, K. (1994). Narrative processes in psychotherapy. *Canadian Psychology, 35*, 190–203.

Beck, A. T., & Ward, C. H. (1961). Dreams of depressed patients: Characteristic themes in manifest content. *Archives of General Psychiatry, 5*, 462–467.

Freeman, A. (1981). Dreams and images in cognitive therapy. In G. Emery, S. D. Hollan, & R. C. Bedrosian (Eds.), *New directions in cognitive therapy* (pp. 224–238). New York: Guilford.

Freeman, A., & Boyll, S. (1992). The use of dreams and the dream metaphor in cognitive-behavior therapy. *Psychotherapy in Private Practice, 4*, 173–192.

Freud, S. (1966). *The interpretation of dreams.* New York: Avon. (Original work published 1900)

Gendlin, E. (1986). *Let your body interpret your dream.* Wilmette, IL: Chiron.

Gonçalves, O. F. (1994). From epistemological truth to existential meaning in cognitive narrative psychotherapy. *Journal of Constructivist Psychology, 7*, 107–118.

Gonçalves, O. F. (1995a). Cognitive narrative psychotherapy. In M. J. Mahoney (Ed.), *Cognitive and constructive psychotherapies* (pp. 139–162). New York: Pergamon.

Gonçalves, O. F. (1995b). Hermeneutics, constructivism, and the cognitive-behavioral therapies: From the object to the project. In R. A. Neimeyer & M. J. Mahoney (Eds.), *Constructivism in psychotherapy* (pp. 195–230). Washington, DC: APA Press.

Gonçalves, O. F. (1997a). Constructivism and the deconstruction of clinical practice. In T. L. Sexton & B. L. Griffin (Eds.), *Constructivist thinking in counseling practice, research and training* (pp. xi–xvii). New York: TC Press.

Gonçalves, O. F. (1997b). Postmodern cognitive psychotherapy: From the university to the multiversity. *Journal of Cognitive Psychotherapy, 11*, 105–112.

Gonçalves, O. F. (1998).*Psicoterapia cognitiva narrativa: Um manual de psicoterapia breve* (Cognitive narrative psychotherapy: A brief therapy manual). S. Paulo, Brazil: Edipsy.

Gonçalves, O. F., & Craine, M. H. (1990). The use of metaphors in cognitive therapy. *Journal of Cognitive Psychotherapy, 4*, 135–149.

Gonçalves, O. F., Korman, Y., & Angus, L. (2000). Constructing psychopathology from a cognitive narrative perspective. In R. A. Neimeyer & J. D. Raskin (Eds.), *Constructions of disorder* (pp. 265–284). Washington, DC: American Psychologist Association Press.

Hill, C. E. (1996). *Working with dreams in psychotherapy.* New York: Guilford.

Hobson, J. A. (1988). *The dreaming brain.* New York: Basic Books.

Hobson, J. A., & McCarley, R. W. (1977). The brain as a dream state generator: An activation-synthesis hypothesis of the dream process. *American Journal of Psychiatry, 134*, 1335–1348.

Jung, C. G. (1974). *Dreams.* Princeton, NJ: Princeton University Press.

Luborsky, L., Barber, J. P., & Diguer, L. (1992). The meaning of narratives told during psychotherapy: The fruits of a new observational unit. *Psychotherapy Research, 2,* 277–290.

Molinari, S., & Foulkes, D. (1969). Tonic and phasic events during sleep: Psychological correlates and implications. *Perceptual and Motor Skills, 29,* 343–368.

Pennebaker, J. W. (1993). Putting stress into words: Health, linguistic, and therapeutic implications. *Behaviour Research and Therapy, 31,* 539–548.

Perls, F. (1969). *Gestalt therapy verbatim.* New York: Bantam.

Rosner, R. I. (1997). Cognitive therapy, constructivism, and dreams: A critical review. *Journal of Constructivist Psychology, 10,* 249–273.

Seligman, M. E., & Yellen, A. (1987). What is a dream? *Behaviour Research and Therapy, 25,* 1–24.

Weishaar, M. E. (1993). *Aaron T. Beck.* London: Sage.

CHAPTER 10

Focusing-Oriented Dream Work

MIA LEIJSSEN

INTRODUCTION

This chapter illustrates how working with dreams therapeutically can be enhanced if the cognitive approach is complemented with the experiential approach. More specifically, the chapter will introduce to cognitive therapists the technique of focusing for use in cognitive dream work. Focusing has been a major innovation and advancement in both client-centered therapy and experiential psychotherapy (Gendlin, 1973, 1981). The person most responsible for introducing and championing focusing is Eugene Gendlin. In this chapter I quote extensively from Gendlin's work, since it has been a central influence on my own research on focusing and dreams.* This chapter, then, is as much a presentation of Gendlin's perspective on focusing and dreams as it is a reflection of my own clinical and research experience.

In the 1950s Gendlin, a graduate student in philosophy, joined Carl Rogers at the University of Chicago in his work on client-centered therapy (Gendlin,

---

*In 1981 Gendlin was guest professor at the University of Leuven, where I worked as a trainer for client-centered therapists. During one month I received an intensive training in focusing from Gendlin and experienced the huge effect of this method. After Gendlin's visit I started a research project on focusing in psychotherapy and made my doctoral dissertation on focusing and experiential psychotherapy.

2002). Gendlin's philosophical work looked at how words and experiencing relate to each other. His work in psychology has been one application of this philosophical agenda (Hendricks, 2002b). Since about 1965, Gendlin has been pushing experiential psychotherapy in the direction of focusing, which he describes as a method of methods, and which can be practiced within different orientations and with many kinds of techniques and diagnoses (Gendlin, 1996). Focusing, like experiential psychotherapy, is rooted in the search for "immediate concreteness." According to this concept, one's sense of immediate experiencing is not emotion, cognition, words, or muscle movements, but a directly felt sense of the complexity of situations. Thus the focusing method is not dependent on which theory one chooses, nor on whether one uses verbal, body, imagery, or interactional techniques, or even all of them, but on *how* one uses these. The desired shift, in the experiential movement, is from *what* to *how* (Gendlin, 1973). Gendlin discovered that successful clients in psychotherapy do not just think about problems and do not drown in emotions. Rather they attend to what is called a *bodily felt sense* of a situation. In other words, they contact their direct experience, what they can sense in the body in the immediate moment. Words or images arise directly from that sense (Hendricks, 2002a).

For cognitive therapists, focusing can be understood as a conversation between the cognitive experience and the bodily felt sense. According to Gendlin, "the role played by cognition cannot be evaluated on the basis of cognition alone. The client must know to sense at the experiential edge. That is where we can find the difference the cognition makes" (Gendlin, 1996, p. 244). The cognitive therapist can point to the felt sense level by asking the client the simple question: "How do these thoughts feel in your body?" This may immediately deepen the process. This integration of experientially based focusing techniques into cognitive psychotherapy is predicated on a holistic mind/body approach to psychotherapy. Through focusing the client can learn to pay attention to the body's holistically registered experience of the cognition and acquire new and valuable information that might not be available from the processes of logic and reasoning alone.

In this chapter I will present an integration of Gendlin's work, the contributions of other focusing-oriented therapists (Lukens, 1992; Dawson, 2001; Kan, Miner Holden, & Marquis, 2001; Hinterkopf, 2002), and my own experience and research using focusing techniques with dreams specifically. For this chapter I have integrated a number of different steps and procedures in focusing-oriented dream work into *five comprehensive processes* that require several skills on the part of the client and specific interventions on the part of the therapist: (1) becoming bodily aware and clearing a space; (2) applying the focusing attitude to the dream and listening to the dream story; (3) developing a felt sense of the dream and getting a felt shift; (4) asking questions or opening up what the dream is about; and (5) exercising bias control or finding new steps. I will indicate how the client can proceed through the different phases and how the therapist—when difficulties arise and the client gets stuck—can be more directive in teaching the necessary skills. In 1986, with the publication of *Let Your Body Interpret Your Dreams* (Gendlin, 1986), Gendlin showed for the first time how focusing techniques could be integrated with different theoretical schools in working with dreams specifically. Gendlin (1986, 1992, 1996) has since presented a number of procedures by which the body can discover meaning and make therapeutic progress from a dream. I will discuss these procedures and highlight how they can be used in conjunction with the techniques of cognitive therapy in the context of enumerating this five-step process.

FOCUSING

Cognitive therapists may not be familiar with the basic principles of the focusing technique more broadly defined. Focusing is a process in which the person makes contact with a special kind of internal bodily awareness (Gendlin,1981, 1984, 1996) that "is not the physiological machine of the usual reductive thinking. Here it is the body as sensed from inside" (Gendlin, 1996, p. 2). The body carries a sense of some situation, problem, or aspect of one's life, felt as a whole complexity, a multiplicity implicit in a single sense. Through interactions with symbols, the felt experience can become more precise, can move and change, and can achieve a felt shift: the experience of a real change or bodily resolution of the issue. Gendlin (1984, pp. 83–84) has described the required attitude for the client in interacting with the felt sense as one of taking the role of "the client's client." The client's "inner therapist" gives friendly attention and silent waiting time, refrains from inter-pretations, and receives and resonates with whatever comes from a felt sense and lets it be at least for a while. Gendlin (1981) has developed a model for teaching focusing that involves six process steps: (1) clearing a space; (2) getting a felt sense; (3) finding a handle; (4) resonating handle and felt sense; (5) asking; and (6) dealing with the inner critic and receiving. Some therapists use that model to guide people through a focusing process. However, it is not necessary to teach focusing during therapy. It can be equally helpful merely if the therapist models the more general focusing attitude of waiting in the presence of the not yet speakable, being receptive to the not yet formed, listening in a gentle, accepting way, honouring and trusting the wisdom that speaks through the body, finding the right symbolizations in which the bodily experience can move further into meaning. The focusing steps can be referred to as "subtasks" or "microprocesses" offered at certain moments in psychotherapy to help establish the conditions that are optimal for facilitating particular kinds of self-exploration (Leijssen, 1998; Stinckens, Lietaer, & Leijssen, 2002).

Cognitive therapists can integrate focusing into their broader treatment plan by employing several "cognitive moves" as part of the focusing technique. First, they can ask the client to say to himself or herself: "Let me make an inventory of my problems" and then welcome what comes experientially. Also, when clients in cognitive therapy get stuck because they are engaged in dead-end discussions and the logic does not change anything, or a strong belief is embedded in an experience that is not touched, the therapist can introduce a focusing microprocess to engender an "actual" experience. If the cognitive side differs from the experienced side, one can ask questions of the felt sense until the two sides become indistinguishable. Cognitive restructuring or reframing, for example, is more effective when it involves a real shift in the concrete bodily experience of the problem, and not *only* a new way of thinking.

In relationships it should be emphasized that focusing can only happen if the interpersonal conditions are right (Gendlin, 1996, p. 297). According to Wiltschko,

> The relational space between client and therapist is the living space in which the client's developmental process can occur. In fact, internal and interpersonal processes are not separate, rather they are two aspects of one process. . . . If the relational conditions are not good, focusing is almost useless because the inner process is very much a function of the ongoing interactional process. (Wiltschko, 1995, pp. 5 and 1)

With dream work the interpersonal relationship needs special consideration because each dream has clearly a personal character, connected with privacy and intimacy; this requires trust.

> When one talks about one's dreams, one gives someone else permission, as it were, to look behind the scenes, even though one does not know oneself what is going on there. . . . The therapist who does not take this delicate aspect into account will soon be punished; but if (s)he is respectful, (s)he will find that the client's trust will increase: this will deepen the relationship and the process. (Vossen, 1990, p. 519)

Becoming Bodily Aware and Clearing a Space

Before working with the content of the dream, some preliminary work with the client is necessary: focusing requires full bodily awareness and the ability to relate to oneself in an open, receiving, friendly way, without being overwhelmed by problems. Finding and keeping a proper way of relating is an important therapeutic process. The therapist will have to intervene differently as a function of the specific difficulties clients can have in this phase.

Some clients do not know *the body* as an internal authority; they look for meaning "outside," such as other authorities (including the cognitive therapist), theories, or books. They concentrate on intellectual processes and speak from there; they explain and rationalize a lot. In such cases, the therapist should actively help the client to discover new ways of relating to himself or herself. Introducing an approach addressed to the body is often a necessary step in bringing such clients in contact with a new source of knowledge: their own inner bodily felt authority. Gendlin (1996, p. 71) offers several instructions therapists can give clients to help them learn to sense the body from inside: Sometimes it is sufficient to use a simple invitation such as: "Take your time to feel how you are inside your body." "Follow your breathing for a moment, simply breathing in and out, without wanting to change anything to it." "What strikes you when your attention scans your body?" The therapist can also ask the client to close his or her eyes for a moment and see how the different areas in the body feel. Breathing and sensations in the throat, chest, stomach, and abdomen receive full attention. Should the therapist choose to let the client start with some form of relaxation, one should see to it that the relaxation does not become too deep; indeed, focusing demands full concentration and keen receptivity. During deep relaxation there is no felt sense. Relaxation is too deep when the body no longer "talks back."

At the other end of the continuum clients can be overwhelmed by too many feelings and sensations so that no "self" remains to relate to what is felt. These clients show, verbally or nonverbally, that too much is coming their way or that their experiences are too intense. The client is then likely to show aversion for what emerges or feel anxiety or tension. When the client feels flooded by problems or totally identifies with some experience, the client's way of relating is too close. Before working with a dream, the therapist should help the client to create a space by sorting out the problems the client is carrying right now. Client and therapist can make an inventory of what's there, noticing each issue and then creating distance from it so that the client can stay related to it and not yet sink in it. It may be very helpful to carry this out concretely, for instance, by having the client write down on a piece of paper the name of the problem or by drawing it and then depositing the paper somewhere in the room. This process of creating space may be continued even further at fantasy level by using various metaphors (for details and illustrations, see Leijssen, 1998).

Let's first look at an example of a therapy session in which one of my clients, who is too close to the dream, is helped to clear the space and to achieve a better way of relating. The client comes for the third therapy session; she is bumping into everything and starts talking immediately.

C: I had a terrible dream last night and I feel extremely tense. During the week I cried a lot (starts crying). There is so much I can't stand any longer.

T: Let's look at that together, quietly. . . . Take your time and follow your breathing for a moment—you may close your eyes if you wish—and simply follow the rhythm as you breathe the air in and out . . . (silence) . . . You said you were very tense . . . ask your body what it is that makes you so tense. . . .

C: Well I have to do an awful lot of things.

T: OK, we will have a look at what it is that demands your attention. . . . Here you have a notepad. . . . Each problem will receive a name which you will write down on a sheet of notepaper, and next, you will assign the sheet—and thus the problem—a place in this room here, at a comfortable distance from yourself. So, what comes to you first?

C: There is a load of work in our house, various things need repairs . . . there is a problem with the heating system, the electrical system needs checking, I have to buy lamps, the curtains need washing. . . .

T: Yes, that is a lot all at once. Take a little sheet for each of these worries . . . and write on each a key word . . . (silence, C. writes on note paper) . . . Now assign each of these a place on the floor or somewhere else in this room but while doing so, try to feel how it is to really put aside each one of these worries for a while. You don't forget them but you let them rest, you give them a place . . . (C. deposits the notes on the floor, within reach, and sighs deeply.) OK, there they are. Now have a look at what else makes you tense. (silence)

C: I urgently have to talk to my son's schoolteacher (C. gives a lengthy explanation of the problem whereby the therapist helps her clarify what exactly she wants to talk about).

T: Make another note of your conversation with the schoolteach-
        er ... and put that down too. (C. deposits the note on the floor on
        the other side; there follows a deep sigh) ... Is there anything else?
        (Several problems follow, all of which are similarly given a place.)
T: And then you also had this dream last night. ... You said it was
        terrible. Can you just make a note for having this dream and give
        it also a place here in the room? ... Now attend again in your body.
        Except for the problems you mentioned and that are deposited by
        the various notes here, can you say you feel fine about how life is
        going? You should find that the overall sense that comes now is
        somewhat relieved compared to the way it was before.
C: I'm surprised it can be that simple to feel much better!
T: Now, we will pick one of these concerns. It can be any of them.
        Give your body a little bit of time to choose which issue to work
        with. ...
C: My attention is drawn towards the dream ... although I'm afraid of
        looking at it.
T: OK, we can work with the dream. I'll give you some explanation
        first.

Whichever way one chooses to create space, in no event is making distance
the same as "putting the problem away," "forgetting it," or "repressing it."
It is rather a friendly search for establishing a better relationship, where the
client gets space to look at problems instead of becoming drawn into them
unaware. "In fact, real progress seems to involve maintaining a part of oneself
that is apart from the intensity, and supporting that part as one explores the
intense emotion" (Iberg, 1996, p. 24). The therapist helps the client to be
with the feelings, not *in* them. Focusing works best when the client can "sit
next to" his or her feelings instead of plunging into them.

Even when the client is not overwhelmed, it makes sense to start with the
process of clearing space in order to grant the body the time to reveal what
it brings along. Otherwise the dream work will be influenced by negative
feelings, moods, judgments, etc. (Dawson, 2001). Everything that comes up
is briefly given attention, but nothing is dealt with. The person extricates
himself or herself from the problems, thus creating room for the observing
self, which becomes free to face the problems and get a hold of the situation.
The disidentification is a step towards gentleness. It brings in the possibility
of empathy and compassion, and it helps the client to develop a healing inner
relationship. The phase of clearing space being completed, one may choose
one issue—a dream in this case—to work with.

Applying the Focusing Attitude to the Dream and Listening to the Dream Story

Clients often feel that their dreams are bizarre, and this scares them. Dreams use a specific language, and often it is this language that scares clients. I believe that modern Western culture has lost the capacity to understand archaic dream language. By sharing some knowledge about the specific nature of dream language and especially by modeling an attitude of interest, welcome, and wonder, the therapist can help the client form a better relationship with the dream. When dream work is new for clients, the therapist can give a little bit of information to help the client overcome prejudices and to deal with the "strange" characteristics of a dream. A therapist using focusing techniques will often explain that dreams are metaphoric like fairy tales; the images point to something; they are not that thing; the dream uses a language that is dramatic and flamboyant; and what is produced is not literal but represents some parts of the self in other persons, animals, objects, or events. Dreams come to help; they can give support and clarity or bring something new in one's life; they offer opportunities to develop.

According to Vossen, dreams ask for a process of *telling*.

> The dream is a series of images which together form a story. And a story wants to be told, requires an understanding ear, a listener. And the funny thing is: however strange, confusing or foolish the dream story may be, it always has a plot and that plot is always neat and clear and completely equal to that of a classic tragedy. There is always an exposition, second a plot, then a culmination and it ends in the denouement, the solution. What is amazing is that we are not consciously there but without knowing it we subconsciously create a product of a higher order, as clear and differentiated in its formal structure as a crystal; even a short dream gives evidence of this. (Vossen, 1990, p. 517)

We love to listen to the story just as children do. We need not interpret it but rather we sit with it, admiring its creativity and enjoying its intricacy. Listening to a dream can result in deep involvement in someone's life, just by receiving the story.

An example provided by Vossen (1990) illustrates how powerful it can be for the client when an empathic listener states the simple facts as they present themselves directly in the dream story and retells the ongoing narrative stream of the dream in terms of first this, then this, then that happened:

> As part of a training I had been working with participants and their dreams. . . . There was a woman, unknown to me, the partner of one of the participants . . . saying: "I don't have very much confidence in working with dreams!" "Why not?" I asked.

She said: "For the last few years I have been dreaming this recurring dream; I once presented it to a psychoanalyst, and later on to another and they both came up with explanations which were useless to me." This roused my curiosity, so I asked: "What was your dream?" She hesitated, looked at me and apparently overcame her hesitation, for she replied: "In this dream I am at a fair: I am holding on to a merry-go-round which is turning round. Then, all of a sudden, it starts to go faster and faster. I cannot hold on any longer and I am hurled away into nothingness. Then I wake up, drenched with sweat." My first reaction was to try and place myself in her position: "It is as if you are hanging on to something (here one should think of the metaphorical meaning) and you feel cheerful and comfortable; and then it seems as if things are speeding up and are taking a direction impossible for you to follow; and then you are lost." Her face turned pale: "Could it be then that I still have not got over my mother's death?" After a while, she recovered and started to talk: when she was five years old, her mother died rather suddenly. She herself was the oldest child and had taken charge of the household. (pp. 516–517)

The charge and the power that is stored in the series of images can sometimes already be elicited if someone joins in, listens carefully, and paraphrases the actions in the different images in an empathic and nonjudgmental way. In this "warm bath" of relating to the dream, the crystallized and frozen product can dissolve and can be brought back to active experiencing. Thus it affects the client and brings meaningful associations. Many clients do not spontaneously tell the whole dream story; they run to the climax in the dream and are overwhelmed by the catastrophe, identifying themselves with the strongest emotional aspect. It is important to keep pulling them back, to invite them to tell the dream in it's own "logic," which arises from its unique progression of images and events, and to go over every detail in the story (as good storytellers always do!).

> If the dream analysis begins by concentrating on one or more of its especially salient aspects, the crucial ever-unfolding contexts of meaning are necessarily lost. In effect the chronology of the dream establishes the context within which all the dream events and images constitute and convey their special meaning. (Jennings, 1986, p. 315)

Clients tend to skip over aspects that manifest themselves as insignificant, dense, secondary, or meaningless. Being respectful to the dream implies "letting the dream speak for itself," listening to the exactness of the dream, following the series of images and the course of the action—first the exposition of the story, then the plot, then the climax, and finally the solution—so as to give the strength and the vividness of the experiential process a chance. One could say that in dream work the therapist has "two clients": the person and the dream. The therapist helps the person (the first client) to take the position of an interested observer and to listen to the dream (the second client) with an open and empathic attitude.

Forming the Felt Sense of the Dream and Experiencing the Felt Shift

Focusing-oriented dream work happens in the client's body, not in verbal conversations. Working in an experiential way involves the client's *bodily felt sense* from (some part of) the dream. According to Gendlin,

> Every aspect of a dream can generate a unique felt sense. Once that unique felt sense has come, it has a life on its own. Even if we wanted to, we could not talk ourselves out of it, nor could we help it if it did not budge in response to some good idea. Then, when the sense finally opens, and the whole stream of details emerges from it, the image is no longer a distant object about which we can only speculate. Only such an opening should count as a successful interpretation, rather than ideas that simply "fit," "click," or generate an intellectual "aha"! (Gendlin, 1996, p. 302)

The felt sense can be invited by instructions or questions such as: "Go inside and ask in your body how this part of the dream feels," or "Wait to see if a vague feeling forms. If only old familiar feelings come, keep on paying gentle attention to the center of your body until a feeling forms which is at least a little bit new and which you cannot at first easily describe." In cognitive therapy more deepening of the dream work can result from inviting the client to form a felt sense about a dream theme or a thematic content. When a cognitive approach succeeds, it changes the deeper layers implicitly. If the dream is restructured with appropriate disputation and rational challenges to the dysfunctional material, it can be a major therapeutic step if the client can also feel in his or her body a positive effect of the new way of thinking.

Lukens (1992) illustrates this unfolding felt sense in a story about how Gendlin was helping him to work on one of his dreams:

> He asked me to find a word to describe a woman in my dream who was getting married. As I put my awareness inside my body, a felt sense of the woman formed. From this sense, the word "delicate" emerged, which felt like the right word to describe it. As I stayed with the feeling, I became aware that this was a quality for which I had no models in my early life. (p. 19)

The felt sense isn't a usual feeling or emotion, like anger, fear, or sadness; in addition to such recognizable feelings a dream leaves one with a unique felt quality that fits no category. It is an indefinable, global, puzzling, odd, uneasy, fuzzy sense in the body; it contains a whole constellation in which emotions can be embedded. Suppose a dream image evokes anger; then one can ask: "What is the whole constellation of which this anger is part?" A vague new feeling may form in the center of the body. This is the felt sense. One can pay attention to it until one feels a definite change in the feeling. This is often accompanied by a new awareness or insight. It is called a *felt shift* or body shift. It is a bodily sensed growth direction that feels unmistakably right. This physical felt shift is a breakthrough, a bit of energy freed up in the body. It is the touchstone of the focusing-oriented dream work (Lukens, 1992).

Paying attention to the felt sense and the bodily felt shift may work in a complementary way with cognitive therapy: Does a given cognitive restructuring bring a step of change in how the dream or the problem is experienced concretely, somatically? If it does, the directly sensed effect must be pursued further. If there is no effect, we can discard what was said or done. If a cognitive effort fails, further listening to the felt sense can tell us what is in it and bring a new opening. A shift in the felt sense brings also new cognitions that move life forward (Gendlin, 1986).

For people who are not used to working with dreams, or for those who do not remember their dreams, it might be a good idea to start in a more general way and pay attention to their felt sense of dreaming (Dawson, 2001). One of my clients in therapy said he never dreamt. I asked him: "Thinking about dreams, what can you experience in the middle of your body?" He felt "uneasiness," "losing control," and "something like sadness." I asked him to stay somewhat longer with this whole indefinable feeling of which sadness might be a part. Then suddenly he had a memory of himself as a child of seven: he had told a dream at breakfast and the whole family had made a fool of him. Since then he couldn't remember having had any dream.

Asking Questions

Different psychological approaches can be of use in understanding dreams. In focusing-oriented dream work, different theories (Freudian, Jungian, gestalt, existential, cognitive) can be used as sources of questions in developing hypotheses. The client is invited to ask questions to his or her inner knowing and to let the answer emerge from the felt sense of the dream. According to Gendlin:

> Instead of saying what a dream means, or what some parts mean, we ask "Does something come if we suppose such and such?" Experientially speaking, different

interpretations are simply hypotheses. Hypotheses are best expressed as questions. We therefore use all the theoretical systems to generate small-scale questions, until the dream is interpreted in terms of concretely experienced steps arising in the client's body. (Gendlin, 1996, p. 202)

Gendlin (1986) offers many questions derived from different theoretical systems. They are simply open-ended questions about different parameters of the dream, grouped in *five categories*: associations, elements of a drama, working with characters, decoding ways, and dimensions of development. The client is invited to sit with each question a while, just long enough (about a minute) to let the question or the cognitive hypothesis touch the felt sense of the dream. Usually some lead to important associations, emotions, or new cognitions; some questions lead to nothing. When the felt sense itself answers, there is a felt shift; this physical signal of relief, opening, or energy is the concretely bodily felt touchstone of the genuineness of the interpretation. The questions can be asked in any order, and one will never need all the questions with one dream. If cognitive therapists work in a focusing-oriented way, they can use the same questions they always ask *and* connect the client's "thinking" to other kinds of experience. At each step the therapist can ask the client how a specific thought affects the experience. If the experience shrivels as a result of the thought, they had better shelve that thought and seek another question that will maximize it. Experientially connected thinking is not "intellectualizing"; it carries the experience forward and brings more psychological change.

I will illustrate how Gendlin's five different categories of questions can be used.

Associations. The only question that needs to be asked every time and that *always comes first* is the open-ended question: "What comes to you in relation to the dream?" By example, a client tells the following dream:

C: I got to my seat on the airplane. Lying right on the seat was a child's ring with different color stones. Someone had just left it there. I knew it wasn't worth anything, it was plastic with glass stones. It was definitely a child's ring. It then slipped down between the seat and the wall, and I left it there.

T: What comes to you, what are your associations in relation to the dream?

C: What comes to me is the airplane. I am soon going on to my new job. The job is temporary. It's just exactly what I'd like to be doing, so I am getting ready not to be disappointed when it's over. I keep having a hope that it would become permanent. Actually it's certain not to. Yes, it's like that ring. It looks like gold and diamonds, but it's a child's toy. (Gendlin, 1986, p. 29)

Asking for associations can have more powerful effects when the client has a felt sense of (some part of) the dream. Then, Gendlin suggests, the therapist can offer questions, such as: "What did you feel in the dream? . . . Pay attention to the middle of your body. Sense what feel-quality the dream-image makes there. . . . Then ask: What in your life feels like that? Or: What does this feel-quality remind you of?" (Gendlin, 1986, pp. 166–167). One can come back to some of these questions to get associations later in relation to any part of the dream.

Elements of a Drama.   Approaching the dream as a drama can translate into questions about the *setting, plot, and characters.* For the setting, Gendlin suggests that the client

> visualize and sense the lay-out of the place in your dream. What does it remind you of? Where have you been in a place like that? What place felt like that? . . . Summarize the events of the dream. Make it more general. Then ask yourself: What in your life is like that story? (Gendlin, 1986, pp. 168–173)

Working with Characters.   Gendlin suggests that the therapist can invite the client to work deeper with characters or objects from the dream by letting the client *play the character or be any object* from the dream:

> Imagine that you are preparing to act in a play. You are going to play that character from the dream. Let the feel quality of being that person come in your body. How would you walk on stage? How would you stand or sit? Don't decide. Let your body do it of its own accord. Exaggerate it. Wait and see what words or moves come from the body feel. (Gendlin, 1986, p. 176)

The agent for interpreting the dream is the physical sense of a new way of being, an inward shift, the new energy-quality in the body.

I will illustrate this process with a fragment from a lengthy therapy (Leijssen, 1999). The client was a single 32-year-old woman who came to therapy after an attempt at suicide. The most important issues she worked with in therapy were the relationship with her demanding and dominant mother and her battle to create more distance between herself and her mother. During the 31st session, she told this dream:

C: I saw my mother drive a car. Next to the car was a green horse trotting, a very beautiful, very big and firm, beautifully shining, well-muscled horse. At a particular moment, it died, it just fell down. I know it is dead.

T: What feeling did this dream give you?

C: Actually none, I simply see the horse drop dead. I wasn't even present in the dream myself.

T: You just find the horse trotting next to your mother dropping dead.

C: Hm.

T: But you stressed how beautiful the horse was in your eyes.

C: Yes, no horse can be so big as the horse in the dream, neither so firmly built.

T: Could you—by way of experiment—crawl into the horse's skin and tell the dream as if you were the horse.

C: Hm (silence) . . . It seems that I have to run very hard and I see the car, but my mother does not see me.

T: Are you running a sort of competition?

C: I have to overtake the car or keep track of it, and yes . . . she doesn't see me.

T: You're not seen, however hard you run to keep track of the car . . .

C: Oh ya, and then there comes this moment. . . . It seems like . . . yes, there was a bridge that only cars can take and I can't go on.

T: She crosses the bridge where you can't go on anymore.

C: Yes, yes I stop.

T: You stop with what?

C: I give up, I surrender. But it has more to do with the fact that she does not see me. . . . That's it, I quit trying, I do not run any further to be seen by her.

T: Take your time to experience that feeling: "I quit running to be seen by her." Sense the feel-quality of that for a while.

C: The battle to be noticed . . . to give that up . . . it brings me peace . . . (silence, sigh).

T: Remain in the horse's skin a little while longer. As you described the horse . . .

C: I still have the image of it being so big and strong.

T: Can you try how it feels to say: "I am big and strong."

C: That's hard for me . . . that is exactly the part that I want to give up.

T: In the dream, that big, strong horse drops dead . . .

C: Yes! I can understand that, that makes sense . . . because I do not want it anymore, the big and the strong . . . yes, it drops dead! . . . (silence, sigh) . . . and it also has to do with what I said before: in reality, no horse is that big, it doesn't coincide with a horse in nature.

T: It wasn't realistic to be so big and strong. Your nature is different?

C: It was how mother wanted me to be, she exaggerated everything to keep up appearances . . . it's weird, but I feel no regrets for the horse dropping dead, while you would expect that it is a sad thing.

T: Dying in a dream often symbolizes ending something. I hear that in the dream, you don't feel sorry to let go of the exaggerated big and strong.

C: Yes, I am in fact ending a period in my life . . . (silence) . . . But reality is also that I have to find out where I'm standing now.

T: That you have to rediscover your own nature.

C: Exactly. It's amazing how much this dream contains. A whole new and rich inner world is opening for me. I feel immensely supported in the feeling that I do not have to be pretentious, but that I have to stay with my own nature.

Sometimes clients *refuse* to "be" a specific character. This strong resistance is interesting to focus on. If you are gentle and understanding with this feeling, it will tell you more about the reasons for rejecting some types of characters. The therapist can also invite the client to work at confronting it and standing his or her ground with it. In general, if it feels wrong for a client to be that character, one can try relating to the character in some way that is new (Gendlin, 1986, p. 180). One can also ask: "If this were a real situation, what would you do? Or what can you imagine doing in such a situation that gives you energy?" Asking a client to *continue* the dream or complete a dream image, can also bring something new (Gendlin, 1986, p. 181).

Decoding Ways.   Gendlin also offers questions about decoding the dream information—questions about symbols, body analogy, and counterfactual information:

> Each person is unique. Therefore "universal" symbols cannot have the same meaning in everyone's dreams. . . . Every common thing is a symbol in that it brings a cluster of common uses, meanings, and functions. These provide a kind of graph paper, a background design, which help us interpret the unique dream. (Gendlin, 1986, pp. 85–86)

Questions about *symbols* can be asked in a very simple way: "What is that kind of thing anyway? What is it used for? Say the obvious. . . . Then substitute that into the story of the dream. See if the dream makes sense when seen or thought of in that way" (Gendlin, 1986, pp. 13–14). I can illustrate this phenomenon with a dream from the lengthy therapy of the same client that in the 31st session told the "horse dream" (Leijssen, 1999). In the 35th session she reported:

C: I needed a new bra and I was in a lingerie shop. All the bras I tried on failed. Eventually I didn't buy one, they were all wrong in the same way: the cups were too round and the straps were too small.

T: So you wanted to buy a new bra, but while trying them on, you noticed they were all wrong and you leave without buying one. . . . I know of course what a bra is, but can you tell me what a bra is to you?

C: I've always had the impression that I wear one despite the fact that I don't need one.

T: Ah yes, why then do you wear a bra if you don't need one?

C: It's a habit. . . . Yes, you put it on in the morning out of the habit. . . . It happens that I forget and then I think that everybody sees it, although I know that isn't the case . . . but a bra . . . yes, theoretically I must say . . . that is support, eh . . .

T: But a support that you actually don't need . . . that you put on out of habit and that you sometimes forget . . . in which case you are worried that others can see it. . . . What is it that the others may not see?

C: I don't know, I think they've never seen it. . . . It is more me feeling not at ease. . . . Those naked breasts. . . . It has to do with something that is proper, all women wear bras.

T: YES?

C: (laughs loudly) Well I think so, I suspect that, and those shops have to survive too . . .

T: It seems like in this case you don't start from your own needs. You seem to start from the way it is supposed to be done.

C: Yes, that's the way it is, women are supposed to wear . . . yes, that has nothing to do with my needs. Because I remember when I was a girl, at a certain moment, my mother bought me my first bra and I said; "What is that? Do I need that?" . . . But my mother insisted, yes I had to. . . . Much later I found out that I was wearing it the wrong way!

T: Your mother gives you a mold that you don't want, but you seem not to be able to sneak out of wearing it and you wear it the wrong way . . . but it is supposed to be like that . . .

C: Yes and it literally did not fit!

T: And in the dream you are in this store with bras that are all wrong . . .

C: That was even funny! It was such a ridiculous sight! Almost a caricature—when you try to wear something that doesn't fit, it becomes ridiculous.

T: And the things that don't fit are the round cups and the short straps . . . I am imagining what you must look like to fit in those.

C: I suddenly have to laugh . . . with those way too short straps . . . (C and T laugh loudly) you have to keep it up high. . . . Ah, I mustn't think about it! And those phenomenal cups, that is real slapstick!

T: You try to fit in that absurd mold . . . but you find it so ridiculous that you don't buy one . . .

C: No! It was obvious, the feeling; they do not fit, I do not need them! (deep sigh)

T: A real relief when you don't try to force yourself into a mold that doesn't fit.

C: I suddenly realize how often I have done that and what a great feeling it is to say; I don't need it. . . . First I thought; do I have to be unhappy because they don't have anything in the store that fits me . . . But now I think; I don't have to be there . . . Why should I wear something that I don't need . . . I feel better without . . .

T: Do you have any idea what the lingerie store stands for, something of which you feel: I don't have to be there? (silence)

C: I think it represents every aspect of the woman my mother tried to make me . . . the unnatural . . . the mold to which I had to adjust myself . . . pretending to be more than you actually are. . . . For such a long time I thought there was something wrong with me because I didn't fit in there. . . . But now . . . it feels so good to be able to say; I do not need these things . . . I won't be forced into it again . . .

T: Wonderful to move so naturally, in your own mold.

C: This is the first time in my life that I become aware of that. It feels so great to be able to feel that I refuse what doesn't suit me. These images give me an inner grip to go on the road not taken.

Something in a dream may make sense if viewed as a *body analogy* and then decoded. Gendlin (1986) gives an example from his work with a female client. She dreamed she owned a motorcycle. There was ice on the motor and the back wheel: "The client discovers: Well, if the motor is frozen, it won't start. My wanting a motorcycle is on ice, I guess. Let me feel that in my body, my wanting a motorcycle. . . . Oh! sure! My sexual desire is on ice, too" (p. 182).

In questions about the *counterfactual* the client is invited to look at what in the dream is especially different from the actual situation. What has the dream changed? In a video demonstration (Focusing Institute, 1992) Gendlin worked with a client who described a room in her dream. The room was a place she knew and it gave her good energy. However, she said: "It has wooden beds and here in the dream these are iron beds." Gendlin put the attention on what the dream changed: "Where have you seen iron beds?" This reminded the client of a hospital situation.

Dimensions of Development. The next set of Gendlin's questions involve aspects of human development: childhood, personal growth, sexuality, spirituality.

> What childhood memory might come in relation to the dream? In your childhood, what had this feel-quality from the dream? . . . How are you developing, or trying to develop? What do you struggle with or wish you could be or do? . . . If it were a story about your ways of being sexual, what would it be saying? . . . What creative or spiritual potential of yours might the dream be about? Are there dimensions of being human in the dream that you don't take much account of in your life? (Gendlin, 1986, pp. 15–16)

The list of questions is a storehouse of *possible moves*; one can generate various versions of each question and also ask other questions that may occur. If one has a great hunch, it can be phrased as a question. With each question it is important to make sure there is a felt sense there, to ask; only the dreamer's body can interpret the dream. The questions are meant to help the dreamer explore his or her felt sense, to sense into the intricate, not yet known place from which movement comes. It is important to notice after each question whether it brings life energy forward or is a new step in the client's process (Hinterkopf, 2002). How the therapist can invite more new steps is worked out in the following procedures.

Exercising Bias Control

Even if the dreamer has already found something new from the dream, bias control can produce a different and even more convincing interpretation of the dream. "Bias" is understood as the way someone would react *usually*. Bias control consists of considering an interpretation opposite to one's usual way of thinking. People tend to apply to the dream the same perspective they always apply to anything in life. For example, if the client experiences an aggressive force as something menacing and bad, his or her usual reaction and feelings would be to run away in fear. Bias control gets *beyond* the client's imposition of his or her *usual conscious attitudes* onto the meaning of the dream. Compared to just asking questions, this part of the method is more challenging and can at times feel inelegant as a therapeutic device.

One procedure of bias control is to look for where there is a disagreement between the dreamer and the dream. The disagreement might be between the dreamer and some other figure in the dream. Or it might be between the dreamer and the trajectory of the dream.

> The dreamer is on a train and realizes he forgot his baggage at the station. He gets off and struggles to go back to get it. But on the way back there is a "distraction." The dreamer keeps saying, "It's a distraction; I've got to get my baggage." But the dream says in effect: "Sorry, you're going this way, over this wall, into a new space." (Gendlin, 1992, p. 25)

There is a juncture in the dream at which the dreamer rejects or denies what the dream says, or conversely, at which the dream refuses to do what the dreamer asks. While conflicts between dream and dreamer need to be worked with, neither side is simply right. The experiential method has this advantage: the client begins dream work automatically feeling one side of the issue, but when the other side is physically experienced the resultant change allows the client to sit at the juncture of both sides of the issue.

The new step or the new direction of growth is often found in something that at first seems bad or *negative*. Bias control invites the client to look at the opposite of what he or she thought, or to what he or she rejects, finds unattractive, wrong, evil, threatening, or undesirable. If the therapist asks how something negative might represent something that the client actually needs emotionally, that which is needed can come into body awareness very quickly, and very positively. The new step is often the opposite of what we value most. This doesn't mean we change our values to the opposite. We merely expand them a little. The new energy can be contacted in the body by trying on for size what comes into the body while role-playing any figure that seems negative in the dream or by simply asking the body about the bad-looking part in the dream: "How might there be something in this which you need?" Attending to the body can provide something new, neither the old way nor the thing in negative form.

"Help" from the Dream. Another focusing procedure is looking for "help" from the dream. "Help" is anything that brings a new and freeing energy, a good or expansive quality, physically in the body; it can be every-

thing positive that we want to take with us when we come to work on the main issue. The therapist goes looking in the odd places and also among the ordinary objects in the dream until "help" is found (see Gendlin, 1996, p. 205 for an example of this strategy). If the client has a dream about something *painful or scary*, Gendlin believes that the dream not only brings an issue to work on, but it also brings some help. He advises not to delve into the issue before finding some help from the dream. If the client hasn't already told of something with positive energy, the therapist asks: "In the rest of the dream is there perhaps an animal or a plant, or a baby, or some living thing or some beautiful thing?" Sometimes there is something in the dream that should be "help," but in the dream *it looks or acts badly*; for instance, an animal acts in some unnatural way.

> At a workshop one participant told of a dream in which there was a sick turtle walking slowly down the road. The image gave the dreamer an awful but familiar feeling. She was asked: "What would a healthy turtle be like?" . . . "A healthy turtle? Well . . . " She inhaled and exhaled a long breath, and her posture and color changed. . . . "That sure feels a lot better." . . . "The good way your body is now, could that be a way to handle that situation that your dream is about?" . . . "Yes! it has a lot of meaning." . . . We see it isn't enough for the dream to be only an accurate metaphor for a dreamer's problem. . . . The turtle image has an incipient energy to engender certain changes. . . . But when something naturally positive is in the dream as sick or negative, we ask what a healthy, natural one would feel like. (Gendlin, 1996, pp. 205–206)

Steps of Resolution

A new step can also come from working further with the problem in terms of the dream images and sensing how they can organically lead to steps of resolution. By way of example, let us take another look at the lengthy therapy in which my client and I discussed the "horse dream" and the "bra dream" (Leijssen, 1999). The excerpt is from the 37th session:

C: There was a big oak tree with a rope hanging from the lowest branch and I was tied with one foot to that rope, hanging with my head down. I could free myself and every time I was free, it started again but then one level more difficult. I also knew there were people watching from the bushes. I didn't see anybody, but I knew there were people watching. I was resting on a branch. I was injured, there was blood on my hands.

T: So you are tied up to a big oak tree and every time you free yourself, there comes a more difficult process of freeing yourself. At the end you stay on a branch, injured, while you know there are people nearby. (In the next part of the therapy, the client finds out that the oak tree is symbol for her family.)

C: That was really tiring, always starting over. . . . I am free and I am resting. . . . I am scared of looking down, the branch on which I am sitting is too high, my feet can't touch the ground. . . . I would hurt myself if I would jump down.

T: You already have a lot of injuries from freeing yourself and then you find out that the branch on which you are sitting is too high. So you are afraid you might injure yourself even more trying to get your feet to touch the ground . . .

C: (cries) That is what I am experiencing. . . . I want to get off that branch but I don't know how. (silence)

T: You said something about people in your dream being in the bushes. . . . Can you tell me a little bit more about that?

C: They were simply there. They were doing nothing special.

T: Did they see that you were injured or how you were sitting in the tree?

C: No, they didn't do anything. . . . I think they didn't know that I was injured. . . . I think they had the impression that I was OK where I was sitting. . . .

T: Were you trying to give them that impression?

C: I was totally absorbed by freeing myself and the wounds. . . . The branch on which I am sitting is too high. Jumping down would be committing suicide.

T: I am surprised that you are only thinking of jumping down as a way out . . . and that would be too painful . . . (silence) . . . Do you really want to get out of that tree?

C: Yes, but I don't know how, the branch is too high.

T: Let's try to think of a way to get out of the tree without having to injure yourself even more. . . .

C: I could call some people from the wood . . . that is the only solution that I see. . . . Else I have to stay on the branch. . . . Yes, asking for help . . . I didn't think of that before. . . .

T: You could ask the people there to help you out of the tree. . . .

C: Yes (smiles), but in my dream I didn't take that step, I am tiring myself and every time I get stuck again . . .

T: You stay alone in your process of freeing yourself. . . . It is striking that you don't think of asking the people around you for help . . .

C: It strikes me that that's the way it is . . . I recognise asking nobody for help. . . . Yes, like in the dream. . . . I just didn't think of it. . . .

While I'm thinking now: of course you can call these people and when someone comes, you just have to step on his shoulder. . . .

T: How does it feel to really imagine that . . . you step out of the tree . . . you go down . . . you use someone's shoulder as support. . . .

C: Yes, that is the way I want to get out of the tree. . . . I still don't understand that I didn't think of that before. . . . In the dream, I was so desperate, I seemed doomed to stay in the tree.

T: You were so absorbed by freeing yourself from your family and also by the injuries you got from doing that, that it slipped out of your mind that you had people nearby to which you could signal that you could use some help.

C: I have been thinking the past week: if I would get sick . . . then I wouldn't have anyone. . . . That made me very sad. . . . That idea made me panic. . . . Now I feel that I can appeal to other people when I'm in need. . . . Funny that I didn't think of that before. . . . I was under the impression that I couldn't get out of that tree without getting hurt. The sudden idea that I can ask for help is really helping and freeing. It makes me want to explore my relationship to others. It is encouraging to enlarge my perspective to people outside my family.

This example also illustrates how the therapist looks for the *point of choice* in the action and invites the client to try to feel through an action different from her problematic reaction, symbolized in the dream images and actions. The images of the dream turned out to have steps to resolution implicit in them. The bodily felt shift brings to consciousness the new action step very organically. What was bodily experienced here at a symbolic level has the power to create real change in the client's actions in daily life.

CONCLUSION

The content of dreams is inherently inexhaustible, and when used with body-awareness and in interaction with the therapist it is possible to discover that dreams and images have an incipient energy for therapeutic movement. The process of dreaming is

> a dimension in which our life unfolds and dissolves, manifests and transforms as an ongoing creative process. Dreaming is answering questions and needs you may have forgotten you asked for. Rather than looking for answers, find your specific question and need that got answered by a certain dream. Dreaming is kind of a

motherly nourishment. Not all of our needs have to be fulfilled on the physical level. To make this more powerful one can ask: What did you do in a dream you once or always wanted to do in real life? Keep the feeling of what it is to have it done, don't limit it down to "it was only a dream." How does the body experience it, what is the emotional experience of this happened event (like travelling somewhere, having a lot of money, quitting your job)? (Dawson, 2001, p. 3)

Finally, I believe that cognitive therapy and focusing-oriented work complement each other because *experiential understanding* is more powerful and effective in achieving therapeutic results than intellectualizing or working only on gut feelings. Steps of actual change are to be found neither in mere verbal discussion nor in mere emotional intensity. Cognitive work uses the mind to see new possibilities; focusing reaches a different level of awareness and pays attention to how one's body feels: "The value of a cognition lies in its experiential effect" (Gendlin, 1996, pp. 244–245). The process of integration can be natural and fluid if clients are invited to recognize whether or not what they are thinking matches what they are experiencing. This results in an increased awareness of self and an enhanced experiential understanding of the constellation of cognitive patterns and disorders that relate to particular problems. Experiential working with dreams integrates conceptual process with bodily felt sense; cognitive arguments are also experientially held. In combining cognitive and focusing-oriented dream work, the body's holistically registered experience of the dream is used as the edge of discovery where thoughts can become fresh, alive, and agents of change.

REFERENCES

Dawson, T. (2001). Dream workshop summary. Focusing-discussion list, November 27. *http://www.focusing.org*

Focusing Institute (Producer). (1992). *Focusing & dreams* (Videotape). Chicago, IL: The Focusing Institute.

Gendlin, E. T. (1973). Experiential psychotherapy. In R. Corsini (Ed.), *Current psychotherapies* (pp. 317–352). Itasca, IL: Peacock.

Gendlin, E. T. (1981). *Focusing* (rev. ed.). New York: Bantam Books.

Gendlin, E. T. (1984). The client's client: The edge of awareness. In F. R. Levant & J. M. Shlien (Eds.), *Client-centered therapy and the person-centered approach: New directions in theory, research and practice* (pp. 76–107). New York: Praeger.

Gendlin, E. T. (1986). *Let your body interpret your dreams.* Wilmette, IL: Chiron Publications.

Gendlin, E. T. (1992, Spring). Three learnings since the dreambook. *The Folio*, 25–29.

Gendlin, E. T. (1996). *Focusing-oriented psychotherapy: A manual of the experiential method.* New York: Guilford Press.

Gendlin, E. T. (2002). Foreword. In C. R. Rogers & D. E. Russell (Eds.), *Carl Rogers. The quiet revolutionary. An oral history* (pp. xi–xxi). Roseville, CA: Penmarin Books.

Hendricks, M. N. (2002a). Focusing-oriented/experiential psychotherapy. In D. J. Cain & J. Seeman (Eds.), *Humanistic psychotherapies* (pp. 221–252). Washington, DC: American Psychological Association.

Hendricks, M. N. (2002b). What difference does philosophy make? Crossing Gendlin and Rogers. In J. C. Watson, R. N. Goldman, & M. S. Warner (Eds.), *Client-centered and experiential psychotherapy in the 21st century: Advances in theory, research and practice* (pp. 52–63). Ross-on-Wye: PCCS Books.

Hinterkopf, E. (2002). How I teach a focusing and dreams workshop: A model. *Staying in Focus. The Focusing Institute Newsletter, 2*(1), 1, 6.

Iberg, J. R. (1996). Finding the body's next step: Ingredients and hindrances. *The Folio: A Journal for Focusing and Experiential Therapy, 15*(1), 13–42.

Jennings, J. L. (1986). The dream is the dream is the dream. A person-centered approach to dream analysis. *Person-Centered Review, 1*(3), 310–333.

Kan, K. A., Miner Holden, J., & Marquis, A. (2001). Effects of experiential focusing-oriented dream interpretation. *Journal of Humanistic Psychology, 41*(4), 105–123.

Leijssen, M. (1998). Focusing microprocesses. In L. S. Greenberg, J. C. Watson, & G. Lietaer (Eds.), *Handbook of experiential psychotherapy* (pp. 121–154). New York: Guilford.

Leijssen, M. (1999). *Gids voor gesprekstherapie*. Utrecht: De Tijdstroom.

Lukens, L. (1992, Spring). The body's role in dreaming. *The Folio*, 17–23.

Stinckens, N., Lietaer, G., & Leijssen, M. (2002). The inner critic on the move: Analysis of the change process in a case of short-term client-centered/experiential therapy. *Counselling and Psychotherapy Research, 2*(1), 40–54.

Vossen, A. J. M. (1990). Client-centered dream therapy. In G. Lietaer, J. Rombauts, & R. Van Balen (Eds.), *Client-centered and experiential psychotherapy in the nineties* (pp. 511–548). Leuven: Leuven University Press.

Wiltschko, J. (1995). Focusing therapy: Some basic statements. *The Folio: A Journal for Focusing and Experiential Therapy, 15*(1), 1–8.

CHAPTER 11

The Hill Cognitive-Experiential Model of Dream Interpretation

CLARA E. HILL
AARON B. ROCHLEN

The Hill (1996) cognitive-experiential model of dream interpretation evolved from a number of different theoretical orientations (e.g., humanistic/experiential, gestalt, psychoanalytic, cognitive, and behavioral theories) and involves three stages: exploration, insight, and action. In the exploration stage, the individual images of the dream are examined and the client is encouraged to reexperience the thoughts and emotions in the dream. In the insight stage, the therapist and client collaborate to construct a new understanding of the dream. In the action stage, the therapist first encourages the client to talk about changes he or she would make in the dream if the dream could be changed in any way the client wanted. The therapist then helps the client bridge from fantasized changes in the dream to thinking about how to translate these to changes in waking life.

To date, about 15 studies have been published on the Hill model. Overall, the research (summarized at the end of this article) has yielded encouraging findings regarding the use of dreams as an effective therapeutic tool with a range of clients and presenting issues. These results are persuasive in suggesting that dream interpretation is useful for helping clients achieve insight and make changes in their lives.

The purpose of the present paper is to describe the model (including some revisions based on our research and training experiences) for cognitive therapists. We revisit the underlying assumptions of the model, describe the three stages of the model, and discuss clinical issues related to using dream interpretation in therapy. We then present a brief overview of the research and provide suggestions for further research.

THE REVISED MODEL

Before describing the steps of the model, several critical assumptions should be noted. First, the meaning of the dream is personal for the client because the dream comes from the client. We assume that dreams are a continuation of waking thinking without input from the external world. Typically, the dreamer is pondering waking issues and figuring out how to fit these into existing cognitive schemas. When existing cognitive schemas are inadequate, it is particularly difficult for clients to deal with the issues, and hence they are more likely to remember their dreams. The goal of therapy, then, is to help clients access existing cognitive schemas and reorganize them to make them more adaptive and functional. Given these assumptions, it follows directly that dreaming is very personal and that standard dream dictionaries and standard symbolic interpretations (such as Freudian sexual symbolism or Jungian archetypes) are not useful because they say very little about the individual's schema. Rather, therapists need to help clients access their personal thoughts and memories about dream images.

The assumption that only the dreamer has the "key" to the meaning of the dream leads to the second assumption, that working with dreams in therapy should be a collaborative process between the therapist and client. The therapist is *not* the expert who knows the meaning of the dream but rather is expert in facilitating the client in exploring the dream, coming to a new understanding of the meaning of the dream, and making decisions about action. The meaning of the dream as well as what the client chooses to do differently in waking life should come as a surprise to both client and therapist.

In addition, we assert that both cognitive and experiential components are necessary for successful dream interpretation. A major task is for clients to examine their cognitive schemas and reorganize them in more adaptive ways. Clients need to be emotionally involved and immersed in the dream and the dream interpretation process, however, to have a complete awareness of what the dream means to them and to be able to use what they have learned to make changes in their lives.

Another assumption is that all three stages are needed for a complete dream interpretation. The stages build on each other, such that a thorough exploration of the images leads to an interpretation of the meaning of the whole dream, which leads to a discussion of what the client can do differently in waking life.

Finally, therapists need to have expertise in using the basic helping skills or therapeutic techniques (see Hill & O'Brien, 1999) before they do dream interpretation. In particular, therapists need to be empathic and skilled at helping clients explore thoughts and feelings (through reflection of feeling, open question, and restatement), construct insights (through interpretation, confrontation, self-disclosure, and immediacy), and develop action ideas (through information and direct guidance) before they work on dreams with clients.

The steps of the dream interpretation process are outlined in Table 11.1. It is important to note that this outline is meant to serve as a guideline rather than as a rigid structure. We suggest that therapists become familiar with the theory behind the model and then try to use the model as presented here with a range of clients. After practicing several times, therapists will find ways to personalize the approach to their own individual styles, to the needs of different clients, and to different types of dreams.

The Exploration Stage

Therapists can start the process by giving clients a brief overview of what to expect in the dream interpretation session to facilitate the development of realistic expectations for what clients can expect in dream interpretation sessions. Clients can be told simply that the structure of this approach to dream interpretation is to explore the individual images of the dream, then put the images together to figure out the meaning of the dream, and then try to decide together what the client would like to do differently in waking life on the basis of what he or she learned about the dream.

Next, the therapist can ask the client to tell the dream in the first-person present tense as if she or he is experiencing it currently. Using the first-person present tense can begin to facilitate immersion into the experience of the dream. After the client tells the dream, the therapist can ask the client to express how he or she felt during and after the dream, again to facilitate reentry into the emotions in the dream. It is important for therapists to encourage clients not only to say feeling words, but to immerse themselves in the emotions involved in the dream experience.

TABLE 11.1   Steps of the Hill Cognitive-Experiential Dream Interpretation Model

A.   Brief overview of model
B.   Exploration stage
    1.   Have client retell dream in first-person present tense
    2.   Have client explore feelings in dream and upon waking
    3.   Explore major images sequentially using DRAW
        a.   **D**escribe
        b.   **R**eexperience Feelings
        c.   **A**ssociate
        d.   **W**aking life triggers
    4.   Summarize exploration process by replacing images with descriptions, feelings, associations, and waking life triggers (optional)
C.   Insight stage
    1.   Ask client for initial understanding of the meaning of the dream
    2.   Collaborate with client to construct a meaning of the dream on at least one level
        a.   Waking life
        b.   Parts of self
        c.   Experience
        d.   Spiritual
        e.   Relationship (if couple's therapy)
    3.   Ask client to summarize the meaning of the dream
D.   Action stage
    1.   Ask client to change the dream
    2.   Bridge to changes in waking life
    3.   Devise a ritual to honor the dream (optional)
    4.   Help client figure out how to continue working with dream (optional)
    5.   Ask client to summarize action plan
    6.   Ask client to title the dream (optional)

When the client first tells the dream, the therapist most often has no awareness of what the dream might mean for the client. For novice therapists, this lack of awareness is sometimes anxiety-provoking because they feel that they have no control over what will emerge in the session. To help quell these anxieties, we suggest that therapists take a client-centered stance of focusing on the client and helping the client explore the dream.

Therapists then move to exploring the major images (objects, people, actions, thoughts, or feelings) as they appear sequentially in the dream. Although it would be luxurious to cover every image in great detail, therapists can typically only do a thorough exploration of a few major images. It is better to do a thorough exploration of a few images than a meager exploration of many images. The acronym "DRAW" (description, reexperiencing, association, waking life triggers) can be used to describe how to help clients explore each major image. The therapist goes through each of the DRAW steps for one image and then moves to the next image, with a thorough exploration of an image taking about 3 to 5 minutes. The therapist's stance during this stage should be one of curiosity, trying to learn about the client's thoughts and feelings in relation to each of the images.

D stands for asking the client to provide a thorough description of the dream image. The client can be asked for all the details that she or he can remember about the image as it appeared in the dream. The therapist can say something like, "Paint the picture for me so that I can see this part of the dream as clearly as you do." Typically, more details of the dream emerge as clients describe the image.

R designates the reexperiencing of the feelings during the segment of the dream in which the image occurs. When the client focuses on the feelings, the images become more immediate, real, and significant. Therapists can use reflections of feelings and open questions to help clients focus on what they were feeling. They can also ask clients to stay with the feeling and try to experience it in their bodies.

A stands for associations. Here therapists might ask clients to say what comes to mind in thinking about the image or about memories related to the image. An effective intervention for facilitating associations, borrowed from Delaney (1991), is for therapists to ask clients to pretend that the therapist is from Mars and has no idea of what the image is. This technique allows clients to explain things that they might think are obvious but, in fact, are idiosyncratic to that person. When the client gives an association, therapists can ask for more details about it (e.g., "Tell me more about what happened when you were a child at the beach") so that clients can explain what the association means to them rather than just saying words. Thorough exploration of the associations is crucial for enabling clients to access the cognitive schemas relevant to the dream so that material needed to understand the dream is available to both client and therapist.

W represents the waking life triggers of the image. In this step, therapists ask clients to think of waking life events that might be related to the particular dream image (rather than what might have triggered the dream as a whole). Often, these waking life triggers have emerged spontaneously during the description, reexperiencing, and association steps, but other times therapists have to probe for them.

An illustration (fictional) of the use of the DRAW methodology may be useful. Marco, a doctor who moved to the United States from Italy to pursue his dream of becoming a physician, had the following distressing recurrent dream.

> "I'm being pursued by a number of men wearing white jackets. They want to catch me and slice off a piece of my nose. I narrowly escape and find myself back in my hometown in Italy."

Using the DRAW acronym, the therapist first asks Marco to describe the men.

> "There are five of them. They are wearing long, white coats. Actually, they look like doctors. Now that I think of it, they look like the five doctors who examined me during my recent test to become a physician in the States."

The therapist then asks Marco to say how he feels when he thinks about the image of the men in white jackets.

> "I feel scared when they are chasing me. They seem to be gaining on me and I am getting out of breath from running so much. They make me mad too. They seem so arrogant and pompous and have this holier than thou attitude."

The therapist then asks Marco to associate to men in white jackets and to say the first thing that comes to his mind when he thinks of this image.

> "I remember the doctors in my hometown in Italy. They were very stern. I was pretty scared of them. It also makes me think about my father. He didn't wear a white coat, but he was very stern. I associate men with masculinity, and I sometimes question how masculine I am, especially compared with my peers. It's funny because as I think about it, my father is very masculine and I never got along with him so well. I also associate white jackets with waiters in restaurants, and I've had to be a waiter since I came over to the States, which has been humiliating. I've been trained to be a physician and am instead serving hamburgers. I thought this was supposed to be the land of milk and honey, what a joke that is."

Finally, the therapist asks Marco to think of things in waking life that might have triggered the image.

> "Well, I wanted to be a doctor here in the States. I went to this examination recently and I didn't get a high enough score to be admitted into a residency program. I haven't decided yet what I want to do about it. I know that I don't want to keep on being a waiter, but I don't know what's coming next in my life."

Once the therapist and client have explored the first image in depth, they move on to the next image. In this case, the therapist would ask Marco to talk about the image of "catching me." Often, therapists find it helpful to pull together the work the client has done in the exploration stage by providing a summary. In this summary, the therapist can retell the dream, inserting the descriptions, feelings, associations, and waking life triggers revealed by the client for the images in the dream. Hearing the dream retold in this manner can be very revealing for some clients, although it is important that the therapist keep this retelling short so as not to take away from the client's immersion in the dream process. For example, the therapist might summarize the exploration of Marco's dream by saying:

> "So you're being chased by five men that look a lot like the physicians who examined you to become a doctor here in the States. The men also remind you of your father because they are very stern, masculine, and unfriendly. These doctors want to catch you, which you associate with suffocating and being punished as a child. They want to cut off your nose, which you associate with your mother's side of the family. You also associate 'nose' with 'knows' and what you feel familiar or comfortable with. Then you narrowly escape from the physicians and find yourself back in your hometown where everything feels peaceful and you can be with your family now that your father has died. What thoughts come to mind when you hear this dream again with your associations?"

The Insight Stage

The insight stage begins with the therapist asking the client to say what she or he thinks the dream might mean. As the client responds, the therapist can listen carefully to indicate a valuing of the client's introspection, to assess the client's current level of understanding of the dream, to assess the client's motivation to hear a different interpretation, and to determine the level of interpretation to which the client is naturally drawn.

In terms of current level of understanding, the client might not understand the dream at all, might understand it partially, or might have a very complete understanding of the dream. If the client has no understanding of the dream and is eager to go further, the therapist has to make a decision about what level of interpretation to pursue (see next paragraph). If the client understands the dream partially, it is important for the therapist to listen for what parts of the dream were left out in the client's interpretation. The initial work is then for the therapist to help the client incorporate the missing pieces into the interpretation to see if that leads to any additional understanding. If the client has a very thorough understanding of the dream, the therapist can ask if the client is happy with that interpretation or whether he or she wants to try to understand the dream at another level, given that most dreams can be interpreted in several ways.

As indicated earlier, the therapist and client can work to understand the dream at a number of levels. First, the dream can be understood in terms of *waking life*. Research indicates that dreams typically reflect waking life concerns (see review in Hill, 1996), and most clients naturally seek out this level of interpretation, so this level makes sense to focus on first. For example, Marco might come to understand that the dream represents his struggles about whether to be a physician or not, whether to live in the States or move back to Italy, how to get along with his parents, or questions about his masculinity. Of course, not all of these themes could be developed fully within a single session, but this list indicates the richness that can be found even in a short dream.

The waking life level of interpretation can include thoughts and feelings about the past and future as well as the present. In the Hill (1996) model, past experiences were considered to be a separate level of interpretation, but we have discovered that past experiences are not easily distinguished from current waking life because the memories of past experiences are typically actively present in waking life. Similarly, although it is somewhat easier to work with recent dreams because the details of events in waking life are more accessible, dreams from the past can be interpreted if clients remember events from the time of the dream clearly or if they can think about the unresolved issues that the dream reflects.

Second, the dream can be interpreted in terms of *parts of self*, such that each image or person in the dream is a part of the client's personality, hence reflecting inner dynamics. Hence, Marco might come to realize that the men in white jackets represent his arrogant, unfriendly side that is similar to his father. The piece of nose that the men want to cut off may represent a part of Marco that he cuts off that is like his mother's side of the family—artistic, into feelings, and sensitive. In putting these ideas about parts of self together, Marco may come to the insight that his masculine and feminine sides of himself are battling with each other and making it hard for him to figure out who he is and what he wants from life. It might be helpful during this discovery process to have Marco play out the different parts of himself using gestalt techniques so that he can come to a deeper understanding of the role of these parts in his life.

Third, the dream can be understood as an *experience in and of itself*, without the need to translate or interpret it into something else. Hence, the therapist might work with Marco to understand what he learns about himself from thinking about living through the experience of this particular dream.

Marco might be surprised to learn that he felt angry that he let the men chase him away without standing up to them and fighting directly. He might also be quite surprised to learn that he really felt better being back in his hometown in Italy as opposed to living in the United States. Marco might begin to see that the dream reflects his way of being in the world—that he is passive about how he approaches the world and that he doesn't pay attention to his feelings. He might become aware that he wants to live more fully in the moment, pay attention to what is going on inside him, and make decisions for himself about what he wants.

Alternatively, the dream can be understood in terms of *spiritual issues,* or what the dream reflects about the person's relationship with a higher power, or existential issues, such as the meaning of life (see also Davis & Hill, 2001). In trying to think about the dream from a spiritual perspective, Marco might realize that the dream reflects his passivity about thinking about spiritual and existential issues. He grew up in the Catholic church and just assumed that the priests had the authority, but he has never questioned what he believes or what he wants. Hence, Marco might realize that he needs to work on his spiritual issues, who he is, and what he wants out of life.

Finally, another level of interpretation can be used if the therapist is working with a couple rather than an individual (see Kolchakian & Hill, 2002). In this *relationship* level, the therapist works with the couple to understand more about what the dream reflects about their relationship. If Marco and his partner were in therapy together, they might begin to discuss how the dream reflects Marco's tendency to run away from problems in the relationship as they arise. The return to Italy might reflect how he automatically runs to his mother when problems arise rather than talking with his partner. By bringing these issues out in the open, the couple can begin talking about their relationship in greater depth. In another session, they can do a similar process with Marco's partner's dream.

Hence, as previously illustrated, the therapist and client work together collaboratively to figure out the meaning of the dream, using at least one of these levels. For most clients, starting with the waking life level is most comfortable. With some clients, it is useful and fun to go on to other levels. The task for therapists in the insight stage is to encourage clients to think about what the dream might mean and to look at other meanings that they might not have thought of before. So, in the first part of this stage, the client might suggest one meaning and the therapist might help the client evaluate whether that interpretation makes sense. The therapist might then offer a variation on the meaning, which the client might alter in some way. Hence, by working together as a team, the therapist and client construct a meaning that makes sense and is acceptable to the client.

Throughout this stage, therapists use their own insights to help clients think about the dream in new ways. However, in doing so, therapists need to remain attuned to the client's feelings and level of comfort. Therapists must remember that they are not the experts who have the answers to what the dream means, but rather they are there to facilitate the client's involvement and understanding of the dream. Therapists must always be aware that they can never know clients completely, and hence their insights are always tentative and subject to revision based on feedback from clients. Therapists need to be creative and flexible and use their intuition and individual therapeutic style to provide clients with possible interpretations, but they also need to be empathic and attentive to what the client can handle. It is also important for therapists to be aware of their own personal issues and how these can negatively impact on the therapeutic process.

Determining the accuracy of interpretations is not possible because we cannot trace back to the exact events in the client's life, nor can we examine how these experiences were stored in the cognitive schemas. In fact, it is doubtful that the "true" meaning ever is attained. Rather, it makes more sense to think about the therapist and the client constructing a meaning of the dream based on the information available at the time. Hence, instead of talking about accuracy, it is more appropriate to think about the value of the dream interpretation for the therapeutic process. The interpretation is good if it fits most of the components of the dream, makes sense to the client, sparks an "aha," provides a sense of newness and satisfaction for the client, leads directly to actions in the next stage, and helps the client do something differently in waking life. In effect, the proof of the interpretation is in whether the client can use it to make changes in waking life.

In ending the insight stage, it is often useful for the therapist to ask the client to summarize the major themes or meanings of the dream in one or two sentences. Summarizing allows clients to consolidate what they have learned about the dream. In addition, hearing the client summarize the interpretation of the dream allows the therapist to hear what the client has taken away from the interpretation process and also to assess the client's readiness to move on to the action stage.

The Action Stage

The purpose of the action stage is for therapists to help clients extend what they have learned during the previous stages to explore the possibility of changing and then working on developing action plans if the client is willing and ready. The action stage can begin with the therapist asking the client what changes she or he would like to make in the dream. Because the client created the dream initially, she or he can change it too. Making changes in the dream is often a fun and creative way to get the client started in thinking about making changes and can lead to specific things that need to be changed.

Encouraging the client to change the dream is important for two reasons. First, because the task emphasizes that clients are the creators and directors of their dreams and hence can change their dreams in any way they like, changing the dream can facilitate a sense of empowerment for the client. Second, hearing what clients say about changing their dreams gives therapists an opportunity to assess readiness for change. If clients act helpless and cannot change their dreams, chances are they are not going to be willing to make changes in their lives. On the other hand, if clients readily think about changes that they could make in their dreams, they are more likely to be willing to make changes in their lives.

Marco, for example, might say that he would want to turn and face the men chasing him and fight them off because he doesn't like it when he runs away. In hearing this, the therapist might determine that Marco is ready to begin working on assertiveness issues (and maybe is less eager to begin working on career and personality issues).

The next step involves bridging from making changes in the dream to making changes in life. The therapist thus helps the client explore how changes in the dream parallel actual changes the client wants to make in his or her life. In the example, Marco might decide that he wants to be more assertive with male authorities in his life. The therapist might then do some assertiveness training with Marco and practice specific situations in which Marco can be more assertive. They might first practice how Marco could have handled the examination situation. Clients often lack specific skills for making changes, so therapists may need to use behavioral techniques (e.g., behavioral rehearsal, feedback, reinforcement) to help clients learn how to behave differently. Hence, therapists must be well versed in behavioral techniques so that they can help clients in making these changes.

If the client is resistant to making changes in waking life or if this additional step seems like it would be helpful, the therapist can discuss with the client how the dream could be "honored" in some way through a ritual (a symbolic act). We have found that often the dream and its interpretation have a very striking impact on the client that can be strengthened and expanded if the therapist emphasizes the importance of using a ritual to honor the dream. Marco might put a picture of a nose above his desk to remind himself that, if he is not careful, his nose (identity) will be chopped off.

In addition, it is sometimes useful for therapists to help clients think about how they might continue to work on the dream. Clients who like to write might be asked to use the self-help manual in Hill (1996) or the upcoming interactive computer software to continue to work on understanding their dream. Other clients who prefer other modalities might be asked to draw a picture of the dream or create a dance. After drawing or dancing, they might be asked to write down their reactions to the experience so that it can be discussed in the next session. Because only a portion of dreams can be discussed in sessions and because therapists want to help clients learn techniques for working with dreams on their own, homework assignments for working with dreams can be helpful.

Finally, therapists can ask clients to summarize what they learned from their dreams and what they want to do differently in their lives based on what they learned from their dreams. Once again, having clients summarize helps them to clarify what they learned and also to make commitments to change. In addition, it helps therapists assess what clients have taken away with them and determine what additional treatment is needed. As a part of the summary process, therapists might ask clients to make up a title that helps them remember the significance of the dream. For example, Marco might title his dream, "The Chase to Save My Nose."

Therapists need to keep in mind during the action stage that they are helping clients explore action rather than dictating action. In other words, therapists need to remain neutral about whether clients make plans to change or actually do anything different in their lives. Their task is to help clients think seriously about whether they actually want to change rather than pushing them to change. Clients are often not ready to change or have very different ideas of what change would involve than their therapists do. The task for therapists is to help clients explore their options, make decisions about whether they want to change, and then help them with specific change strategies if they want to change.

USING DREAM INTERPRETATION IN THERAPY

Therapists can let clients know at the beginning of therapy that they are willing to work with dreams. If dreams are brought up at the end of sessions, therapists can ask clients to bring them in again at the beginning of the next session so that they can spend a concerted amount of time dealing with the dream.

A thorough interpretation of a single dream often takes about 90 to 120 minutes. The majority of the time (about 30 to 45 minutes) is typically spent in the exploration stage, with approximately equal amounts of the remaining time spent in the insight and action stages. A substantial amount of time spent in the exploration stage is critical because that is where the data for the insight and action stages are gathered. It is important, however, for therapists to allot enough time for both the insight and action stages, since both are typically necessary for giving clients a sense of completion about the dream interpretation process.

Although it is ideal to interpret a dream in one 120-minute session, most therapists do not have this luxury. Within the more typical 50-minute sessions, we suggest that therapists do all three stages with a smaller part of the dream. They can always come back to the dream in subsequent sessions to gain additional insight and action. But we have found that it is hard to regain momentum if therapists come back to the interpretation process in subsequent sessions after only having completed some of the process.

Therapists can use dream interpretation in the first session of therapy. Working with dreams in this manner helps therapists gain a great deal of information in a manner that circumvents client defenses because clients tell all kinds of information that they had not planned on telling. Therapists learn about clients in a very nonthreatening way, and clients leave feeling that they have accomplished something specific—they brought in a dream and now understand it and have specific ideas for things to do differently.

The question often comes up about whether there are certain clients with whom dream interpretation is not advisable. Our research and experience suggest that the choice about whether to use dream interpretation depends on attitudes of the therapist and client toward working with dreams. Therapists and clients with positive attitudes toward dreams are the ones who are most likely to want to work with dreams. The one caveat is that therapists probably will not want to do dream interpretation with clients who have a tenuous grasp on reality (i.e., who cannot distinguish dreams from waking life), who are psychotic, who cannot tell a coherent dream, or who cannot concentrate on the dream interpretation process.

BRIEF SUMMARY OF RESEARCH ON THE HILL MODEL

A number of studies have now been conducted on the Hill dream interpretation model (Cogar & Hill, 1992; Diemer, Lobell, Vivino, & Hill, 1996; Falk & Hill, 1995; Heaton, Hill, Hess, Hoffman, & Leotta, 1998; Heaton, Hill, Petersen, Rochlen, & Zack, 1998; Hill, Diemer, & Heaton, 1997; Hill, Diemer,

Hess, Hillyer, & Seeman, 1993; Hill et al., 2001; Hill, Nakayama, & Wonnell, 1998; Hill et al., 2000; Rochlen, Ligiero, Hill, & Heaton, 1999; Wonnell & Hill, 2000; Zack & Hill, 1998). The majority of this research has involved individual client-therapist dyads (both in single sessions and in brief therapy) with volunteer clients and advanced graduate student therapists. Effectiveness of dream interpretation has most often been assessed through client postsession ratings on the Gains from Dream Interpretation (Heaton, Hill, Petersen, et al., 1998), the Mastery-Insight Scale (Kolden, 1991), Session Impacts Scale—Understanding Scale (Elliott & Wexler, 1994), Session Evaluation Questionnaire—Depth Scale (Stiles & Snow, 1984), and Working Alliance Inventory (Horvath & Greenberg, 1989) measures. The major results can be summarized as follows:

1.   The most impressive finding, which has been replicated across 10 studies, is that dream interpretation resulted in client ratings of session process (quality of sessions, insight, and understanding) that were about a standard deviation higher than for therapy not involving dream interpretation. These findings have emerged for single sessions of dream interpretation as well as for dream interpretation conducted within ongoing therapy. For example, Hill and colleagues (2000) found that brief therapy focused on dream interpretation (at least 5 of 12 sessions, including the first session) had higher client ratings of process (quality of session, insight, and working alliance) throughout the entire therapy process than did a comparison therapy that used a similar model focused on working on loss events for clients who had recent losses and good dream recall.

2.   A comparison of the effects of interpreting one's own dream, interpreting someone else's dream as if it were one's own, or interpreting one's own recent event indicated that interpreting one's own dream resulted in higher client ratings of session outcome (Hill et al., 1993). Hence, dream interpretation seemed to be effective because clients worked with their own personal dreams rather than because they were projecting onto some ambiguous stimulus (another person's dream) or because they went through the process of interpretation (used the same interpretation model to work on a recent waking life event).

3.   People with positive attitudes toward dreams expressed more interest in participating and gained more from dream interpretation than people who had more negative attitudes (Hill et al., 1997). Clients with negative attitudes toward dreams also had low recall of their dreams, were less open to their experiences, and were less emotionally responsive. Some clients with negative attitudes have expressed doubt about dream interpreta-

tion because they equated it with "fringe" psychology (palm reading, numerology, etc).

4.   In single sessions of dream interpretation, volunteer clients reported better session outcome from discussing pleasant rather than unpleasant dreams (Hill et al., 2001; Zack & Hill, 1998). We do not know whether this finding would replicate in ongoing therapy. It might be that clients would gain more from working with more troubling dreams when they have ongoing relationships with their therapists and have more time to work with material that emerges from dream interpretation.

5.   A comparison of conditions in which clients received description, association, or a combination of description and association indicated that clients reported significantly more exploration/insight gains from association than from description, but there were no differences in terms of client-rated session quality, judges' ratings of cognitive complexity of client dialogue, judges' ratings of insight gained in written dream interpretations, or judges' ratings of the quality of clients' written action plans (Hill et al., 1998). Hence, both description and association seem to be helpful components of the exploration stage.

6.   A comparison of waking life and parts-of-self levels of interpretation revealed no significant differences in terms of client-rated session process and outcome (Hill et al., 2001). Furthermore, both types of interpretation were equally effective with different types of clients and different types of dreams. Hence, therapists are justified in using either level of interpretation.

7.   A comparison of a condition including the exploration and insight stages with another condition including all three stages (exploration, insight, and action) indicated that inclusion of all three stages was important for helping clients develop ideas for changes they want to make (Wonnell & Hill, 2000). Therapists, however, did not feel equally competent in using the action stage with all clients.

8.   A comparison of sessions with therapists facilitating dream interpretation with sessions in which clients followed the same procedures by themselves indicated that clients gained more from and preferred therapist-facilitated sessions to self-help sessions (Heaton, Hill, Petersen, et al., 1998). Volunteer clients, however, expressed that writing out all the stages was boring. It may be that using a computer program, such as we are developing, would be more interactive and engaging.

9.   A comparison of three training conditions (teaching skills involved in the Hill dream interpretation model, teaching methods for increasing dream recall, teaching about various approaches to counseling) with stu-

dents who had low attitudes toward dreams and low dream recall revealed no differences in terms of attitudes toward dreams or dream recall (Rochlen et al., 1999). However, students who received training in the skills involved in the Hill model (description, association, etc.) had better session outcome after dream interpretation than students in the other two conditions. These results suggest that dream interpretation was effective even with students who had low attitudes toward dreams and poor dream recall and that therapists might want to train clients in dream interpretation skills.

    10.   Dream interpretation is effective in single sessions of individual therapy (Heaton, Hill, Petersen, et al., 1998; Hill et al., 1993, 1997, 1998, 2000; Rochlen et al., 1999; Wonnell & Hill, 2000; Zack & Hill, 1998), brief individual therapy (Diemer et al., 1996; Heaton, Hill, Hess, et al., 1998), group therapy (Falk & Hill, 1995), and couples therapy (Kolchakian & Hill, in press). Changes are most consistently in insight and self-understanding rather than in symptoms.

FUTURE RESEARCH

The research on this model and on dream interpretation in general is still in its infancy. At this point, what can be said with reasonable certainty is that the model appears to be a promising therapeutic tool leading to increased insight, self-awareness, and understanding. Several promising areas of research can be offered:

1.   It seems critical for researchers to investigate the differences between dream interpretation used in single sessions versus that used within therapy.

2.   It would be useful to compare the Hill model of dream interpretation with other dream interpretation models (e.g., Freudian, Jungian, gestalt) as well as with other expressive, creative therapeutic techniques (e.g., art therapy techniques, gestalt techniques, projective testing). Results of such studies could shed further light on the question of what it is about dream interpretation that yields changes in insight and self-understanding.

3.   It would be useful to test the effects of having people complete the dream interpretation process using interactive computer software.

4.   It is critical to continue testing the Hill model on a range of clients and dreams to see what the limits of application are of this therapeutic approach.

5. A very exciting area is to chart the actual cognitive changes that occur during successful dream interpretation, a task that seems more possible with improvements in cognitive psychology.
6. Studies need to be conducted to determine whether attitudes toward dreams can be changed so that more people would be amenable to working with their dreams.

In conclusion, we hope that inclusion of this updated cognitive-experiential dream interpretation model and accompanying research findings will encourage more therapists to begin to use dream interpretation in therapy. Dream interpretation does seem to be effective in increasing client insight, so it can be useful for therapists to know when and how to use it. Furthermore, we hope that more researchers will begin to study this model and other models of dream interpretation so that we can improve the delivery of dream interpretation and discover more about its uses.

REFERENCES

Cogar, M. M., & Hill, C. E. (1992). Examining the effects of brief individual dream interpretation. *Dreaming, 2,* 239–248.

Davis, T. L., & Hill, C. E. (2001). Dream interpretation from a spiritual perspective. In L. VandeCreek & T. L. Jackson (Eds.), *Innovations in clinical practice: A source book,* Vol. 19 (pp. 79–94). Sarasota, FL: Professional Resource Press/Professional Resource Exchange, Inc.

Delaney, G. (1991). *Breakthrough dreaming.* New York: Bantam Books.

Diemer, R. A., Lobell, L. K., Vivino, B. L., & Hill, C. E. (1996). Comparison of dream interpretation, event interpretation, and unstructured sessions in brief therapy. *Journal of Counseling Psychology, 43,* 99–112.

Elliott, R., & Wexler, M. M. (1994). Measuring the impact of sessions in process-experiential therapy of depression: The Session Impacts Scale. *Journal of Counseling Psychology, 41,* 166–174.

Falk, D. R., & Hill, C. E. (1995). The process and outcome of dream interpretation groups for divorcing women. *Dreaming, 5,* 29–42.

Heaton, K. J., Hill, C. E., Hess, S., Hoffman, M. A., & Leotta, C. (1998). Assimilation in therapy involving interpretation of recurrent and nonrecurrent dreams. *Psychotherapy, 35,* 147–162.

Heaton, K. J., Hill, C. E., Petersen, D., Rochlen, A. B., & Zack, J. (1998). A comparison of therapist-facilitated and self-guided dream interpretation sessions. *Journal of Counseling Psychology, 45,* 115–121.

Hill, C. E. (1996). *Working with dreams in psychotherapy.* New York: Guilford Press.

Hill, C. E., Diemer, R., & Heaton, K. J. (1997). Dream interpretation sessions: Who volunteers, who benefits, and what volunteer clients view as most and least helpful. *Journal of Counseling Psychology, 44,* 53–62.

Hill, C. E., Diemer, R., Hess, S., Hillyer, A., & Seeman, R. (1993). Are the effects of dream interpretation on session quality, insight, and emotions due to the dream itself, to projection, or to the interpretation process? *Dreaming, 3*, 269–280.

Hill, C. K., Kelley, F. A., Davis, T. L., Crook, R. E., Maldanado, L. E., Turkson, M. A., et al,. (2001). Predictors of outcome in dream interpretation session: Volunteer clients' characteristics, dream characteristics, and type of interpretation. *Dreaming, 11*, 53–72.

Hill, C. E., Nakayama, E., & Wonnell, T. (1998). A comparison of description, association, and combined description/association in explorating dream images. *Dreaming, 8*(1), 1–13.

Hill, C. E., & O'Brien, K. (1999). *Helping skills: Facilitating exploration, insight, and action*. Washington, DC: American Psychological Association.

Hill, C. E., Zack, J., Wonnell, T., Hoffman, M. A., Rochlen, A., Goldberg, J., et al. (2000). Structured brief therapy with a focus on dreams or loss for clients with troubling dreams and recent losses. *Journal of Counseling Psychology, 47*, 90–98, 101.

Horvath, A. O., & Greenberg, L. S. (1989). Development and validation of the Working Alliance Inventory. *Journal of Counseling Psychology, 36*, 223–233.

Kolchakian, M. R., & Hill, C. E. (2002). A cognitive-experiential model of dream interpretation for couples. In L. VandeCreek & T. L. Jackson (Eds.), *Innovations in clinical practice: A source book*, Vol. 18 (pp. 85–101). Sarasota, FL: Professional Resource Press/Professional Resource Exchange, Inc.

Kolchakian, M. R., & Hill, C. E. (in press). Working with unmarried couples with dreams. *Dreaming.*

Kolden, G. C. (1991). The generic model of psychotherapy: An empirical investigation of patterns of process and outcome relationships. *Psychotherapy Research, 1*, 62–73.

Rochlen, A., Ligiero, D., Hill, C. E., & Heaton, K. (1999). Preparation for dreamwork: Training for dream recall and dream interpretation. *Journal of Counseling Psychology, 46*, 27–34.

Stiles, W. B., & Snow, J. (1984). Counseling session impact as viewed by novice counselors and their clients. *Journal of Counseling Psychology, 31*, 3–12.

Wonnell, T., & Hill, C. E. (2000). The effects of including the action stage in dream interpretation. *Journal of Counseling Psychology, 47*, 372–379.

Zack, J., & Hill, C. E. (1998). Predicting dream interpretation outcome by attitudes, stress, and emotion. *Dreaming, 8*, 169–185.

PART **IV**

Future Directions

CHAPTER 12

To Dream, Perchance to Sleep: Awakening the Potential of Dream Work for Cognitive Therapy

RACHAEL I. ROSNER

WILLIAM J. LYDDON

One of the significant challenges that cognitive therapists face in adding dreams to their clinical repertoire involves recognizing and acknowledging their own metatheoretical and epistemological commitments. It becomes much less difficult for a cognitive therapist to envision using dreams therapeutically after he or she has found a suitable epistemology and language system with which to understand them. From that perspective, the discussions about cognitive therapy and dreams in this volume also require some summary discussion of how cognitive therapists can translate them into their own language framework. As we have demonstrated here and elsewhere (Lyddon, 1990; Lyddon & Weill, 2002; Rosner, 1997), the larger landscape of cognitive therapies may be viewed as reflecting two different epistemologies (or theories of knowing): objectivism and constructivism. The challenge for objectivist cognitive therapists who are considering dreams is to find a mechanism for working with them consistent with their general commitments to directive and relatively short-term treatment programs. From this perspective, the dream is often viewed as a mirror of the client's schema—one reflecting the same cognitive distortions that may be at work in his or her waking life. For constructivist cognitive therapists the task may prove less daunting because constructivism is predicated on the human capacity for creative and imaginative thought and the notion that humans actively construct their personal (and social) realities via a multitude of symbolic means (language, metaphor, narrative, myth, etc.). From a constructivist perspective, dreams represent yet another symbolic vehicle for personal meaning making. In either case, however, the field is sufficiently young that cognitive therapists will need to continue to experiment clinically and conceptually to discover which particular approach is consistent with their own epistemological inclinations.

CLARIFYING METATHEORETICAL COMMITMENTS

One potential integrative solution to the problem of bridging this "epistemological divide" may be related to the type or level of change being addressed in therapy. As Lyddon and his colleagues have noted (Lyddon, 1990; Lyddon & Satterfield, 1994; Lyddon & Alford, 1993), objectivist and constructivist therapies may be more or less appropriate depending on whether the goals of therapy are designed to facilitate first- or second-order change. In brief, first-order change is essentially "change without change," or change that does not produce a change in the structure of the system (Lyddon, 1990; Watzlawick, Weakland, & Fisch, 1974). As Hanna (2002) notes, "*first-order change* is linear, surface, uncomplicated, straightforward change that takes the form of an adaptation or adjustment" (p. 13). Clients for whom first-order change is indicated typically are comfortable with their core assumptions about self and world and tend to require only peripheral adjustments in their personal systems. Clinical goals consistent with first-order change include the learning of new coping skills designed to produce relatively immediate symptom relief and/or the reestablishment of some sense of personal equilibrium. Often these individuals are experiencing a life crisis (loss of job, ended intimate relationship, conflict with a supervisor, etc.) and their current coping strategies are being taxed. Objectivist approaches may find their greatest utility in these situations by helping clients learn to better regulate their cognitive and emotional responses to such life events.

By way of contrast, second-order change is "change of change," a type of change that alters the fundamental structure or organization of a system (Lyddon, 1990; Watzlawick et al., 1974). Constructivists refer to second-order change as "deep" (Guidano, 1987) or "core" (Mahoney, 1990) and suggest that it (a) entails a restructuring of a client's personal identity and most basic assumptions about self and world and (b) is often accompanied by intense and sometimes painful emotions. As Hanna (2002) elaborates:

> *Second-order change* . . . is profound. It can be defined as a sweeping, deep structure or core change in an individual (Lyddon, 1990). This kind of change affects a person's core self or mode of being or his or her essential worldview. Second-order change radiates into and transfers across the wide array of a person's personality traits, compartmentalizations, activities, and interests. Our research findings agreed with Lyddon's in that second-order change often initially involves intense turmoil or stress that is directly related to internal conflicts of considerable magnitude. (p. 13)

Second-order change may be indicated when a client exhibits a history or pattern of difficulty in addressing some developmental life challenge. In such instances clients' core beliefs about self and world are no longer functional and their presenting problems appear more pervasive (e.g., a *pattern* of job losses, a *history* of relationship difficulties, and/or *long-standing* problems with regulating emotion). Because constructivist approaches tend to emphasize (a) a developmentally focused reconstruction of the history and patterning of the problem, (b) gradual elaboration of the client's tacit working models of self and world that are no longer viable (clues to which may emerge in the dream work process), (c) full exploration of the emotions related to this newly accessed experiential information, and (d) therapist support for the client's construction of new meaning structures, they seem well suited to addressing second-order change.

One implication of placing the distinction between first- and second-order change at the intersection of objectivist and constructivist approaches to therapy and working with dreams is that neither approach—objectivist or constructivist—is right or wrong, good or bad. Rather, each approach may be more or less appropriate to employ based on the type or level of change being considered.

Following from the above metatheoretical issues and distinctions, in the remaining pages of this concluding chapter we examine some of the theoretical, scientific, and clinical implications of introducing dreams formally into cognitive therapy.

CLARIFYING THEORETICAL COMMITMENTS

The Concept of Dream-Work Cognates for Cognitive Therapy

From a theoretical point of view, we have found it helpful to conceptualize the different contributions to this volume as reflecting "cognates" in related languages, rather than as representing distinctly different languages without any etymological relationship. As suggested by the previous discussion regarding the distinction between first- and second-order change, it may be the case that an emergent metatheory of dreams can provide for conceptual "cognates" that bridge the constructivist and objectivist perspectives. For instance, virtually all of the authors advocate the technique of manipulating the dream imagery to help the client gain a feeling of mastery and "working through" of the issues involved in the dream. Objectivist cognitive therapists who work in a manner akin to Krakow, Doweiko, and Freeman and White might describe what they're doing as visual rehearsal in the context of exposure and desensitization, or as simple cognitive restructuring. The identical technique in the hands of constructivists might be understood as working with root metaphors of the client's core, self-organizing, and organismic process. Leijssen's focusing technique, in contrast, can be understood as a supplemental source of information useful to either approach. In all these cases, constructivists and objectivists would agree that the therapeutic objective is to transmute threatening or painful imagery into imagery that is more easily assimilated into the client's emergent and more effective coping style—to give the client a sense of mastery and competency in managing and working through threatening feelings and thoughts.

Primary and Secondary Process Theory

Conceptualizing the different perspectives contained in this volume as cognates simultaneously helps clinicians retain respect for the differences— differences in culture, in theory, in intentions for the use of language—in the context in which these cognates are being used. Thus, in addition to distinguishing themselves over whether they prefer to make first-order or second-order change, which portray differences in metatheoretical commitments about what the goal of therapy should be, these contributors can also be distinguished by theoretical differences over the exact intrapsychic mechanism they claim to be manipulating with dream work. Generally speaking, they tend to claim that dream work manipulates mechanisms either in the primary process or in the secondary process. The concepts of primary process and secondary process derive from psychoanalysis, where Freud conceived of them as representing the id and libidinal drives, on the one hand, and the reality-testing functions of the ego, on the other hand. Beck, when he rejected the motivational model of psychoanalysis in the 1960s, recast primary and secondary processes as primitive/irrational (primary) and mature/rational (secondary) modes of interpreting stimuli (Beck, 1970a,

1970b; Rosner, 1999). In his cognitive model Beck argued (Rosner, 1999) that a healthy secondary system was capable of evaluating rationally the stream of irrational, primitive, and childlike thoughts that emanated from the primary (and more primitive) system. Automatic thoughts, daydreams, and dreams were all the byproducts of this secondary system. When the secondary system was faulty, as evidenced by the presence of cognitive distortions, primitive and irrational cognitions emanating from the primary system took over the cognitive field.

Consistent with the metatheoretical distinction between first- and second-order change, then, we suggest that objectivists like Beck, Doweiko, and Freeman and White (who are committed to making first-order change in therapy) conceive of clinical dream work on a theoretical level as facilitating change in the secondary process, just as, in the case of challenging automatic thoughts, the goal is to reshape the cognitive mechanism that evaluates irrational and primitive thoughts, rather than to change the mechanism that generates automatic thoughts in the first place. Their emphasis on secondary process can also explain why they don't emphasize the differences between verbal material (automatic thoughts) and visual material (dreams) in their treatment of dreams. They are less interested in the dream images as in helping clients challenge the faulty assumptions embedded within them.

Constructivist cognitive therapists, in contrast (who conceive of therapy as making second-order change), are more inclined to conceptualize dreams (and dream work) as the product of a primary process, or in cognate form what they prefer to call "core schemas" or "root metaphors." Ottens and Hanna (1998), experiential therapists who have advocated for an integration of experiential therapy and cognitive therapy, suggest that these root metaphors or core schemas are ontological in nature, based on fundamental conceptions of who we are in the world that extend far beyond specific schemas about specific situations. Narrative constructivists, like Gonçalves, as well as early constructivists like George Kelly, add that these core schemas are preverbal in nature, the products of a prelogical visual system that predates the logic of verbal syntax. As constructivists have noted (Lyddon, Clay, & Sparks, 2001), metaphor may function as a core organizing principle for this pre-verbal system. If one assumes that dreams are prelogical and preverbal products of a primary process, then they cannot be accessed by the tools of logic and rationality and cannot be manipulated effectively if one's goal for therapy is to work on secondary process in order to make first-order change.

Constructivists tend to understand dream work as a process of manipulating the core organizing principles, or manipulating the primary process, by employing, entering, and inhabiting its own language structure in the waking state (for a discussion of the metaphorical syntax of dreams, see Lakoff, 1997). We argue that this work delves deep into the dream generator itself. Leijssen's emphasis on bodily felt sense, Barrett's emphasis on symbols and messages embedded within dreams, Gonçalves and Barbosa's emphasis on narrative restructuring, and Hill and Rochlen's emphasis on insight and action all tap into this metaphorical, ontological structure—even though each of their systems has conceptual ties to different therapeutic traditions (psychoanalytic, narrative, and experiential).

ARTICULATING SOME RESEARCH HYPOTHESES

Following from the above, we may ask, then: Is it more useful to understand dreams as a product of the primary system, the secondary system, a preconscious system somewhere in between, or a combination of them all? Can empirical research help to clarify which system is at work? How might an appreciation of the difference between primary and secondary process facilitate working with dreams in cognitive therapy if one's goal is to make first-order change, on the one hand, or second-order change, on the other? These theoretical and metatheoretical considerations, in other words, create the foundation from which hypotheses can be generated about cognitive therapy and dreams and then tested empirically. The theoretical issues are complex, making it difficult to generate data that can't be explained using either theoretical position. One could argue, for instance, that if dream themes of depressed patients are full of depressed, negative content, then the primary system is the active mechanism (because it generates the negative affect). An experiment designed to discover if dream themes change from negative to neutral in someone undergoing cognitive therapy could be used to support the hypothesis that the primary system is the object of therapeutic manipulation, because it is the generator of negative thoughts. In other words, if dream themes change, then the generator has changed. In contrast, Beck's research implies that cognitive therapy helps an individual to test and authenticate reality better, in which case an equally plausible interpretation of the data would be that the therapy succeeded in bolstering the secondary system; in other words, changes in dream themes reflect the more efficient interventions of the secondary system.

Further complicating the task of generating research questions, empirical research on dreams to date offers mixed results from which to build new hypotheses. Doweiko's and Krakow's work suggest that at least a client's waking experience of dreams—the degree to which dreams intrude upon and influence someone's life—can change dramatically over the course of treatment, irrespective of whether or not the dream themes change (Krakow et al., 2001). Krakow's work raises the important question, then, of what exactly is the object of therapeutic manipulation—the image in the waking state or the dream itself. It still remains an open question, despite Beck's findings about the themes of depressed patients, whether or not dream themes are reliable indicators of the state of a client's cognitive and affective experience; Sauteraud, Menny, Philip, Peyré, and Bonnin (2001), for instance, found no differences between the dreams of obsessive-compulsives and controls containing themes of anxiety, sadness, failure, or rituals.

In terms of whether or not dream themes change during the course of therapy, and if so why, research results are equally mixed. Armitage et al. (1995) found no change in dream content with reduction of depressed symptoms, although patients in their study were treated with antidepressants rather than therapy. Beck and Hurvich (1959) and Beck and Ward (1961) left an ambiguous legacy. Beck and Hurvich (1959) rated 240 dreams of depressed patients undergoing psychoanalytic psychotherapy on their newly created Masochism Scale (created specifically for this project) to assess the frequency of "masochistic" dream themes. They reported that the dreams of depressed patients showed a relatively high frequency of unpleasant affect relative to those of nondepressed patients. They speculated from these results, based on additional anecdotal evidence, that masochistic dream content may reflect habitual patterns of "masochistic" behavior both in and outside of depression. From this perspective, dream themes would be likely not to change once patients had remitted from their acute episodes of depression. In a second study designed to expand and improve on the first one, Beck and Ward (1961) reiterated the possibility that the "masochistic dream cannot be construed as being associated only with the state of depression. It may more properly be regarded as related to certain personality characteristics of individuals who may develop depressions" (p. 466). They argued that the persistence of these themes was useful data for personality research: "This approach is within the same methodological framework used to measure motivations as reflected in imaginative responses to standardized stimuli, such as the Thematic Apperception Test" (p. 466).

Armitage et al. (1995) suggested that cognitive therapies, because they manipulate the system that generates and shapes dreams, might result in more changes in dream themes than antidepressant treatment. But the implication of Beck and Hurvich (1959) and Beck and Ward (1961) is that negative dream themes would persist beyond acute depression. One hypothesis worthy of further study for objectivist cognitive therapists, then, would be that negative dream themes of depressed patients in a standardized protocol of cognitive therapy will not change over the course of treatment. The theoretical basis of this hypothesis would lie in the argument that dream themes, like other fantasy-based narratives such as stories to TAT cards, are the products of implicit (nonconscious) processes that cannot be accessed through objectivist cognitive therapy techniques (for a discussion of implicit and self-attributed motives, see Peterson & Ulrey, 1994). In contrast, measures of explicit (self-attributive, conscious) processes, according to this hypothesis, would decrease as a result of cognitive therapy. This is because, it might be argued, standard cognitive therapy targets conscious, explicit processes that are reflected in individuals' beliefs about themselves (Teasdale, 1993).

Constructivist cognitive therapists, in contrast, might hypothesize that dream themes in constructivist treatments *will* change because those treatments are designed to work at the level of implicit, or motivational, processes (Guidano, 1987; Mahoney, 1990). Rosner, quoting George Kelly's personal construct theory, has suggested that dream themes

> can be used as a check to see if new thematic metaphors are operating at a deeper level, a suggestion that builds on Kelly's concept of "mile-post" dreams, dreams that "mark a transition in the underlying construction system of the client" and that "express new behaviors which are about to emerge spontaneously." (Rosner, 1997, p. 267, quoting Kelly, 1991, p. 339).

The empirical task facing constructivist therapists, who prefer to use grounded theory and other qualitative methods, would be to develop a system of benchmarks, or predetermined intervals, for checking in with clients about their dream experiences to be sure to capture the dream data during the course of treatment. In sum, future research in cognitive therapy and dreams might test empirically these twin propositions, namely, that cognitive interventions with dreams that target the evaluative system which makes meaning out of the dream images (as the objectivists would argue) will not result in changes in dream themes but will result in changes in conscious or self-attributed experiences, whereas cognitive interventions with dreams that target the dream generator will result in changes in dream themes (as constructivists would argue).

CLINICAL APPLICATIONS OF DREAM WORK IN COGNITIVE THERAPY

For many clinicians, theory and research are of less consequence than the pressing reality of the therapy room. Cognitive therapists may be asking:

What do I do when a client brings dreams into my office? I see clients in short-term symptom-reduction focused treatment. How can I integrate dreams into a highly structured treatment protocol? How can I use dreams to reduce my client's symptoms?

Listening With an Ear to Dreams

First, we suggest that cognitive therapists interested in using dreams will need to prime their ears for them, which in turn requires bringing to dreams a framework for making use of them. One of the most important steps in discovering the clinical utility of dreams is for cognitive therapists to develop an appreciation of the clinical utility of other therapeutic systems. In other words, working with dreams in cognitive therapy, at least at this early date, necessitates integrating cognitive therapy with other schools and, as has been suggested herein, even integrating objectivist and constructivist points of view. For instance, Drew Westen (2000), a psychodynamic researcher who has advocated for the benefits of remaining open to alternative orientations, argues that

> integrating psychodynamic and cognitive-behavioral theory and practice may at times be essential for optimal treatment because the two perspectives have complementary strengths and weaknesses. . . . Psychotherapy integration can occur at the level of technical eclecticism, common factors, and theoretical integration. Theoretical integration is the most thoroughgoing form of integration. (Westen, 2000, p. 237)

If Crook's research (chapter 4) is truly representative of the broader community of cognitive therapists, where they take the position that "I don't ask about dreams and people don't volunteer in my experience," then adopting Westen's perspective may be crucial to bringing dreams into the cognitive system.

This may be difficult to do. It means shifting therapists' own cognitive frames in order to assimilate the idea that cognitive therapy does possess different theories of dreams and that there are specific techniques that can be used to work with them. Therapists interested in making first-order change can employ the suggestions of Krakow, Doweiko, and Freeman and White by conceptualizing short-term, solution-focused cognitive therapy as a manipulation of the secondary processes (including manipulating dream images) that, in turn, help clients reduce and better manage symptoms of anxiety and depression. If the goals of therapy are second-order in nature (and one has the luxury of doing longer-term work with clients), it is possible to move beyond secondary process work into the deeper, core schemas and primary process material. Using dreams in this context involves the same skills used in therapy for creating new narratives, or entering the subjective experience of intense emotional memories.

The goal of this book has been to begin the process of building a clinical framework from which cognitive therapists can make use of dreams if and when they materialize in the therapy room. Where cognitive therapists choose to go with dreams from here will depend very much on the degree to which they discover that dreams can be used practically. In other words, a new field of cognitive therapy and dreams will blossom if dreams can be incorporated into the technical framework of preexisting schedules for cognitive therapy sessions. Nonetheless, while cognitive therapists tend to be more pragmatic than theoretical, there are both practical and theoretical issues at stake if dreams are to become fully assimilated into the repertoire of objectivist and constructivist cognitive therapies.

REFERENCES

Armitage, R., Rochlen, A., Fitch, T., Madhukar, T., & Rush, A. J. (1995). Dream recall and major depression: A preliminary report. *Dreaming, 5*(3), 189–198.

Beck, A. T. (1970a). Cognitive therapy: Nature and relation to behavior therapy. *Behavior Therapy, 1*, 184–200.

Beck, A. T. (1970b). Role of fantasies in psychotherapy and psychopathology. *Journal of Nervous and Mental Disease, 150*(1), 3–17.

Beck, A. T., & Hurvich, M. S. (1959). Psychological correlates of depression: 1. Frequency of "masochistic" dream content in a private practice sample. *Psychosomatic Medicine, 21*(1), 50–55.

Beck, A. T., & Ward, C. H. (1961). Dreams of depressed patients: Characteristic themes in manifest content. *Archives of General Psychiatry, 5*, 462–467.

Guidano, V. F. (1987). *Complexity of the self.* New York: Guilford.

Hanna, F. J. (2002). *Therapy with difficult clients: Using the precursors model to awaken change.* Washington, DC: American Psychological Association.

Kelly, G. A. (1991). *The psychology of personal constructs: Volume Two—Clinical diagnosis and psychotherapy.* London and New York: Routledge.

Krakow, B., Hollifield, M., Johnston, L., et al. (2001). Imagery rehearsal therapy for chronic nightmares in sexual assault survivors with posttraumatic stress disorder: A randomized controlled trial. *Journal of the American Medical Association, 286*(5), 537–545.

Lakoff, G. (1997). How unconscious metaphorical thought shapes dreams. In D. Stein (Ed.), *Cognitive science and the unconscious: Progress in Psychiatry No. 52* (pp. 89–120). Washington, DC: American Psychiatric Press.

Lyddon, W. J. (1990). First- and second-order change: Implications for rationalist and constructivist therapies. *Journal of Counseling and Development, 69*, 122–127.

Lyddon, W. J., & Alford, D. J. (1993). Constructivist assessment: A developmental-epistemic perspective. In G. L. Neimeyer (Ed.), *Casebook of constructivist assessment* (pp. 31–57). Newbury Park, CA: Sage.

Lyddon, W. J., Clay, A. L., & Sparks, C. L. (2001). Metaphors and change in counseling. *Journal of Counseling and Development, 79,* 269–274.

Lyddon, W. J., & Satterfield, W. A. (1994). Relation of client attachment to therapist first- and second-order change assessments. *Journal of Cognitive Psychotherapy: An International Quarterly, 8,* 233–242.

Lyddon, W. J., & Weill, R. (2002). Cognitive therapy and postmodernism: Emerging themes and challenges. In R. L. Leahy & E. T. Dowd (Eds.), *Clinical practice of cognitive psychotherapy* (pp. 189–208). New York: Springer.

Mahoney, M. J. (1990). *Human change processes.* New York: Basic Books.

Ottens, A. J., & Hanna, F. J. (1998). Cognitive and existential therapies: Toward an integration. *Psychotherapy, 35*(3), 312–324.

Peterson, C., & Ulrey, L. M. (1994). Can explanatory style be scored from TAT protocols? *Personality and Social Psychology Bulletin, 20*(1), 102–106.

Rosner, R. (1997). Cognitive therapy, constructivism and dreams: A critical review. *Journal of Constructivist Psychology, 10,* 249–273.

Rosner, R. (1999). *Between science and psychoanalysis: Aaron T. Beck and the emergence of cognitive therapy.* Unpublished dissertation, York University, Toronto.

Sauteraud, A., Menny, J., Philip, P., Peyré, F., & Bonnin, J. (2001). Dreams in obsessive-compulsive disorder: An analysis of semantic and emotional content compared to controls. *Journal of Psychosomatic Research, 51*(2), 451–457.

Teasdale, J. D. (1993). Emotion and two kinds of meaning: Cognitive therapy and applied cognitive science. *Behavioural Research and Therapy, 31,* 339–354.

Watzlawick, P., Weakland, J. H., & Fisch, R. (1974). *Change: Principles of problem formation and problem resolution.* New York: W. W. Norton.

Westen, D. (2000). Integrative psychotherapy: Integrating psychodynamic and cognitive behavioral theory and technique. In C. R. Snyder & R. E. Ingram (Eds.), *Handbook of psychological change: Psychotherapy processes and practices for the 21st century* (pp. 217–242). New York: John Wiley & Sons, Inc.

Index

Springer Publishing Company

Journal of Cognitive Psychotherapy
An International Quarterly
John H. Riskind, PhD, Editor
E. Thomas Dowd, PhD, International Editor
William Lyddon, PhD, Assistant Editor

The *Journal of Cognitive Psychotherapy* is an international journal that publishes clinical, theoretical and empirical articles on cognitive psychotherapy. Because cognitive therapy emphasizes the importance of testing theory and practice, this journal is unique in its emphasis on both research and clinical practice. Cutting-edge recent advances in social phobia, panic disorder, depression, mania, and personality disorders are presented. Empirical studies are published which have relevance to theory and practice. In addition, the journal publishes numerous book reviews in order to keep readership abreast of recent publications in the field.

SAMPLE ARTICLES:

* Treatment Integrity Concerns in Cognitive-Behavioral Therapies for Depression, *J. B. McGlinchey and K. S. Dobson*

* A Cognitive Therapy Approach for Adult Attention-Deficit/Hyperactivity Disorder, *J. R. Ramsay and A. L. Rostain*

* Dysthymia and Major Depression: Distinct Conditions or Different Stages Along a One-Dimensional Continuum?, *P. Possel*

* Childhood Emotional Maltreatment, Cognitive Vulnerability to Depression, and Self-Referent Information Processing in Adulthood: Reciprocal Relations, *J. A. Steinberg, B. E. Gibb, L. B. Alloy, and L. Y. Abramson*

* The Relationship Between Core Beliefs and a History of Eating Disorders: An Examination of the Life Stories of University Students, *S. Sarin and J. R. Z. Abela*

* Group CBT for Clients With a First Episode of Psychosis, *T. Lecomte, C. Leclerc, T. Wykes, and J. Lecomte*

Volume 18, 2004 • 4 issues annually • ISSN 0889-8391

536 Broadway, New York, NY 10012• (212) 431-4370 • Fax (212) 941-7842
Order Toll-Free: (877) 687-7476 • *www.springerpub.com*

Empirically Supported Cognitive Therapies

Current and Future Applications

William J. Lyddon, PhD
John V. Jones, Jr., PhD, LPC, NCC, ACT, Editors

"This volume moves the field of psychotherapy from the pre-scientific era...to the scientific era... The therapeutic principles, strategies, and techniques for each of the disorders have been validated in clinical trials. This volume is a must for practitioners, neophytes, and teachers."
—**Aaron T. Beck**, MD
University of Pennsylvania, School of Medicine

Empirically validated cognitive techniques for depression, bipolar I disorder, OCD, PTSD, and other common clinical disorders, including anger management and antisocial behavior in children and adolescents, are presented. Case examples are integral to each discussion. Encompassing recent trends, current limitations, and new directions and developments, this text offers a fundamental knowledge base for students and practitioners alike.

Empirically Supported Cognitive Therapies
Current and Future Applications

William J. Lyddon
John V. Jones, Jr.
Editors

Ⓢ Springer Publishing Company

Contents:
An Introduction, *W. J. Lyddon & J. V. Jones*
Section I: Mood Disorders
  • Depression, *I. Blackburn & S. Moorhead*
  • Bipolar I Disorder, *M. R. Basco*
Section II: Anxiety Disorders
  • Phobias, *E. T. Dowd & D. Fahr*
  • Panic Disorder, *W. C. Sanderson & S. A. Rego*
  • Obsessive Compulsive Disorder, *S. Wilhelm*
  • Posttraumatic Stress Disorder, *S. A. Falsetti & H. S. Resnick*

Section III: New Directions and Developments
  • Anger Management, *E.R. Dahlen & J. L. Deffenbacher*
  • Antisocial Behavior in Children and Adolescents: Expanding the Cognitive Model, *L. Hanish & P. H. Tolan*
  • Eating Disorders: Enhancing Effectiveness Through the Intergration of Cultural Factors, *N. L. Wilson & A. E. Blackhurst*
  • Empirically Supported Treatments: Recent Trends, Current Limitations, and Future Promise, *W. J. Lyddon & D. K. Chatkoff*

2001   272pp   0-8261-2299-X   hard

536 Broadway, New York, NY 10012 • Telephone: 212-431-4370
Fax: 212-941-7842 • Order Toll-Free: 877-687-7476
Order On-line: www.springerpub.com

Springer Publishing Company

Adlerian, Cognitive, and Constructivist Therapies
An Integrative Dialogue
Richard E. Watts, PhD, Editor

"With this collection of dialogues, Richard Watts and colleagues make it clear that Adler's work shines its own clear light, and that light has timeless relevance for psychotherapy."

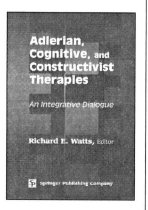

—Michael J. Mahoney, PhD
University of North Texas, Denton

Over the past 20 years, interest in integration has increased among psychotherapy theorists and practitioners. This book demonstrates that Adlerian theory/therapy soundly resonates with contemporary cognitive and constructivist therapies, and is indeed a significant "voice" in contemporary dialogue regarding integration.

Partial Contents:
- Introduction to the Dialogue, *R. E. Watts*

Part I: Adlerian and Constructivist Psychotherapies
- Integrating Adlerian and Constructivist Therapies: An Adlerian Perspective, *R. E. Watts and B. H. Shulman*

Part II: Adlerian and Cognitive Psychotherapies
- Commonalities Between Adlerian Psychotherapy and Cognitive Therapies: An Adlerian Perspective, *L. Sperry*

Part III: Cognitive, Adlerian, and Constructivist Responses
- Adlerian, Cognitive-Behavioral, and Constructivist Psychotherapies, *E. Thomas Dowd*
- Where's the Thinking in Cognitive? *M. P. Maniacci*
- Cognitive/Constructivist Contrasts and the Future Evolution of Adlerian Psychology, *R. A. Neimeyer*

2003   160pp   0-8261-1984-0   hard

536 Broadway, New York, NY 10012
Order Toll-Free: 877-687-7476 • Order On-line: www.springerpub.com